The Midnight Court: Eleven Versions of Merriman

For Jane

The Midnight Court:
Eleven Versions of Merriman

Gregory A. Schirmer

The Lilliput Press
Dublin

First published 2015 by
THE LILLIPUT PRESS
62–63 Sitric Road, Arbour Hill,
Dublin 7, Ireland
www.lilliputpress.ie

A CIP record for this title is available
from The British Library.

10 9 8 7 6 5 4 3 2 1

ISBN 978 1 8435 1 6392

Set in 12 pt on 15.3 pt Jensen by Marsha Swan
Printed in Navarre, Spain, by Castuera

Contents

Acknowledgments   VII

Introduction   XI

Denis Woulfe: Cultural Loss and Metrical Finesse   3

Michael C. O'Shea: Nationalism Unleashed   14

Arland Ussher: On Behalf of the Ascendancy and Liberal Humanism   22

Frank O'Connor: Restoring the Nation   32

Lord Longford: Merriman and the Theatre   44

David Marcus: Marginality and Sexuality   53

Patrick C. Power: Scholarship and Poetic Translation   62

Cosslett Ó Cuinn: The Footprint of Sectarianism   69

Thomas Kinsella: 'A Dual Approach'   78

Seamus Heaney: Ovid, Feminism and the North   89

Ciaran Carson: 'Wavering between Languages'   98

Appendix: Text of *Cúirt an Mheán Oíche* with literal translation   III

Bibliography   173

Notes   179

Index   195

Acknowledgments

First and foremost, thanks are due to Antony Farrell of The Lilliput Press for his enthusiasm, generosity and editorial savvy throughout the process of translating manuscript into finished book. I'm also grateful to Tom Dunne for advice and camaraderie and to the late Robert Welch for contributions in print and in general. Thanks also to Frank Clune, Michael Kelleher, Hilary Lennon, Dónal Ó Conchubháir, Hallie O'Donovan, Patrick O'Shea, Kathleen Shields, Alan Titley and Helen Walsh. For various kinds of research assistance, I'm grateful to the National Library in Dublin, the Boole Library at University College Cork and the University of Mississippi Library, and for grant support to the College of Liberal Arts and Department of English at the University of Mississippi.

Ciaran Carson, excerpts from *The New Estate and Other Poems* (Oldcastle, Co. Meath: Gallery Press, 1976) and *The Midnight Court: A New Translation of 'Cúirt an Mheán Oíche'* (Oldcastle, Co. Meath: Gallery Press, 2005) reprinted with permission of the author and The Gallery Press.

Seamus Heaney, excerpts from *The Midnight Verdict* (Oldcastle, Co. Meath: Gallery Press, 1993) reprinted with permission of Faber and Faber Ltd.

Frank O'Connor, excerpts from *The Midnight Court: A Rhythmical Bacchanalia from the Irish of Bryan Merryman* (London, Dublin: Maurice Fridberg, 1945) reprinted with permission of Harriet O'Donovan Sheehy.

Patrick C. Power, excerpts from *Cúirt an Mheán-Oíche: The Midnight Court* (Cork: Mercier Press, 1971) reprinted with permission of Helen Walsh and Ann Farrell.

Every reasonable effort has been made to secure permission to quote specific passages. The author would be grateful to hear from any copyright holders not acknowledged here.

To a greater or lesser degree, every language offers its own reading of life. To move between languages, to translate, even within restrictions of totality, is to experience the almost bewildering bias of the human spirit towards freedom. If we were lodged inside a single 'language-skin' or amid very few languages, the inevitability of our organic subjection to death might well prove more suffocating than it is.

—George Steiner, *After Babel: Aspects of Language and Translation* (1975)

Introduction

B rian Merriman's *Cúirt an Mheán Oíche* (*The Midnight Court*) is the best-known and most admired narrative poem in the Irish language.[1] It's also the most frequently translated. Since the poem was written, presumably around 1780,[2] at least twelve complete translations into English verse have been made, beginning with a metrically ambitious version done early in the nineteenth century by a bilingual schoolmaster living in Merriman's part of east Clare, and running up to a self-consciously postmodern translation published in 2005 by the Belfast poet Ciaran Carson. In between, Merriman's poem has attracted as translators some of the most esteemed writers in modern and contemporary Ireland: Frank O'Connor, Thomas Kinsella and Seamus Heaney, as well as Carson.

Cúirt an Mheán Oíche has received its fair share of scholarly attention, much of it (perhaps too much) speculating as to sources and influences, but the translations of the poem have, with a few exceptions, been mentioned only in passing.[3] *The Midnight Court: Eleven Versions of Merriman* attempts to fill that gap by providing detailed critical, historical and comparative analyses of eleven poetic translations of Merriman's poem composed over the course of nearly two centuries.[4] Not only has no such study of the work of Merriman's translators been done, but also, although poetic translation from the Irish has been going on steadily since the beginning of the eighteenth century, and constitutes a significant body of poetry in its own right, no such study has been made of the translations of any poem, or group of poems, in Irish. By focusing on a number of translations of a single poem, *Eleven Versions of Merriman* sheds light on the process of poetic translation itself, offering a view from the translator's workshop. It investigates such questions as how Merriman's translators attempt – or don't attempt – to carry over into their translations *Cúirt an Mheán Oíche*'s principal themes, how their translations negotiate between those themes and issues contemporary to the translators, and how they address the problem of rendering into English verse Merriman's intricate prosody and exuberant diction and imagery, all of it deeply rooted in the Irish-language tradition. And because any translation is inevitably an interpretation, these translations constitute in effect a body of criticism of *Cúirt an Mheán Oíche* as revealing as some of the conventional critical commentary that the poem has elicited.

Translation is always a form of negotiation – between two languages, between two cultures, between two historical moments. The analyses in *Eleven Versions of Merriman* attempt to show how translation from the Irish has engaged and contributed to the relationship between the Irish- and English-language traditions in Ireland, and so between the country's two principal cultures. *Cúirt an Mheán Oíche* is particularly suited to this process, being both the final, culminating expression of the Irish-language tradition before the relative silence of the nineteenth century, and a poem very much aware of the tradition of English poetry; its use of tetrameter owes something to eighteenth-century English verse, especially that of Jonathan Swift, and its 'court of love' structure can be found, as W.B. Yeats argued, in Swift's 'Cadenus and Vanessa'.[5] Also, as the translations occur over a relatively long period, they reflect changes in social, political and aesthetic issues, many of which bear on the often fraught relationship between Ireland's two main traditions. Looking at that relationship, for example, from the viewpoint of colonialist analysis, translation from Irish into English is generally seen as an act of cultural and political appropriation, resting on the assumptions that the Irish-language tradition can – and perhaps should – be known adequately in English translations, and that the English language, because of a presumed superiority, has proved uniquely able to harbour all kinds of foreign texts in translation. But one inevitable implication of translating Irish-language texts into English is to concede the significance of the tradition to which they belong. As George Steiner has said, 'To class a source-text as worth translating is to dignify it immediately and to involve it in a dynamic of magnification,'[6] and Merriman's poem has been dignified and magnified again and again by its many translators; indeed, its status inside as well as outside the Irish-language canon has much to do with it having been translated so often.

As an act of negotiation, translation is inevitably bound up in the translator's historical and cultural moment. A detailed study of various translations of one poem over a relatively long period not only addresses changing cultural realities and issues, but also analyzes how those realities and issues are made manifest, and at what cost in terms of fidelity to the original. The existence of so many translations over nearly two centuries itself argues that there is something inherent in *Cúirt an Mheán Oíche* that encourages multiple and widely varying translations; the poem, which has enjoyed a considerable reputation almost from the day it was written,[7] is able, as Seamus Heaney has said, 'to subsume into itself the social and intellectual preoccupations of different periods'.[8] And Merriman's poem undoubtedly has presented to its translators as well as to its readers a wide range of issues readily capable of reaching beyond the specific culture of Merriman's day: the promotion of sexual and imaginative freedom, the questioning of various kinds of hierarchy, a profound but also often parodic view of the Irish-language tradition, a realistic representation of rural life in Ireland, and the creation of an alternate reality inside a dream-vision in which society's injustices can be reversed. The poem's remarkable formal and narrative qualities – its dramatically effective use of a courtroom setting, its ability to negotiate between a highly developed literary style and *caint na ndaoine* (the speech of the people), the vitality of its imagery and language and the wonder of its intricate, complex prosody – have also had much to do with its attraction for poetic translators.

The poem's generally subversive nature, appealing to so many of Merriman's translators, surfaces early in the narrative. Following a fairly conventional opening describing the narrator walking along a river and then falling asleep, Merriman introduces into the narrator's dream-vision a character who rebelliously recycles one of the staples of the *aisling* (vision) poem in the Irish-language tradition: the appearance of a *spéirbhean*, literally 'sky-woman', but also, since in Irish folklore the sky is often peopled with fairies and spirits, a fairy-woman. In the typical *aisling* poem, a form that flourished in the eighteenth century, the young and beautiful *spéirbhean* predicts the success of the Stuart cause and the demise of English rule in Ireland. Merriman's *spéirbhean*, a towering, glowering, and hideous-looking bailiff, is anything but fairy-like or lovely. And far from prophesying an end to

Ireland's sufferings, she complains of the numerous ills affecting Irish society –
a passage that many of Merriman's translators have found convenient as a forum
for their own social and political critiques. The bailiff then drags the narrator
to a court presided over by a local fairy queen named Aoibhill, and convened to
address the problem of the sexual inadequacies of Irish men and the consequent
sexual frustrations suffered by Irish women.

From this point on, the poem's structure is largely dramatic, organized
around three major speeches, two by a young woman and one by an old man.
The young woman opens her first speech by saying that men in Ireland either
marry only when they're too old to satisfy their wives sexually, or they marry old
women. She lists her own attractive qualities, and describes everything that she's
tried, including the use of various folk remedies, to secure a husband. Near the
end of her speech, she expresses, in plangent tones, a fear of growing old without
husband or children.

The temperature of the poem rises sharply when the second speaker appears
before the bar, an old man who, in responding to the young woman's complaints,
relies principally on personal insult, *ad hominem* argument, and vitriolic attacks
on women in general. The old man also provides an account of his marriage to
a young woman who gave birth to a child that was not his, and then, somewhat
surprisingly, makes a short speech in defence of bastards.

The young woman returns to the witness stand to describe in unblinking
detail the sexual frustrations that the old man's young wife experienced. She then
delivers a set piece questioning celibacy, making deliberately shocking comments
about the sexual attractions of the clergy – a passage that appealed especially
to translators intent on using Merriman's poem as a vehicle for critiquing the
Catholic Church's power in modern Ireland and especially its puritanical teachings. Aoibheall then delivers a judgment in favour of the young woman, and
calls for various kinds of punishment to be inflicted on men who avoid marriage,
including the narrator. But just as the young woman invites the other women
in the court to help her torture the narrator, he awakes from his dream-vision,
and the poem ends.

The various 'social and intellectual preoccupations', in Heaney's words, of
Merriman's many translators are generally grounded in a liberal, humanistic view
of *Cúirt an Mheán Oíche*.[9] This world-view manifests itself in many different
ways, from the modern philosophical humanism that finds its way into Arland
Ussher's translation of 1926, to the attacks on a puritanical Catholic Church

found in the translations of Frank O'Connor (1945) and David Marcus (1953), to an historically grounded argument for the rights of women informing the translation of Patrick C. Power in 1971, to the celebration of female empowerment and poetic freedom that governs Seamus Heaney's partial translation, published in 1993. The question of how far a translator should stray from the original to advance his or her own agenda is not easy to answer. The most accomplished translators of Merriman's poem manage to express issues close to them while staying within the orbit of the original – to negotiate effectively between the world of the translator and the very different world that Merriman inhabited. In less effective translations, contemporary issues tend to displace the themes and ideas in Merriman's poem. Michael C. O'Shea's version of 1897, awash in the discourse of nineteenth-century Irish nationalism, provides one example; Cosslett Ó Cuinn's version of 1982, in which wholly invented passages attacking the Catholic Church are inserted at will, provides another.

The poet-translator coming to *Cúirt an Mheán Oíche* faces problems other than questions of loyalty to Merriman's themes and ideas. One of these is how – or whether – to render into English verse the prosodic intricacies that root Merriman's poem in the Irish-language tradition, and provide so much of its dazzling panache. While Merriman's tetrameter couplets are conscious of English-language verse, particularly of Swift's favoured octosyllabic line, Merriman's prosody comes straight out of the Irish-language tradition; Merriman's couplet, constructed on an abbc/abbc pattern of internal and terminal assonance on the four stressed syllables of each line, is derived from the *caoineadh* measure in the Irish-language tradition.[10] Also, as Liam P. Ó Murchú has shown, the pattern is often extended over four lines, forming quatrains rather than couplets, and there are places in which couplets and quatrains are linked by assonance as well; indeed, according to Ó Murchú, passages constituting quatrains or quatrains joined to couplets account for more than two-thirds of the poem.[11] Direct imitation in English verse of Merriman's basic pattern of assonance over two lines is difficult enough, but extending it over four or six can be done, if at all, only with awkwardness or tedium, or both.

Merriman's translators have tried various strategies – with varying degrees of success – to represent some of the prosodic qualities of the original. Denis Woulfe's translation, the closest in time to *Cúirt an Mheán Oíche*, is probably the most ambitious in trying to imitate Merriman's assonantal patterns, but it often pays a price in unwieldy diction or phrasing. Some translators, like Ussher,

O'Connor and Marcus, translate Merriman into tetrameter couplets using terminal rhyme rather than terminal assonance, with internal assonance relied on only occasionally and with little or no adherence to the original's abbc/abbc pattern. Kinsella, acknowledging that much of Merriman's prosody is simply untranslatable, renders Merriman into English verse informed by what he calls 'ghosts of metrical procedures',[12] and avoids both terminal assonance and terminal rhyme. Patrick C. Power's translation, on the other hand, uses terminal assonance, and Seamus Heaney employs a variety of terminal links, most frequently half-rhyme, enabling him to vary the pitch of his couplets to reflect the variety and auditory nuances of Merriman's terminal assonance. Finally, Ciaran Carson says he based his translation of Merriman's poem on the rhythms of a jig tune, 'Paddy's Panacea,' that he'd heard from a singer in County Clare.[13]

Merriman's diction and imagery pose another set of problems. At times extravagant, copious, and parodic – 'the fine surprising excess of poetic genius in full flight', in Seamus Heaney's words[14] – the language of the poem is also, appropriately enough for a work made up primarily of dialogue, very closely tuned to *caint na ndaoine* (the speech of the people); indeed, part of the miracle of the poem is Merriman's ability to write in a language that is both literary and ordinary, poetic and earthy.[15] *Cúirt an Mheán Oíche* also contains numerous passages in which lists of related nouns or adjectives run on for several lines, a practice that doesn't translate readily into English verse.[16]

Of Merriman's translators, Kinsella and Carson, in different ways, are the most sensitive to Merriman's diction and imagery. Kinsella has said that in his work in translation from the Irish in general, 'all images and ideas occurring in the Irish are conveyed in translation and images or ideas not occurring in the Irish are not employed'.[17] Carson's translation, although less conservative than Kinsella's, seeks to imitate what Carson sees as the primary, underlying quality of Merriman's diction, something that reflects, in his view, the 'deep structure' of the Irish language itself: the multiple layers of meanings and implications, often quite different, embedded in a single word or phrase.[18] Not surprisingly, given the mastery of dialogue that characterizes his short stories, O'Connor is particularly adept at translating the *caint na ndaoine* of Merriman's Irish into 'the speech of the people' in English. At the other end of the spectrum, O'Shea's and Ó Cuinn's translations tend to rewrite Merriman's language into the discourse of their political and religious views, and Marcus' translation was specifically written, he says, in the English spoken in Ireland in the 1950s.

There are some puzzling lacunae in the history of the translations of *Cúirt an Mheán Oíche*. Setting aside O'Shea's version, published privately in Boston in 1897, no translations were produced in England or Ireland between Woulfe's early in the nineteenth century and Ussher's in 1926, despite the great flowering of translation from the Irish in the middle decades of the nineteenth century as well as during the Irish literary revival. The poem was widely available in manuscript form immediately after its composition and well into the nineteenth century, and it was first published, in Dublin, in 1850. Although Merriman's poem would probably have held little appeal for romantically inclined nine-teenth-century translators like J. J. Callanan and James Clarence Mangan, or for the leading lights of the literary revival, given their own generally romanti-cized sense of Gaelic culture, the lack of any translation, even a partial one, from writers deeply invested in the folk tradition – Douglas Hyde, Padraic Colum, James Stephens, for example – is difficult to fathom. Finally, although one of the poem's primary themes is the empowerment of women, even if the argu-ment is delivered in terms not always likely to win the unqualified enthusiasm of modern or contemporary feminists, no woman has undertaken to translate *Cúirt an Mheán Oíche*.[19]

Setting out to render a complex and difficult poem deeply rooted in the Irish-language tradition at the end of the eighteenth century into accomplished poetry written in English for readers often living in worlds at a great distance from Merriman's, the poetic translators examined here faced a task that was undeniably problematic. The same might be said for any effort to assess the work of those translators. As Jackson Mathews has argued: 'Just as every way of translating poetry is partial, every way of judging the results is partial. It is one of the most hazardous … of all literary judgments.'[20] But like translation itself, the critical analysis of translation gets done, even if the critic rarely finds firm ground to stand on. *Eleven Versions of Merriman* takes to heart George Steiner's view that, at best, what the critic writing about translation can provide are 'reasoned descriptions of processes',[21] and the 'reasoned descriptions of processes' that this book provides of eleven translations of *Cúirt an Mheán Oíche* do not pretend to be definitive, and they cannot, of course, be neutral. They are, however, moti-vated by some of the desires that drive translators themselves – in the words of Umberto Eco, 'loyalty, devotion, allegiance, piety'.[22]

The Midnight Court: Eleven Versions of Merriman

Denis Woulfe: Cultural Loss and Metrical Finesse

The destruction of Gaelic civilization in the seventeenth century was still very much alive in the country's cultural memory when Merriman was writing *Cúirt an Mheán Oíche*, and the social, political and cultural consequences of that catastrophe were all too evident in Merriman's rural Co. Clare. Denis Woulfe's translation of Merriman's poem, probably written early in the nineteenth century, is particularly sensitive to that memory and those consequences. A schoolmaster in east Clare and Co. Limerick in the early decades of the nineteenth century, Woulfe knew the ground of Merriman's poem – its landscape, its people, its culture, its language. (It's also possible that he knew Merriman himself.) As someone who wrote poetry in both Irish and English, Woulfe would have been acutely conscious of the question of audience, and his translation was no doubt intended, in part at least, to make an English-speaking readership aware of the lamentable realities of rural Irish life around the turn of the nineteenth century. Woulfe's bilingualism also may account for his ambitious efforts to reproduce in English verse the assonantal patterns that root *Cúirt an Mheán Oíche* in the Irish-language tradition, as well as carrying over into English the lively, colloquial diction of Merriman's dialogue. Indeed, Woulfe's translation, in edging so close to the formal qualities of the original, both embodies and argues for a symbiotic relationship between the English- and Irish-language traditions at this moment in Irish history.

Little is known about Woulfe (Donncha Ulf) himself. According to one account, he was from Sixmilebridge, Co. Clare, and was working as a school-master between 1817 and 1826.[1] In addition to writing poetry in English and Irish, he put together three collections of poetry from Clare and Limerick. Little is also known about the date of his translation of Merriman's poem. Although there are four manuscript copies extant, none, according to Liam P. Ó Murchú, who included Woulfe's translation in his 1982 edition of *Cúirt an Mheán Oíche*, is in Woulfe's hand. But it's likely that the translation was done sometime in the early decades of the nineteenth century. For one thing, it includes the phrase 'my love of Union' – a reference not in Merriman's poem – and the Union, if that is what Woulfe is referring to, did not come into existence as a political institution until 1801.[2] The translation was published twice in the nineteenth century, once in a Clare newspaper of unknown date, and in 1880, the supposed centenary of the composition of the original, in the weekly journal *The Irishman*.[3]

Perhaps because of Woulfe's shared geography and history with Merriman, his translation is often particularly sensitive to Merriman's representation of various social and political problems of the time, such as rural poverty, the powerlessness of the Irish peasant, a shrinking population, cultural and linguistic marginalization and corruption in the administration of justice – all arguably consequences of the collapse of Gaelic civilization in the seventeenth century and its replacement in the eighteenth by the Anglo-Irish Ascendancy. Despite the view of some critics that Merriman's poem is not particularly interested in political and social issues,[4] these kinds of questions surface often enough in *Cúirt an Mheán Oíche*, most notably perhaps in the bailiff's recounting, early in the poem, of the various ills afflicting Ireland at the end of the eighteenth century:

> Gan sealbh gan saoirse ag síolrach seanda,
> Ceannas i ndlí ná cíos ná ceannphoirt,
> Scriosadh an tír is níl 'na ndiaidh
> In ionad na luibheanna acht flíoch is fiaile,
> An uaisle b'fhearr chum fáin mar leaghadar
> Is uachtar lámh ag fáslaigh shaibhre
> Ag fealladh le fonn is foghail gan féachaint
> D'fheannadh na lobhar 's an lom dá léirscrios.
> Is dochrach dubhach, mar dhiú gach daoirse,

Doilbheadh dúr an dúcheilt dlíthe,
An fann gan feidhm ná faighidh ó éinne
Acht clampar doimhin is loighe chum léirscris,
Falsacht fear dlí agus fachnaoide airdnirt,
Cam is calaois, faillí is fábhar,
Scamall an dlí agus fíordhath fannchirt,
Dalladh le bríb, le fís, le falsacht.[5]

(Without property, without freedom for an ancient race,
Sovereignty in law or rent or rules,
The land destroyed and nothing after it
In place of the herbs but chickweed and weeds,
The best nobility wandering as they faded away to nothing
And rich upstarts have the upper hand
Deceiving with inclination and pillaging without regard
Skinning the leper and the naked in their devastation.
It's distressing and sorrowful, like the worst of every oppression,
A hard affliction [is] the dark denial of the law,
The weak without influence who get nothing from anyone
But great deceit and submitting to destruction,
Falseness from the man of law and derision from high power,
Crookedness and fraud, neglect and favouritism,
The law [is] a darkness with nothing of [even] weak justice,
Blinding with bribe, with fees, with falseness.)[6]

Woulfe's translation of this telling passage is deeply grounded in the distressing political and social realities of Ireland at the turn of the nineteenth century:

No land or store the old possessing,
No friends in court their wrongs redressing,
In lieu of herbs and fragrant seed
There grew wild rape and chicken weed.
The ancient nobles fast decaying,
And sordid clans in grandeur swaying,
Foul deceit and fell oppression,
Feuds create and rank aggression.
Alas too direful to detail

The woeful ills that now prevail,
A dreary tribe by tyrants goaded
With woes and wiles and anguish loaded,
The lawyers frown the proud's reflection,
Frauds through power and foul rejection,
The law obscured the poor oft cheated,
By fees and bribes our rights defeated.[7]

The contrast drawn between the 'ancient nobles' and the 'sordid clans' that replaced them, as well as the reference to the transformation of the Irish nobility into a 'dreary tribe', locate the source of Ireland's political and social malaise at the time Woulfe was writing in what happened to Ireland's Gaelic civilization during the seventeenth century.

A few lines later, the bailiff contrasts Aoibheall's court to the corrupt English courts the people had to become used to:

Geallimse anois nách clis ná comhachta,
Caradas *Miss* ná *Pimp* ná comhalta
Shiúlfas tríd an dlí seo 'o ghnáth
Sa gcúirt 'na suífe an síolrach neámhdha. (127–30)

(I promise now that neither tricks nor influence,
The friendship of *Miss* nor *Pimp* nor companions
Will march through this law as usual
In their court in which the heavenly tribe will be seated.)

Woulfe translates:

No pander pimp or concubine
The law should stem or undermine
Through party power or friendly aid
Where Royalty will be displayed. (127–30)

The tetrameter couplet compresses the argument effectively, in the best tradition of eighteenth-century satirical verse in English, and the final reference to 'Royalty', which is Woulfe's invention, reminds the reader of the lost Gaelic aristocracy and its system of justice – the 'Royalty' of the old Gaelic leadership – and points as well to the forces of colonization under an English monarch that brought down that leadership.

Woulfe's translation also goes to some lengths to bring to the attention of his English readers the specific details of rural poverty in the Ireland of the late eighteenth and early nineteenth centuries. When, for example, the young woman makes her final appeal to Aoibheall for help, at the end of her second speech, she laments how many unmarried young women there are in Ireland, and how many more there will be if nothing is done to light a fire under Ireland's men. In translating this passage, Woulfe departs from the literal meaning of Merriman's text to delineate the sufferings of Irish children because of poverty. In the original, the young woman says:

Meáigh an t'intinn díth na mbéithe
Is práinn na mílte brídeach aonta
Is toicibh mar táid ar bhráid a chéile
Ag borradh is ag fás mar ál na ngéanna.
An t-ál is lú atá ag siúl na sráide,
Garlaigh dhubha tá giúnnach gránna,
An aga dá laghad má gheibhid a ndóthain
Glasra, meidhg is bleaghdair, borrfaid
D'urchar nimhe le haois gan éifeacht. (833–41)

(Weigh in your mind the deprivation of women
And the need of the thousands of single maidens
And falling as they are on the necks of each other
Increasing and growing like a brood of geese.
The smallest progeny who are walking the street,
Dark urchins who are close-cropped, ugly,
In a small period of time, if they get their sufficiency
Of green stuff, whey and curdled milk, will grow
Like a bolt from the blue in an inconsiderable space of time.)

Woulfe's translation shifts the emphasis; the young woman's argument about the need to do something about the plight of women without husbands or prospects of marriage is translated into a graphic depiction of poverty, overcrowding, and illness, and also into a plea to rescue the poor from hunger and the many ills that attend it:

With wisdom weigh our train declining
And countless maids each day repining

How youngsters heaped and crowded lie
Like goslins green they multiply.
The smallest breed that move around
Of ghastly hue and looks unsound
If mainly fed would spread and grow
And soon emerge from wretched woe. (735–42)

Woulfe is the only translator of Merriman's poem to have made a concerted effort to reproduce in English verse the original's abbc/abbc pattern of terminal and internal assonance. The result is inevitably uneven and imperfect, if the effort is admirable. Woulfe usually ignores the assonantal link between the first stressed syllables in each pair of lines in Merriman's text, and replaces terminal assonance with terminal rhyme. Also, the regular rhythm of Woulfe's relatively strict tetrameter lines, as opposed to that of the highly variable four-stress line used by Merriman, becomes monotonous over the long haul. More important, the inherent difficulties in constructing in English assonantal links within every line and between every two or every four lines leads to awkward diction and phrasing. Still, at their best, Woulfe's attempts to mirror the metrical intricacies of *Cúirt an Mheán Oíche* do manage to get admirably close to the distinctive music of Merriman's Irish. For example, when the old man, in replying to the young woman's first speech, turns characteristically to a class-based and *ad hominem* argument, saying that the young woman grew up in extreme poverty, Merriman has:

I gcomhar bhotháin gan áit chum suí ann,
Sú sileáin is fáscadh aníos ann,
Fiaile ag teacht go fras gan choimse
Is rian na gcearc air trasna scríofa. (409–12)

(In a communal shack without a place in it for sitting,
Soot shedding and pressing down on it,
Weeds flourishing without moderation
And the track of the hens written across it.)

Although Woulfe's translation overlooks the striking image of 'Is rian na gcearc air trasna scríofa', it's sensitive enough to the internal assonantal patterns that lie at the heart of Merriman's prosody:

Your cabin sluiced from soot and rain
And springing fluids that oozed amain

Its weed-grown roof so rudely shaped
By hens at roost all scooped and scraped. (387–90)

As happens when Woulfe is translating well, his mirroring of Merriman's asso-nantal music here is functional as well as imitative, reinforcing aurally, espe-cially in the links between 'sluiced' and 'soot' and 'fluids' and 'oozed', the images of poverty set forth by the old man.

Although Woulfe is always writing with sensitivity to Merriman's Irish-language prosody, his translation also at times reminds his reader that Merriman's poem is itself notably conscious of the English-language tradition, especially of eighteenth-century verse satire. As seen earlier, the compression generated by Woulfe's tetrameter couplet often furthers his own satiric inten-tions, but Woulfe's mastery of that form is at times compounded by an ability to hold the English- and Irish-language traditions in a symbiotic relationship within his translation. When, for example, Merriman has the old man say of a young woman of his acquaintance, 'Ise bheith seang nuair theann gach éinne í / Is druidim le clann nuair shantaigh féin é' (465–6) ('She being slender when everyone squeezed her / And moving with a child when she strongly desired it'), Woulfe translates: 'Her womb so light when primed by all / To swell so high at Hymen's call' (443–4). It's a couplet worthy of Pope or Dryden, but it also carries within it the richness of Merriman's prosody, particularly in the assonantal link between 'light' and the perfectly chosen 'primed', which echoes Merriman's equally inspired link between 'seang' and 'theann', where 'seang' brings together a number of relevant additional meanings, such as 'virginal', 'subtle' and 'cunning', and 'theann' also can mean 'stiffened' and 'assailed'.

Daniel Corkery has argued that the language of Merriman's poem contains not a trace of romanticism: 'no luxuriance in it, nothing flowing, sinuous, gentle or efflorescent. Its accent is, rather, boorish, abrupt, snappy; it is taut and well-articulated.'[8] Although Woulfe occasionally lapses into numbing conventional poetic diction, especially in his rendering of the poem's opening description of nature, peppered with phrases such as 'dewy meads' (1), 'charming sight' (5), 'woodland gay' (12), 'finny tribe' (15), and 'bounding doe' (20),[9] his diction is on the whole well-tuned to the 'snappy' accent of Merriman's speakers. When, for example, the young woman tells the court how a friend of hers managed to get a husband by a peculiar kind of ritualistic fasting, Merriman has:

Is d'inis sí dhomhsa, ar ndóigh tré rún,
Um Inid is í pósta ó bhord na Samhan

Nár ibh is nár ól an fóntach fionn
Acht cuile na móna dóite ar lionn. (349–52)

(And she told me, of course in secret,
Around Shrovetide, and she married since the verge of Hallowe'en
That there was neither eating nor drinking for the fair person
But *cuile na móna* burned in ale.)

Woulfe translates:

But she to me in secret told
That Planksty fair her mate so bold
Was booked at once though strong and hale
By boggy roots infused in ale. (349–52)

Although it's not precisely clear what *cuile na móna* is, possibly some kind of herb, Woulfe's 'boggy roots infused in ale' is certainly an inspired bit of poetic translation,[10] and 'booked at once' for Merriman's 'pósta' is perfectly in keeping with the colloquial diction of *Cúirt an Mheán Oíche*. Later, the old man, in responding to the young woman's complaint about the sexual failings of Irish men, reveals details of the young woman's supposed sexual exploits:

Acht bheirim don phláigh í lá mar chínn í
Leagaithe láimh le Gáras sínte,
Caite ar an ród gan orlach fúithi
Ag gramaisc na móna ar bhóithre Dhúire. (459–62)

(But a plague on her the day that I saw her
Laid down close by Gáras, stretched,
Thrown on the road without an inch of anything under her
By the turf-gang on the Doora road.)

Woulfe translates:

But plague be on her one day I viewed
By Garus Mills the game renewed
To Doora road she next retreated
Where ass boys roared and rusticated. (437–40)

'The game renewed' is regrettable, but 'ass boys' for 'gramaisc na móna', although not literally accurate, is certainly in character – and certainly unromantic – and

'rusticated', suggesting both 'rustic' and 'rutted', and helped along by the consonance with 'roared', is a nicely resonating term for what those 'ass boys' were
getting up to on the Doora road.

In those many passages in which Merriman's characters indulge in lengthy
lists of descriptions and insults, Woulfe is usually quite up to the mark in imitating
Merriman's often bombastic diction. When the young woman, in her first speech,
describes the old women that young men tend to marry, Merriman has:

> Ní suairle caile ná sreangaire mná me
> Acht stuaire cailce tá taitneamhach breá deas.
> Ní sraoill na sluid na luid gan fáscadh
> Ná smíste duirc gan sult gan sásamh,
> Lóiste lofa ná toice gan éifeacht
> Acht óigbhean scofa comh tofa is is féidir. (241–6)

> (I am not a slattern of a girl or an ungainly woman
> But a handsome, chalk-white woman who is pleasing, fine, nice.
> Not a slattern nor a bad woman nor a slut without tidiness
> Nor a boorish female without enjoyment, without satisfaction,
> A rotten sluggard nor a hussy without sense
> But an excellent young woman as choice as is possible.)

Woulfe translates:

> Count me not a cranky stake
> A drowsy gad or rank old rake
> A haughty hulk or humdrum hateful
> Brawling butt or slut deceitful
> Or sluggish ape devoid of glee
> But loveliest maid that eyes could see. (239–44)

The slightly off-beat terms here – 'cranky stake', 'drowsy gad', 'rank old rake',
'haughty hulk' – depart considerably from the literal meaning of the original,
but they are true to Merriman's rich and playful style in these kinds of passages.

For all his loyalty to the themes and techniques of *Cúirt an Mheán Oíche*,
Woulfe shies away from the original in one important area, that of sexuality,
especially female sexual desire. It's impossible to know why Woulfe blunted or
avoided altogether passages with specifically sexual content, but it may have

had to do less with personal squeamishness than with a belief that his English-speaking audience would have been more distressed by Merriman's sexual candour than were Merriman's Irish-speaking readers.

Woulfe's unwillingness to allow his English reader to see the full extent of that candour often takes the form of translating specific sexual images in the original into abstractions, generalizations or euphemisms. When Merriman has the young woman, early in her testimony, describe her sexual frustration – '… gan suaimhneas sínte / Ar leabain leamh fhuar dár suaitheadh ag smaointe' (189–90) ('… without peace stretched / On an impotent cold bed disturbed by thoughts'), Woulfe translates: '… tossing turning all alone / All social pleasures from me flown' (189–90). Later in the same speech, when the young woman says that men wait to marry until they're too old, 'An t-am nár mhéin le éinne góil leo, / An t-am nárbh fhiú bheith fúthu sínte' (196–7) ('The time no one would desire to conceive with them, / The time it would not be worth it to be stretched under them'), Woulfe translates: 'When no soft maid would them admire / When no fond pleasure would proceed' (196–7).

Woulfe seems particularly eager to sidestep sexual innuendo, one of the hallmarks of Merriman's writing. When the young woman describes the kind of young man she'd like to marry, Merriman has her say, 'Nó buachaill basta-lach beachanta bróigdheas, / Cruacheart ceannasach ceapaithe córach –' (215–16) ('Or a boy showy, vigorous, with a nicely shaped boot, / Rightly hardy, commanding, determined, shapely – '). Woulfe translates these suggestive images into the vague and the harmless: 'A dashing sightly scion allured / Of handsome size and mind matured' (215–16). And near the end of the poem, when Aoibheall outlines the sexual shortcomings of old men in no uncertain terms – 'An gabhal gan gotha ná an gola gan geall suilt, / Toll gan toradh ná an tormach falsa' (893–4) ('The groin without a spear or the penal orifice without promise of pleasure, / The hole without issue or the false swelling') – Woulfe passes. He leaves out as well a passage of nearly sixty lines in which the young woman, in questioning the church's policy of celibacy, describes in detail the sexual attractions of the clergy. It is by far the largest lacuna in Woulfe's translation of *Cúirt an Mheán Oíche*, which, at 936 lines, is ninety lines shorter than the standard version of the original.

On the whole, however, Woulfe's translation sails well within the orbit, formally and substantively, of *Cúirt an Mheán Oíche*, and in so doing it provided a useful model for translators of Merriman who came after him. The translation also serves as a reminder of how close the Irish- and English-language traditions were in the decades before the Great Famine of the 1840s, and before the rise of a militant, romantic nationalism that tended to see Ireland's two principal traditions as existing in a relationship more adversarial than complementary.

Michael C. O'Shea:
Nationalism Unleashed

ichael C. O'Shea's translation of *Cúirt an Mheán Oíche* was published in Boston in 1897 in a private run of two hundred copies. In his introduction, O'Shea says the translation was done 'many years ago',[1] and so, although there's evidence that it couldn't have been done before 1850,[2] it may have been completed not too many decades after Denis Woulfe's version. The two translations are, however, poles apart. O'Shea, an ardent nationalist in the romantic mode – and living in America most of his adult life – translates Merriman's poem into a work notably shaped by the language and concerns of nineteenth-century nationalism, whereas Woulfe's translation is generally faithful to Merriman's engagement with the political, cultural and social realities of Irish rural life in the late eighteenth century. Also, O'Shea's translation is written in a style strongly influenced by mid-nineteenth-century writing in English – in Ireland, the work of writers like Gerald Griffin (anachronistically mentioned in O'Shea's translation), or Aubrey de Vere, as well as the patriotic verse of Thomas Davis and *The Nation* poets – and paying little or no attention to the distinctively Irish-language qualities of Merriman's poem, to which Woulfe's version attends closely. Nevertheless, for all its failings as a work of poetic translation, and precisely because of its many deviations from Merriman's text and world, O'Shea's version of *Cúirt an Mheán Oíche* is of interest as an illustration of how – and at what cost – a poetic translation can transform a text belonging to one historical and literary world into one set in a very different one.

O'Shea was considerably farther removed from Merriman's world, in place as well as time, than was Woulfe. There's some evidence that he was born in Co. Kerry,[3] but he was living in the USA when he completed his translation of Merriman's poem.[4] He was also extremely active in Irish-American nationalist circles. Between May 1889 and July 1890, O'Shea edited *The Irish Echo*, published in Boston by the Philo-Celtic Society, and, as stated in the prospectus published in the first issue, dedicated to 'the vindication of the character of the Irish race from the foul slanders of centuries by English writers'.[5] When O'Shea took over as editor, he promised to continue the magazine's efforts 'towards the revival, dissemination, elucidation and vindication, of the long proscribed, maligned, and vilified language of our learned and valorous ancestry'.[6] O'Shea also served as president of the Philo-Celtic Society, which was organized in 1873 to advance the cause of the Irish language. He contributed frequently to *The Irish Echo*, publishing poems in English, poems in Irish accompanied by his own verse translations, and numerous essays, often quite detailed, on the Irish language. Most of O'Shea's poetry in *The Irish Echo* is heavily marked by the clichés of romantic-nationalist verse,[7] and the views expressed in his many essays are fiercely anti-English.

O'Shea imports these nationalist sentiments, sometimes wholesale, into his translation of *Cúirt an Mheán Oíche*. They appear even in his introduction, in which he remarkably describes Merriman's narrator as someone who 'enters dreamland in the role of an ardent patriot, deploring the wrongs and woes of his country'.[8] When he comes to the passage early in the poem in which the bailiff gives an account of the ills plaguing the country – a passage that Woulfe translates with considerable sensitivity to Merriman's representation of rural Irish life at the end of the eighteenth century – O'Shea injects into the speech prefabricated phrases from nineteenth-century nationalist discourse: 'Erin groans beneath a load of wrong' (p. 5), 'greedy robbers from a foreign coast' (p. 5), 'how cruel war and meaner guile / Have ruined – crushed – our fair and fertile Isle' (p. 5).[9] And later, when, the young woman is praising Aoibheall at the beginning of her first monologue – 'A shaídhbhrios saoghalta a ngéibheann daoirse, / A cheanasach, bhuadhach, o shluaightibh aoibhnis, / Dob' easnamh mór tu d-Tuamhain 'sa d-Tír Loirc[10] ('Treasure long lived in distress and in bondage, / Powerful, victorious from hosts of pleasure, / You were greatly wanted in Thomond and in

Tír Loirc') – O'Shea translates:"Twere sad wert thou like others to us lost / Who would our woes redress, but that the foe / By war and wile in blood has laid them low' (p. 9). Even the old man's set speech defending bastards, which in the original contains not a trace of politics, nationalist or otherwise, comes in for a strong gust of patriotic rhetoric in O'Shea's hands. In the original, the old man says:

Cá bh-fuil an gádh le gáir ná bainse,
Cárta biotaille's pádh lucht seínnte,
Sumaig air bórd go fóiseach, taídhbhseach,
Glugar's gleó'co,'s ól dá shaígheada.
O d'aibig an t-óghar-so bhronn mac Dé dúinn,
'S gan sagart air domhan dár d-tabhairt dá chéile,
Is leathan-mhar, láidir, lán-mhar, léadmhar,
Fairsing le fághail an t-álmhach saor so. (p. 19)

(Where is the need for the commotion of the wedding,
Quarts of spirits and pay of the musicians,
Plump youngsters at table, self-indulgent, vain,
Gurgling and noise from them and drink voraciously swallowed,
Since this embryo that the Son of God bestowed on us ripened
Without a priest in the world giving them [the parents] to each other,
Broad, strong, fully active, bold,
Generous is this noble progeny to be found.)

O'Shea translates:

When nature prompts and perfect parts incite,
No cleric law should baulk the rule of right.
Were freedom given, cramping shackles rent,
And gushing fervor close no longer pent –
A copious offspring, strong and fair and free,
Would throng the land, and banish o'er the sea
Oppression's minions, glorious freedom's smile
Would bless each one upon our seagirt isle. (p. 25)

This kind of misrepresentation has serious consequences, at times erasing values and attitudes that are central to Merriman's poem. Later in the old man's argument on behalf of bastards, a critique of class distinctions is made:

Leis sin ná h-iarsadh a Ríoguin réaltach,
Milleadh na d-triath le riaghail gan éifeacht,
Sgaoil a chodla gan cochall, gan cuíbhreach,
Síol an bhoduig 'san mhogul-fhuil mhuíghteach,
Sgaoil fá chéile do réir nádúra,
An síolrach séimh 'san braon labúrthadh,
Fógair féilteach tré gach tíortha,
D'óg, 's d'aosda, saor-thoil síolraig,
Cuirfig an dlígh-so gaois a ngaodhluibh,
'S tiocfaig an brígh mar bhí iona laochaibh,
Ceapadh sé cóm, 's drom, 's dóirne,
D'fhearaibh an domhain mar Gholl mac Móirne. (p. 20)

(With that, do not ask, starry Queen,
The destruction of the nobles by means of a rule without sense,
Make free to sleep without a cloak, without fetters,
The seed of the churl and of the boastful noble blood,
Make free together according to nature
The seed of authority and the base drop,
Declare regularly through every country,
For the young and for the mature freewill to propagate,
This law will put wisdom in the Gaels,
And strength will come as it was in their warriors,
It will compose waist and back and fist,
Into men of the world like Goll Mac Móirne.)

Woulfe's version of this passage is sensitive to the appeal for basic human equality
that informs it:

Therefore Oh Queen this law repeal
Destruction to our common weal
And let the dusty dunghill race
With gentlefolks unite apace,
Let rich and poor without rejection
Join henceforth in stout connection
And let your mandate truly paint
That young and old with no restraint.

For marriage laws if abrogated
Our tribes would be invigorated
Our Irish heroes soon would spread
Like warlike Goll who knew no dread.[11]

This egalitarian plea, part of the larger fabric of Merriman's poem, disappears in O'Shea's version, displaced by nationalist cliché and fantasy:

Then queen, refulgent as the star sent ray,
Annul this blighting rite and rend away
All galling shackles and let love be free,
Give men and maidens nature's liberty,
Soon o'er the land will manly youth abound,
The peers of ancient heroes will be found
In thews and sinews, stature, make and might,
The battle of their native land to fight.
Mac Moirna's son and Oscar of the lance,
From Ghaodhal's descendants will again advance
Against the foe, and gloriously renew
Those brighter days our hero fathers knew. (p. 26)

Judging from his political writings, O'Shea loathed all things English, and believed that the Irish language was threatened with a calculated annihilation at the hands of the English; in an address given in 1887, and reprinted in *The Irish Echo*, O'Shea said: 'It has been the settled policy of the Saxon to extinguish the language and the literature of the Gael, thereby obliterating his history and destroying his distinctive race and nationality.'[12] And yet O'Shea's translation of *Cúirt an Mheán Oíche* is unabashedly indebted to English poetics. It converts Merriman's flexible four-stress line, governed by patterns of internal and terminal assonance deeply grounded in the Irish-language tradition, into conventional heroic couplets that pay no attention to the distinctively Irish qualities of Merriman's prosody; also, the extra foot in each of O'Shea's lines produces a rhythm that is badly out of tune with Merriman's.

In addition, O'Shea frequently elaborates on the original – his translation runs to 1292 lines, or 223 lines more than are in the version of the original that he was translating from – and the resulting leisurely pace is more characteristic of Victorian poetry in English than of the compressed, energetic language and imagery of Merriman's writing. Comparison with Woulfe's relatively taut translation reveals how much of the poetic energy in Merriman's poem is drained out of O'Shea's version. When Merriman's young woman, in her first speech, describes how she keeps an eye out for men while attending various social occasions, she says, 'Aonach, margadh, 's Aifrionn Dómhnaig, / Ag éiliomh breathnaighthe, ag amharc, 'sa togha fir' (p. 10) ('[At] fair, market, and Sunday Mass, / Courting observation, looking at every choice man'). Woulfe translates: 'At market fair and Sabbath meeting / Courting gazing glancing greeting' (277–8). O'Shea extends the passage to four limp and awkward lines:

> Now, fair and market, race and raffle, ball,
> Bonfire and goal game, church and dancing hall
> I have attended, gazing at the men,
> Culling in mind, the kind I fain would win. (p. 12)

O'Shea's version of Merriman's narrator, who in fact doesn't say much once he arrives at Aoibheall's court, at times bears the marks of an intrusive and garrulous Victorian narrator. When the old man rises to respond to the young woman's attacks on the sexual failings of men, Merriman's narrator says, 'Budh dheireóil an radharc go deímhin do'n chúirt é, / Air bórd na taídhbhse am éisteacht dúbhairt sé') (p. 13) ('Wretched was the sight indeed for the court, / At the [witness] table in his vanity in my hearing he said'); O'Shea converts this couplet into six lines in which the narrator comments on the subject of the old man's speech before he gives it:

> Like a charred fire brand on the dais this grim
> Old fellow looked, he spoke with fearful vim;
> The lengthy speech he in my hearing made
> Was but a scorching, blighting vile tirade
> Against the women, all who seemed to him
> The plague of man and nature's weakest whim. (p. 16)

Despite all these shortcomings, O'Shea's translation is not entirely without poetic merit; there are a few occasions, for example, in which O'Shea's tendency to elaborate on Merriman's text produces some effective verse. For example, in her second speech, the young woman, arguing against celibacy, describes the prosperity and sexual attractiveness of the clergy in these terms:

Arradh 'gus ór chum óil's aoibhnis,
Clúmh chum luíghe, 'gus saíll chum bídhe 'ca,
Plús, 's meídhir, 's mílseacht fíonta,
Is gnáthach cumasach iomadach óg iad,
'S tá fhios aguinne gur fuil agus feoil iad. (p. 25)

(Goods and gold for drink and delight,
They have feathers for lying on, and they have meat for food,
Flour, and mirth, and the sweetness of wines,
Generally vigorous, proud, young they are,
And we know that they are blood and flesh.)

O'Shea's translation overlooks some of those sumptuous details, and goes off on its own direction; but its closing image is pointed and amusing enough:

... the very best
Of meats and wines they have at their behest;
Good cheer and mirth and leisure is their lot,
And some know well that cleric blood is hot, –
That vigor quickens through the manly frame
Begetting fire unlike the vestal flame. (pp. 35–6)

And O'Shea's version of one of the young woman's tirades against the old man expands two lines in Merriman – 'Acht seanduine seannda, crannda, créimtheach, / Feamarie feannta, 's feamm gan féile' (p. 24) ('But an aged, withered, decayed old person / An infirm, weak-loined person and a stalk without pleasure') – into a run of quite forceful and Merriman-like images:

But thou! a weak and trembling shaky wight,
A cold companion through a winter's night,
A faded, sapless, crumpled autumn leaf,
A skinny shade whose lease of life is brief,
An aged fungus near its final day,
Whose spent out strength and hastening decay –
No vital gush, no juices can produce,
But rancid rot to nought on earth of use. (p. 35)

Such moments are, however, rare, and O'Shea's version of Merriman's poem is generally far too insensitive to the world and style of *Cúirt an Mheán Oíche* to constitute an effective poetic translation. Later translators of Merriman's poem like Frank O'Connor and Seamus Heaney will be able to do what O'Shea plainly could not do – create a poetic translation that manages to express social and cultural realities substantially different to Merriman's without betraying the integrity of the original.

Arland Ussher: On Behalf of the Ascendancy and Liberal Humanism

rland Ussher's translation of *Cúirt an Mheán Oíche* appeared in 1926, just three years after the establishment of the Irish Free State, a moment in which, in the view of many cultural and political leaders, there was a particular urgency about establishing a distinctively Irish identity. The effort to construct that identity around Gaelicism and Catholicism effectively marginalized the Anglo-Irish Ascendancy, the class to which Ussher belonged, and Ussher's translation can be seen as an effort not just to forge a link between the English- and Irish-language traditions, but also to insist that the Anglo-Irish still had a role to play in the culture of post-independence Ireland. Also, Ussher's decision to translate into English one of the centrepieces of the Irish-language canon – Merriman's poem had been published six times between 1850 and 1912 – implicitly called into question attempts being made at the time to cordon off the Irish-language tradition from Irish writing in English, and, in extreme instances, for example the views of Daniel Corkery, whose study *The Hidden Ireland* was published just two years before Ussher's translation of Merriman's poem, to claim that only literature written in the native language could be considered genuinely Irish. Finally, Ussher was a serious student of philosophy – he published a collection of philosophical essays in 1948[1] – and his translation brings to bear on Merriman's poem a point of view grounded in liberal humanism and scepticism.

Ussher was born in 1899 into a well-established Ascendancy family, and grew up on his grandfather's estate of Cappagh in western Co. Waterford. Irish was still spoken in the region then, and Ussher picked up the language quite quickly, 'to the uncomprehending amazement of my "County neighbours",' he once said.[2] He attended Trinity College Dublin and St John's College Cambridge, but abandoned the life of a university student to give himself wholly to writing, especially philosophical writing. Since leaving university, he wrote in his journal, 'I have lived on a small income in Waterford and Dublin – with intervals abroad – trying to hammer out a new esthetic philosophy.'[3]

Given these interests, it's not clear what motivated Ussher to translate, quite early in his career, *Cúirt an Mheán Oíche*. He did say once that, when a young man, he 'gave my first love to the Gaelic among the languages'[4], and in the 1940s he published two volumes of Waterford folklore in 'the traditional speech of my neighbourhood'.[5] Also, there was a tradition in Ussher's family of seeing Irish-language texts into print; in 1571 his ancestor John Ussher published the first book to be printed in Irish, a translation of the Protestant Catechism, and John's son William was responsible for the first Irish-language version of the New Testament.[6] Finally, Merriman's poem could be said to accord generally with Ussher's characterization of Irish literature as a kind of writing that 'wavers continually between fantasy and farcicality; its most successful *genre* – from the Cuchulainn epic to *Ulysses* – is a sort of surrealistic extravaganza which has no precise parallel elsewhere'.[7]

But translating Merriman no doubt had more than a little to do with how Ussher saw his own position as an Anglo-Irish Protestant deeply interested in the Irish-language tradition, a position that resisted narrow definitions of Irish identity.[8] Indeed, Ussher has been regarded as an important figure in Irish cultural politics in modern Ireland because of his ability, as evidenced primarily in two books of essays, *The Face and Mind of Ireland* (1949) and *Three Great Irishmen* (1952), to see at least two sides of the question of what it means to be Irish.[9] In *The Face and Mind of Ireland*, Ussher describes the various ambiguities surrounding his background and interests:

> I have never been able to associate myself completely with any Irish or Anglo-Irish group. Though an Irishman by birth and ... by choice also, I have a good

quarter of English blood; though not a Roman- or even an Anglo-Catholic, I have always taken a deep interest in Catholic philosophy and the Catholic life; though a student of Gaelic, I am no revivalist; and though an offspring of the form 'Ascendancy', I never felt any sentimental ties to that class when it was in the ascendant.[10]

Ussher's assertion of his claim on the Irish-language tradition is evident in his choice of W.B. Yeats to write the preface to his translation of Merriman's poem. By the 1920s, Yeats was increasingly identifying himself with the Protestant Ascendancy and attacking middle-class Irish Catholics newly empowered in the Free State as being overly materialistic and out of tune with the spirit of the nation. In his introduction to Ussher's translation, Yeats argues that *Cúirt an Mheán Oíche* is grounded less in Irish folklore or in such elements of the Irish-language tradition as the *aisling* poem or poems about informal courts of poets, or even in the great wealth of Irish-language satirical poetry, as it is in Jonathan Swift's 'Cadenus and Vanessa'. Even if Ussher might have been a bit uneasy with some of the attitudes that Yeats strikes in the preface – at one point he says, astonishingly, given the widespread following of Merriman's poem almost since the day it was written, that Ussher's translation would introduce Merriman 'to the Irish reading public'[11] – the link that Yeats argues for between Swift and Merriman provided support for Ussher's view that an Anglo-Irishman like himself had every right to translate *Cúirt an Mheán Oíche* into an English-language poem. And Ussher, if not Yeats, might well have been counting on his readers to remember that Swift himself produced one of the first important poetic translations from the Irish, 'The Description of an Irish Feast', based on Aodh Mac Gabhráin's 'Pléaráca na Ruarcach', and that he did so without nearly as much Irish – if indeed he had any at all – as Ussher himself had.

Ussher once described his parents as 'liberal intellectuals', and said that he had 'inherited ... their sense of responsibility, without their optimism'.[12] Ussher was certainly sceptical of social and political conservatism in general, and he saw the Irish society of his day as 'deeply and warily conservative'.[13] Not surprisingly, his generally liberal social values find their way into his translation of *Cúirt an Mheán Oíche*.[14] Early in the poem, for example, when the bailiff praises Aoibheall's court in part by contrasting it to the practices of courts in the real world, Merriman has her say:

Ní cúirt gan acht gan reacht gan riaghail,
Ná cúirt na gcreach mar chleacht tu riamh
An chúirt seo ghluais ó shluaighte séimhe –
Cúirt na dtruagh na mbuadh is na mbéithe.[15]

(Not a court without decree, without law, without rule,
Or a court of the plunderers as you are ever accustomed to
This court that sprang from gentle crowds –
A court of mercy, of virtue, and of women.)

Ussher translates:

No court of robbers and spoilers strong
To maintain the bane of fraud and wrong,
But the court of the poor and lowly-born,
The court of women and folk forlorn.[16]

While maintaining the original's implication that mercy and virtue are generally the province of women, Ussher replaces Merriman's 'shluaighte séimhe', a reference to the women in Aoibheall's court, with 'the court of the poor and lowly-born', and in the last line, links the court of women with 'folk forlorn', for which there is no corresponding phrase in the original. And when the young woman, at the beginning of her opening speech to the court, first addresses Aoibheall, Ussher has her admire the queen not as someone, as she's represented in the original to be, 'shaoghalta i ngéibhinn daoirse' (170) ('long-lived in distress and bondage'), but rather as someone who would 'pity the poor and relieve their plight / And save the brave and retrieve the right' (p. 22).

Ussher also reads *Cúirt an Mheán Oíche* as a poem that strongly advocates the rights of women. From this point of view, the dream-vision form allows Merriman to create a world in which the marginalized position of women in Irish society in the late eighteenth century is reversed; in the narrator's dream, women are empowered to speak freely, and, through Aoibheall's position as judge and jury, to make binding decisions that affect men. The need for society to empower women is generally in keeping with Ussher's liberal values, but the argument is also tied specifically to the politics of Ussher's age, as he was working on his translation at a time when women's rights were a particularly urgent political issue; women's suffrage took effect in Great Britain, for women over thirty, in 1918, just eight years before Ussher's translation was published, and in Ireland with the establishment of the Free State in 1923.

These politics are clearly evident in certain moments in Ussher's translation of *Cúirt an Mheán Oíche*, as, for example, when Aoibheall, near the end of the poem, encourages the women of her court to punish the narrator. In his translation of this passage, Ussher gives the young woman four additional lines that, whatever their poetic qualities, register the hope for gender equality that inspired many women in the early decades of the twentieth century:

> To-day a new reign is begun
> Of peace since Women's Rights are won;
> Our waiting and our weeping past,
> Our tears and prayers prevail at last. (p. 58)

Since women are identified in the poem as advocates of mercy and virtue, this 'new reign' in the modern world, Ussher seems to be suggesting, is one in which the injustices and failures of past male-dominated societies might well be reversed, as they are inside the narrator's dream-vision.

One sign of Ussher's efforts to infuse specifically humanistic values into his translation of *Cúirt an Mheán Oíche* is his strongly sympathetic treatment of the character of the young woman and of her suffering. The prospect of loneliness and spinsterhood, a real one for many young women in rural Ireland in Merriman's day, and in Ussher's, is set forth by Merriman's character in her first speech in moving, and very human, terms:

> A Phearla ó Pharrthas screadaim is glaedhim ort,
> Éiric m'anma ort, aitchim thu is éighim ort,
> Seachain ná scaoil me im shraoill gan áird
> Ná im chailligh gan chrích gan bhrígh gan bhláith,
> Gan charaid gan chloinn gan choim gan cháirde
> Ar theallacha draghain gan feidhm gan fáilte. (313–18)

> (Pearl from Paradise, I implore and I call on you,
> Ransom my soul, I beseech and I appeal to you,
> Take care, don't dismiss me as a useless slattern
> Or as a hag unmarried, without virtue, without bloom,
> Without friends, without children, without protection, without credit
> At inhospitable firesides without use, without welcome.)

Ussher's particular sensitivity to the young woman's fears can be seen by comparing his translation of this passage with that of Denis Woulfe, who overlooks the highly effective specific details in the original:

> O heavenly gem of radiant light
> My soul forfend from fell affright
> Dispel with speed my deep decay
> Reflection keen on me pourtray
> The scowling brow if doomed to roam
> No soothing spouse or friendly home.[17]

Ussher, paying more attention to the details in the original than Woulfe, translates:

> O matchless maid, have mercy, pray,
> E'er my freshness fade and my charms decay
> And you see me left in plight forlorn
> My beauty's prime and pride to mourn,
> With bleaching hairs, by cares oppressed,
> On unfriendly hearths an unwelcome guest. (p. 28)

Also, Ussher expands one line of complaint spoken by the young woman near the end of her second speech – 'Is deacair dam súil le súbhchus d'fhagháil' (845) ('It's difficult for me to hope to find joy') – into four despairing lines that express forcefully the plight of young women in a society that provides so few options for fulfilment:

> Ah woe is me! my words are vain
> And to what end do I thus complain?
> What are my tears and entreaties worth
> Or how can I hope in the face of this dearth? (p. 50)

The Censorship Act of 1929 was passed just three years after Ussher's translation of *Cúirt an Mheán Oíche* appeared, and Ussher, from his liberal humanist viewpoint, saw the law as an unfortunate expression of sexual conservatism in Irish society. 'Sometimes one really wonders', he said in *The Face and Mind of Ireland*, 'why we do not erect a statue of Oliver Cromwell, since the Puritan has become our Patron Saint.'[18] Given that view, and Ussher's engagement with the issue of feminist empowerment in *Cúirt an Mheán Oíche*, his tendency to shy away from Merriman's candid representations of sexuality, and especially female sexual desire, is puzzling. At times Ussher's translation simply omits suggestive passages; his version of the 1026-line original that he was presumably working from comes to just 892 lines, and most of the cuts and compressions have to do with passages describing sexual behaviour or desire. Ussher also frequently waters down suggestive language in Merriman. When, for example, the old man recounts the lively sexual history that he attributes to a girl married to an older man whom he knows, Merriman has him say at one point:

> Do b'fhuiris dam innsin cruinn mar chuala
> An chuma n-a mbíodh sí sraoillte suaidhte,
> Stracaithe ar lár is gáir 'n-a timcheall,
> Sraithte ar an sráid nó i stábla sínte. (445–8)

> (It would be easy for me to tell exactly as I heard it
> The way she used to be plucked, kneaded
> Dragged on the floor and laughter about her,
> Spread out in the street or stretched in a stable.)

Displaying a bit of puritanism in his own right, Ussher renders the passage in bland generalities:

> So grave her carriage, who would guess
> What light repute, what evil fame,
> The country gave her whence she came,
> Or that the name of that wild wench
> Made every matron blush and blench?[19] (p. 35)

And when Merriman's young woman, in her second speech, recounts in considerable detail the unsuccessful efforts that the old man's wife undertook to arouse him – a passage that runs on for thirty-four lines bristling with such details as 'Béal ar bhéal 's ag méaracht síos air' (706) ('Mouth on mouth and fingering down him'), 'Is chuimil a bruis ó chrios go glún de' (708) ('And rubbed her brush from thigh to knee of him'), and 'Ag fáscadh an chnaiste, ag searradh 's ag síneadh' (714) ('Squeezing, shaking and stretching the stout lump') – Merriman boils down the passage to six lines marked by nothing more graphic than ''Tis sure from her share she ne'er would shrink' (p. 45).

Whatever effect Ussher's humanistic, liberal values may have had on his treatment of specific issues and themes in Merriman's poem, his consciousness of his Anglo-Irish background certainly influenced the style and poetic qualities of his translation. For one thing, Ussher seems at ease with the language and culture into which he is translating, less enslaved than is Woulfe to trying to reproduce in English the various poetic effects of Merriman's Irish. Ussher is sensitive to the assonantal patterns in *Cúirt an Mheán Oíche*, but at the same time seems aware that any attempt to reproduce those patterns faithfully in English verse is doomed to the kind of awkwardness that at times mars Woulfe's translation. Ussher relies on a combination of assonance and consonance in flexible four-stress lines, while frequently varying the placement of the assonantal links within a given line. For example, Merriman's poem opens with a characteristic couplet governed by internal and terminal assonance – 'Ba ghnáth me ag siubhal le ciumhuis na habhann / Ar bháinseach úr 's an drúcht go trom' (1–2) ('It was usual for me to be walking along the edge of the river / On a fresh green and the dew heavy'); Ussher translates: "Twas my wont to wander beside the stream / On the soft greensward in the morning beam' (p. 15), where in the first line, the first two stressed syllables carry the assonantal link (they are connected as well by consonance), and in the second line the two stressed syllables in the middle:'green*sward*' and'*morn*ing'. There is also a terminal-medial echo between 'stream' and '*green*sward', a practice that, while not employed by Merriman with any consistency, is characteristic of much Irish-language poetry. Woulfe's version of these two lines follows the abbc/abbc assonantal pattern in Merriman more closely; but it lacks the fluency and confidence of Ussher's English, and requires two poetic inversions to match Merriman's metrics: 'Through dewy meads by streamlets clear / I often strayed the greenwoods near' (1–2).

At times, Ussher's use of consonance and assonance in a relatively flexible tetrameter line achieves a metrical richness that, while generally based on Merriman's Irish verse, draws attention to the poetic effects possible in English: 'She clapped her claw on my cape behind / And whisked me away like a wisp on the wind' (p. 21) for Merriman's description of the bailiff dragging the narrator off to Aoibheall's court ('Do bhuail sí crúca im chúl 'san chába / Is ghluais chum siubhail go lúbach láidir') (135–6) ('She stuck a crook in my back and in the cape / And set me moving to walk vigorously, firmly'); 'And wring your stringy windpipe well / And pitch your soul to the pit of hell' (p. 44) for the young woman's threats following the old man's speech ('Go stróicfinn sreanga do bheathadh le fonn ceart, / 'S go seólfainn t'anam go Acheron tonntach') (655–6) ('I would tear the cords of your life with a right pleasure, / And I would send your soul to billowy Acheron')'.

Ussher also strays readily and confidently from the literal meaning of Merriman's poem, often using diction and phrasing that, while sensitive to the original, is clearly rooted in the English language. In the opening description of nature, for example, where Merriman has, 'Ar maidin indé bhí an spéir gan cheó, / Bhí *Cancer*, ón ngréin, 'n-a caorthaibh teó' (23–4) ('Yesterday morning the sky was without fog, / *Cancer*, of the sun, was a warm glowing mass'), Ussher translates, 'Yesterday morn the sky was clear / In the dog-days' heat of the mad mid-year' (p. 16). Later, when Merriman's narrator describes the bailiff's face as 'héadan créachtach créimeach, / Ba anfadh ceanntair, scannradh saoghalta, / A draid 's a drandal mantach méirscreach' (54–56) ('her gashed, corroded face, / They were a terror of the district, a real fright / Her mouth and her fissured, toothless gums'), Ussher translates: 'Her features tanned by wind and air / Her rheumy eyes were red and blear, / Her mouth was stretched from ear to ear' (pp. 17–18). In her first speech, the young woman complains that attractive, lively young men end up marrying old, loathsome women:

Ag fuaid ag cailligh ag aimid nó ag óinmhid,
Nó ag suairle salach de chaile gan tionnscal,
Stuaiceach stailiceach aithiseach stanncach
Suaidhteach sodalach foclach fáidhmhail
Cuardach codlatach goirgeach gráinmhail. (218–22).

(To a witch, to a hag, to a foolish woman, or to a simpleton,
Or to a dirty whelp of a girl without industry,
Obstinate, starchy, shameful, self-willed
Haughty, arrogant, verbose, gossiping
Acquisitive, sleepy, irritable, hateful.)

In Ussher's version, the young woman laments that young men 'Of noted parts and proved precocity' are:

Sold to a scold or old hidiosity,
Withered and worn and blear and brown,
A mumbling, grumbling, garrulous clown,
A surly, sluttish and graceless gawk
Knotted and gnarled like a cabbage's stalk,
A sleepy, sluggish decayed old stump,
A useless, juiceless and faded frump. (p. 24)

There are no corresponding phrases in Merriman for 'old hidiosity', nicely rhymed with 'precocity', or for the image of the 'cabbage's stalk', or for that very English word 'frump'.

This kind of inventive phrasing, rendering with confidence Merriman's Irish into distinctively English words and phrases, runs throughout Ussher's translation: 'A slummocky scut of cumbrous carriage' (p. 25) for Merriman's 'Ní sraoill ná sluid ná luid gan fáscadh' (243) ('Not a slattern, nor a bad woman, nor a slut without tidiness'); 'A stark and crooked and stiff old stake' (p. 25) for Merriman's 'Lóiste lobhtha ná toice gan éifeacht' (245) ('A rotten sluggard nor a hussy without sense); 'It makes my heart to smart with passion / To see her flounced out in the fashion' (p. 34) for Merriman's 'Is searbh lem chroidhe nuair chím im radharc í – / A gradam, a críoch, a poimp's a taidhbhse' (435–6) ('Bitterness is in my heart when I see her – / Her showiness, her married state, her pomp and her vanity'); 'With drink till each guest was stretched speechless and sick' (p. 38), based on just one phrase in Merriman, 'is ól gan choimse' (509) ('and drink without moderation'); 'Tingling and taut with nature's crave' (p. 42) for Merriman's 'Le fonn na fola is le fothram na sláinte' (628) ('With desire of the blood and with the lustiness of health').

Merriman's poem ends with the narrator waking just in time to escape the various tortures with which he's threatened inside his dream. It all happens very quickly, in just two lines: 'Do scaras lem néill, do réidheas mo shúile, / 'S do phreabas de léim ón bpéin 'om dhúiseacht!' (1025–6) ('I started from my sleep, I cleared my eyes, / And I jumped with a bound from the pain upon my awaking'). Ussher's version of this represents one last effort to bring to bear on *Cúirt an Mheán Oíche* the humanism of his own day: 'I broke from sleep, forgot my pain, / And woke to light and life again' (p. 58). The narrator's return 'to light and life again' suggests, in the manner of Leopold Bloom's emergence from Glasnevin Cemetery in the 'Hades' episode of *Ulysses*, a humanistic embracing and celebration of everyday life, of the material and physical world rather than the world of visions and spirits. It's a fitting conclusion to a poetic translation that asks the modern reader to see this late-eighteenth-century poem written in Irish as capable of speaking to him or her nearly a century and a half removed from it, and of doing so in English, and in the hands of a member of the Protestant Ascendancy to boot.

Frank O'Connor: Restoring the Nation

F rank O'Connor (1903–1966) is best known as one of Ireland's finest short-story writers, but he's also one of the country's most prolific and accomplished poetic translators from the Irish.[1] Translation figured in his career from beginning to end; he published his first collection of translations early in his working life, in 1932, and his fifth, and last, in 1963, three years before his death. O'Connor's dedication to translation from the Irish was inspired, in part at least, by dissatisfaction – first, with the way that the Irish-language tradition had been represented in largely romantic terms during the Irish literary revival, and, then later, in the years following the establishment of the Irish Free State in 1923, with efforts to construct a distinctively Irish identity based on the twin pillars of Gaelicism and Catholicism. Those efforts – and especially the idea that a puritanical Catholicism and the Gaelic tradition could sit side by side easily and fruitfully – were anathema to O'Connor, and his translations, including that of *Cúirt an Mheán Oíche*, published in 1945, were intended to set the record straight about the nature of literature in Irish.

Merriman's poem also provided O'Connor with an effective platform for railing against the hold that the Catholic Church had over modern Irish life, and particularly against the church's puritanical attitudes toward sexuality. (Official

Irish society repaid O'Connor's hostility by banning his translation under the terms of the Censorship Act of 1929, although Arland Ussher's translation and Merriman's poem itself were left untouched.[2]) O'Connor's translation of *Cúirt an Mheán Oíche* is also marked in places by a sense of lost political and social possibility, something experienced by many of his generation and political convictions – O'Connor fought on the anti-Treaty side in the Civil War – who believed that the Ireland that emerged from the decades of struggle for independence had betrayed the promise of the revolution to produce a society not only independent of British rule, but also constructed on liberal values. Both O'Connor's critique of a Church-dominated Irish society in post-independence Ireland and his lament for the vanished ideals of the revolution are enabled in his translation of *Cúirt an Mheán Oíche* by some of the same qualities that distinguish his fictional accounts of life in rural and provincial Ireland, most notably his great gift for character and dialogue.

O'Connor's parents did not speak Irish. He was introduced to the language at the local grammar school in his native Cork, where Daniel Corkery was teaching. In part because of Corkery's belief that the Irish-language tradition constituted the only valid Irish literature, O'Connor's early feelings about the language were inevitably associated with nationalism; he once said that he turned to a thorough study of the language just after the Easter Rising, when he discovered that Patrick Pearse had written poems in Irish.[3] But his passion for translation was grounded in a love of language as well. In his memoir *An Only Child*, O'Connor says of his youth:

> All I could believe in was words, and I clung to them frantically. I would read some word like 'unsophisticated' and at once I would want to know what the Irish equivalent was. In those days, I didn't even ask to be a writer; a much simpler form of transmutation would have satisfied me. All I wanted was to translate, to feel the unfamiliar become familiar, the familiar take on all the mystery of some dark foreign face I had just glimpsed on the quays.[4]

By the time he was nineteen, and being held in Gormanstown Internment Camp for his part in the Civil War, he was teaching Irish to the staff in the camp, and, later, when released, he taught Irish at St Luke's, a Protestant school in Cork. Not long after the end of the Troubles, he published a translation of a French poem into Irish, presumably his first published verse translation, and one that led Corkery to encourage him further in his study of the Irish language.[5] It was around this time that O'Connor began translating Irish poetry into English verse. He said that his friend Geoffrey Phibbs, for whom he worked at the Wicklow Town library in the 1920s, 'read my poems … and marked them all "Rubbish" except a few translations from the Irish.'[6]

O'Connor was not a scholarly translator, and never represented himself as such.[7] But he had an uncanny ability to translate the spirit of a poem in Irish, even when not following its literal meaning with much fidelity. The scholar D.A. Binchy, who worked with O'Connor on some of his translations, once said that O'Connor's approach to scholarship was 'primarily intuitive, and his intuition was at times so overwhelming as to leave a professional scholar gasping with amazement.'[8] At the same time, O'Connor's translations are never neutral or objective renderings of the original, but the work of a strongly felt subjective presence. 'Behind every poet he translates we can clearly hear his own integral voice growling unmistakably away,' Alan Titley has said. 'Whatever gets lost in translation, Frank O'Connor certainly does not.'[9]

It may well be that it was Merriman's audacity that attracted O'Connor to him in the first place.[10] Certainly, Merriman's willingness to take on the subject of sexual relations in eighteenth-century Ireland, his various critiques of the social and religious institutions of that time and the freewheeling nature of his style appealed to a writer who saw himself as suffocating in a society dominated by philistinism and puritanism. O'Connor himself said of Merriman: 'here he was in the eighteenth century writing, in an Irish village in the back of beyond, things that very few men would dream of writing in Dublin of the twentieth … To say the man was 150 years ahead of his time would be mere optimism.'[11]

By the time O'Connor came to translate it, Merriman's poem was indeed viewed by the more conservative elements in Irish society as morally dangerous. It was too popular and too important to be ignored entirely, but it could be made safe for loyal Irish Catholic readers; two bowlderized editions of the poem, for use in the schools, were published in the early decades of the twentieth century.[12] Even the subtitle that O'Connor assigns to his translation – *A Rhythmical Bacchanalia from the Irish of Bryan Merryman* – alerts his readers to his interest in undermining the timid and repressive values that lay behind those abbreviated editions.

Especially when he is using *Cúirt an Mheán Oíche* as a vehicle for attacking the force of puritanism in the Ireland of the 1930s and 1940s, O'Connor often departs freely from the literal meaning of Merriman's text.[13] In the young woman's second speech, when she is arguing against celibacy, she says there are some priests who hate women; O'Connor's translation of this passage adds in a specific reference to the kind of hellfire-and-brimstone preaching found in much Catholic teaching at that time, and rendered so memorably nearly thirty years earlier in James Joyce's *A Portrait of the Artist as a Young Man*. In Merriman, the passage reads:

> Cuid aca bíodh gur rícígh riamh
> 'S cuid eile bhíos gan ríomh gan riaghail,
> Cinntigh chruadha gan truagh gan tréithe,
> Fíochmhar fuar is fuath dho bhéithe.[14]

> (Some of them there are who were ever wastrels
> And some of them not to be accounted for, without regulation,
> Hard, mean persons without pity, without accomplishment,
> Cruel, cold, and with hatred of women.)

O'Connor translates:

> And though some as we know were always savage
> Gnashing their teeth at the thought of marriage,
> And, modest beyond the needs of merit,
> Invoked hell-fire on girls of spirit.[15]

In his speech defending bastards, Merriman's old man says that the strong, hearty child that his wife has just given birth to could not have been sired by a feeble old husband like himself:

> Ní deacair a mheas nách spreas gan bhrígh
> Bheadh ceangailte ar nasc ar teasc ag mnaoi,
> Gan chnámh gan chumus gan chumadh gan chom,
> Gan ghrádh gan chumann gan fuinneamh gan fonn,
> Do scaipfeadh i mbroinn d'éanmhaighre mná
> Le catachus draghain an groidhre breágh
> Mar chuireann sé i bhfeidhm gan mhoill gan bhréig
> Le cumus a bhaill 's le luigheamh a ghéag
> Gur crobhaire é crothadh go cothrom gan cháime
> Le fonn na fola is le fothram na sláinte. (619–28)

(It's not difficult to think that it's not a dry branch without force
Who would be tied on a chain for a task by a woman,
Without a bone, without ability, without a figure, without a waist,
Without love, without friendship, without vigour, without desire,
Who would beget in the womb of any healthy woman
With passionate concupiscence the fine, hearty fellow
As he demonstrates at once, without falsehood
With the power of his member and with the cut of his limbs
That he is a strong, able person created justly without fault
With desire of the blood and with the lustiness of health.)

As does the original, O'Connor's translation of this passage revels in a sequence of suggestive images, but it also specifically gives expression to the unrestrained force of human sexuality, culminating in one of the most striking images in the translation:

No sleepy, good-natured, respectable man
Without sinew or bone or belly or bust
Or venom or vice or love or lust,
Buckled and braced in every limb,
Spouted the seed that flowered in him;
Back and legs and chest and height
Prove him in the teeth of spite
A child begotten in fear and wonder
In the blood's millrace and the body's thunder. (p. 34)

In translating the many passages in Merriman describing sexual desire, O'Connor often insists on the naturalness of sexuality, calling into question by implication the views advanced by the church in his own day. (When he revised the translation for inclusion in *Kings, Lords and Commons*, he capitalized every reference to nature.) For example, in the young woman's second speech, she says that a woman of her acquaintance who is married to a sexually inadequate elderly husband would be justified in taking a lover: 'Má d'imthigh an mhodhm-hail bhí trom 'n-ghábha / 'S gur deineadh an fhoghail seo gabhaimse a páirt' (721–2) ('If the gentle lady who was seriously in need strayed / And this trespass was done, I take her part'). O'Connor adds two lines to this assertion that locate the justification for such an action in the naturalness of sexual desire:

If the creature that found him such a sell
Has a lover today, she deserves him well;
A benefit nature never denies
To anything born that swims or flies. (p. 38)

Although by the time the Civil War ended, O'Connor could be quite sceptical about the Irish struggle for independence,[16] he never abandoned the liberal
social and political values that were, in theory, part of the revolutionary cause,
and his commitment to translation from the Irish in general can be seen as a
means of protesting against cultural and political leaders who he thought had
allowed the country's native tradition to be placed in the service of attitudes
and values that were anything but liberal.[17] *Cúirt an Mheán Oíche* came readily
to hand for this purpose, as Merriman had used the dream-vision framework
commonly found in the Irish-language *aisling* tradition in part to mock the
failure of his society to achieve any kind of meaningful social justice, and to
envision a different, revolutionary future.[18]

In O'Connor's translation, references to the idea of lost manhood often
have political as well as sexual implications.[19] When Aoibheall, near the end of
the poem, attacks men who boast of supposed sexual conquests of women to
enhance their own standing, Merriman has her say:

An chuid aca atá go táir n-a smaointe,
Fuireann nach fuláis leó a gcáil bheith sínte,
Mhaoidheas le fothram a gcothrom ar bhéithe,
Chífe an pobul a gcogair's a sméide.
Is taitneamhach leó's is dóth gur laochus
Scannal na hóige pósta is aonta,
Mian a dtoile ní sporann a gcionta,
Bréantus fola ná borradh na drúise,
Taitneamh don ghníomh ná fíoch na féithe
Acht magadh na mílte, maoidheamh a n-éachta.
Ní sáinnt dá sógh bheir beó na céadta
Acht caint is gleó agus mórtus laochuis. (927–38)

(Some of them who are vile in their thoughts,
A group for whom it's necessary that their renown be extended,
Who boast with lustiness of their treatment of women,

The public will see through their whispers and their winking.
It pleases them and it seems that it's heroism
The disgrace of the young, married and single,
The desire of their will does not spur their passions,
Sensuality or the swelling of lust,
Pleasure in the act or fury of the vein
But mockery of the thousands, boasting of their deeds.
Fierce desire for their pleasure does not at all grip hundreds
But talk and clamour and boasting of heroism.)

O'Connor's translation frames the passage in the political climate of his own day by representing not only the ruin of women at the hands of such men, but also the loss of manhood that those men experience through this kind of treatment of women:

And mostly those who sin from pride
With women whose names they do not hide,
Who keep their tally of ruined lives
In whispers, nudges, winks and gibes.
Was ever vanity more misplaced
Than in married women and girls disgraced?
It isn't desire that gives the thrust,
The smoking blood and the ache of lust,
Weakness of love and the body's blindness,
But to punish the fools who show them kindness.
Thousands are born without a name
That braggarts may boast of their mothers' shame,
Men lost to nature through conceit,
And their manhood killed by their own deceit. (p. 45)

The images of destroyed manhood here have no corresponding references in the original.

At times, O'Connor specifically adds in material advancing some of the ideals that once fuelled the revolution. In the old man's speech in defence of bastards, Merriman has him say of the healthy child his wife has given birth to out of wedlock:

Deisigh anall i dteannta an bhúird é.
Breathain go cruinn é, bíodh gurab óg é
Is dearbhtha suidhte an píosa feóla é,
Is preabaire i dtoirt i gcorp's i gcnámh é,
Cá bhfuil a locht i gcois ná i láimh dhe? (610–14)

(Bring him here near the table.
Look at him attentively, although he is young
It's certainly certified that he is a piece of flesh,
He's a hearty person in size, in body and in bone,
Where is the flaw in foot or in hand of him?)

O'Connor extends Merriman's text to place the argument about the physical vitality of bastards in a context that argues for disregarding rank and religious affiliation:

Let him come here for all to view!
Look at him now! You can see 'tis true.
Agreed, we don't know his father's name,
His mother admires him just the same,
And if in all things else he shines
Who cares for his baptismal lines? (p. 34)

O'Connor once described Merriman as 'supremely a realist',[20] something that might well be said of O'Connor himself. By 1945, when his translation of *Cúirt an Mheán Oíche* appeared, O'Connor had achieved considerable renown as a short-story writer often praised for his realistic representations of the life of rural and provincial Ireland, and for his ability to create convincing characters and dialogue. That ability figures importantly in his translation of *Cúirt an Mheán Oíche*.

In O'Connor's characterization of Merriman's young woman, for example, the principal figure in the poem, she emerges as far more than a vehicle for O'Connor's attacks on puritanical Ireland; O'Connor's portrait of her, and of the plight of women in rural Ireland in general, in his own day as well as in Merriman's, is genuinely and forcefully sympathetic. In the preface to his translation, O'Connor says that Merriman finds his true voice as a poet only when the young woman begins talking: 'As always, when he deals with women's human needs, he puts real tenderness and beauty into the writing.'[21] Praising in particular the young girl's second speech, O'Connor says that the speech expresses 'the tenderness Merryman always shows in dealing with women.'[22] In his translation, O'Connor takes the full measure of the suffering of Merriman's young woman. In her first speech, for example, she voices a fear of loneliness that was all too real for many unmarried women in rural Ireland in the eighteenth century:

'S é fáth mo scéil go léir's a bhrígh dhuit
Mar táim gan chéile tar éis mo dhíchill,
Fáth mo sheanchus' fhada, mo phianchreach,
Táim in achrann dhaingean na mbliadhnta,
Ag tarraing go tréan ar laethibh liaithe
Is eagal liom éag gan éinne'om iarraidh. (307–12)

(It is the reason of my entire story and its meaning for you
That I am without a spouse after doing my best,
The reason of my long story-telling, woe is me,
I am in the firm fastness of the years,
Approaching rapidly the grey days
And I fear a death without anyone asking for me.)

Denis Woulfe's use of double rhyme in his translation of this passage, along with generalized diction, waters down the feelings expressed in Merriman's lines:

O baneful strife Oh dire reflection
No marriage rite or kind protection
My sad relation annalized
My years increased unharmonized
To silver locks I am fast approaching
And no fond spark his passion broaching.[23]

Although Ussher's translation of *Cúirt an Mheán Oíche* is generally committed to a humanistic representation of the young woman's situation, his version of these lines is no more poignant, and even more abstract, than is Woulfe's:

'Tis why I am laying my case before ye
That I'm single still at the end of the story,
And age draws near with outrageous pace
To rob my form of former grace.[24]

[40]

O'Connor's version, on the other hand, grounded in a realistic rendering of spoken English, expresses with conviction the weight and emotional urgency of the woman's fears:

> For here I am at the place I started,
> And that is the cause of all my tears,
> Fast in the rope of the rushing years
> With age and want in lessening span
> And death at the end and no hopes of a man. (p. 23)

Later, in the young woman's second speech, in which she describes the frustration that the old man's wife experiences when trying to rouse him sexually, O'Connor expands two lines in Merriman into four lines that specifically focus attention on the wife's suffering. In Merriman, the passage reads: 'Is nár dham aithris mar chaitheadh sí an oidhche / Ag fáscadh an chnaiste, ag searradh 's ag síneadh' (713–14) ('It's a shame for me to tell how she spent the night / Squeezing, shaking and stretching the stout lump); O'Connor translates:

> But she'd nothing to show for all her pain,
> His bleary old eyes looked just the same;
> And nothing I said could ever explain
> Her sum of misery and shame. (p. 38)

In a review of Ussher's translation of *Cúirt an Mheán Oíche*, O'Connor identified as one of the salient qualities of Merriman's poem its ability to give voice to the 'speech of the people',[25] and it's fair to say that O'Connor's translation comes most alive as poetry when the characters start to speak. Moroever, for O'Connor, giving voice to the 'speech of the people' had strong political and cultural implications for an Ireland in which freedom of expression was, in his view, being compromised by church and state, most evidently in the Censorship Act, the force of which he himself had felt.

O'Connor's general indifference to reproducing in his translation the prosodic qualities of the original, something that both Woulfe and Ussher had thought very much worth doing, can be explained by his commitment to translating Merriman into the 'speech of the people' in English. O'Connor's penchant for dialogue is evident in his version of the first words spoken in Merriman's poem, those of the bailiff, addressed to the narrator as the dream-vision gets under way: 'Múscail! corruigh! a chodlataigh ghránna; / Is dubhach do shlighe bheith sínte it shliasta / Is cúirt 'n-a suidhe is na mílte ag triall ann' (62–4) ('Awake! move! ugly sleeper; / It's sad your way to be stretched on your side / And a court sitting and the thousands travelling there'). Woulfe's version fails to capture the colloquial force of Merriman's lines, in large part because of awkward poetic inversions resulting from his attempts to be true to Merriman's prosody:

> 'You wretch' she cries 'arise in haste
> Our precious time no longer waste,
> The court is thronged with maids despairing
> And thousands still to it repairing.' (61–4)

Ussher's translation of this passage also stumbles, and for much the same reason: 'You lazy laggard, arise! awake! / Is this the way for you, wretch, to be, / When the court is seated for all to see?' (p. 18). O'Connor's version, by comparison, is direct and concrete, and governed by the rhythms and diction of ordinary speech in English as it's spoken in Ireland: 'Get up out of this, you lazy thing! / That a man of your age can think 'tis fitting / To sleep in a ditch while the court is sitting!' (p. 15).

Indeed, to read O'Connor's translation of *Cúirt an Mheán Oíche* is, perhaps above all, to experience the force of vigorous, living speech. There's nothing like it in any of the translations that come before or after it: Merriman's 'D'fheannadh na lobhar's an lom dá léirscrios' (84) ('Skinning the lepers and the naked in their devastation') becomes, in O'Connor's translation, 'To pick the bones of the Irish clean' (p. 16); 'Is buaireamh suidhte fíor 'n-a féachaint' (154) ('And true vexation settled in her look') is rendered as 'But the cut of her spoke of some disgrace' (p. 18); 'Gan codladh gan suan gan suairceas oidhche' (188) ('Without sleep, without rest, without a night's mirth') becomes 'Unable to sleep for the want of a man' (p. 19); 'Créad an t-adhbhar ná tabharfaidhe grádh dham / Is me chomh leabhair, chomh modhmhail, chomh breagh so?' (227–228) ('What is the reason that I would not be given love / And I as slender, as modest, as fine as this?') is translated as 'Couldn't some man love me as well? / Amn't I plump and sound as a bell' (p. 21); 'Is ca bhfios don tsaoghal nach *stays* é 'ot fháscadh?' (396) ('And who in the world knows it is but stays confining you?') becomes 'Or is it the stays that gives you the waist?' (p. 26); 'Aithris cá bhfuair tu luach an húda, / Is aithris cá bhfuair tu luach do ghúna' (423–4) ('Relate where you got the price of the hood, / And relate where you got the price of your gown') is rendered as 'The frock made a hole in somebody's pocket, / And it wasn't yourself that paid for the jacket'

(p. 27); 'Ar lár 'n-a lóiste ag pósta is aonta' (518) ('On the floor a drone for married and single') becomes 'Flattened herself to married and single' (p. 30).

Because it's so closely tuned to the 'speech of the people', O'Connor's translation also often achieves comic effects lost on other of Merriman's translators. In the young woman's description of the various cures she undertook to enhance her chances of finding a husband, she says at one point: 'Chuirinn an tsúist fé chúil na gaibhle, / Chuirinn an ramhan go ciúin fén adhairt chugham' (299–300) ('I would put the flail in the corner of the hearth, / I would put the spade silently under my pillow'). Woulfe and Ussher render this quite faithfully, both in terms of literal meaning and metrical form, but both are insensitive to the *double entendre* in Merriman's 'gaibhle', which is the genitive form of 'gabhal', meaning, among other things, 'groin' or 'crotch'. Woulfe's version has 'The flail I placed upraised from earth, / The spade concealed behind the hearth' (297–298); Ussher translates it as 'Beneath the hearth the flail I laid, / Below my pillow placed the spade' (p. 28). O'Connor's translation is fully alert to the sexual innuendo in the original: 'Up the chimney stuck the flail, / Slept with a spade without avail' (p. 23).

In her speech early in the poem, the bailiff describes the meeting of fairies in Moy Graney palace that led to the establishment of Aoibheall's court. Among the many regrets about the state of Ireland outlined at that gathering is a decline in the male population; as Merriman's bailiff puts it, 'An cogadh is an bás gan spás dá ndíogadh, / Uabhar na righthe 's ar imthigh tar sáile / 'Nuair ná deineann sibh tuilleadh 'n-a n-áit díobh' (100–102) ('War and death without reprieve draining them, / The pride of kings that went over the sea / When you are not making any more in their place'). O'Connor's translation of the first two of these lines is accurate enough – 'Since famine and war have struck the village / And a flighty king and the emigration' – but his third line departs considerably from the literal meaning of the original: 'And what have you done to restore the nation?' (p. 16). That's a question that, for O'Connor, writing in the decades following the establishment of the Free State, every Irish writer worth his salt had to consider. And one answer to that question for O'Connor is that he translated *Cúirt an Mheán Oíche*.

Lord Longford: Merriman and the Theatre

L ord Longford was a director of the Gate Theatre in the 1930s, and later of his own production company, as well as the author of a number of successful plays. His translation of *Cúirt an Mheán Oíche*, published in 1949, just four years after Frank O'Connor's version had appeared, calls attention to the dramatic qualities of Merriman's poem, especially in its rendering of Merriman's often complex dialogue into relatively straightforward speech that often seems written more for the stage than for the private reader. In his introduction to Longford's translation, Padraic Colum said: 'Lord Longford as a dramatist has felt the situation, put his pair on the witness stand and made them speak as they would from there, dramatically.'[1] Although much is lost in Longford's theatrically conscious translation – the effects of Merriman's intricate prosody, many of the social and political implications that attracted O'Connor to the poem, and most of the sexual vigour and candour of the original – there are moments in which his version of Merriman achieves an admirable forcefulness and clarity. Moreover, in its failings as well as its strengths – and the former certainly outnumber the latter – the translation not only foregrounds the inherently theatrical nature of *Cúirt an Mheán Oíche*, but also testifies to the importance of the theatre in Irish culture in the first half of the twentieth century.

Longford's considerable interest in the Irish language – he published three collections of translations from Irish bardic poetry before he turned to Merriman[2] – was bound up with his fiercely nationalist politics, both of which put him very much at odds with his Anglo-Irish family. Longford was born, in 1902, Edward Arthur Henry Pakenham, and became the sixth Earl of Longford in 1915, when his father was killed at Gallipoli. The Pakenhams had been established in Ireland for nearly three centuries; one of Longford's ancestors had served as an officer under Cromwell, and, like many of those who supported Cromwell's campaign in Ireland, was rewarded with Irish land – a large holding in Co. Westmeath, where the Longford family residence, first known as Pakenham Hall and now as Tullynally Castle, still stands. Longford's mother and his brother Frank, who became the seventh earl upon Edward's death in 1961, were fiercely pro-unionist,[3] and his father had little interest in Ireland or, for that matter, in Pakenham Hall.[4]

But when Longford was at Eton, where Irish nationalism was regarded with scepticism, to say the least, he declared himself a supporter of Arthur Griffith, Michael Collins and Sinn Féin, and took up the study of Irish, working on his own.[5] By the time he went to Oxford, he was signing himself Eamon de Longphort, and alienating many of his fellow students because of his support for the Irish cause.[6] Among other things, he opposed a motion at the Oxford Union condemning as murderers the Irish nationalists who had assassinated Field-Marshal Sir Henry Wilson, who had been responsible for attacks on Catholics in Belfast in 1920; the night of his speech against the motion, Longford was manhandled by a group of students and hurled into the pond known as 'Mercury'.[7] By the end of the 1920s, following a trip to Poland that fed his nationalist convictions, he had committed himself fully to the Gaelicization of Ireland, and was frequently asked to speak at functions around the country supporting the language.

In the 1930s Longford's attentions were directed to the cause of Irish theatre. When the Gate Theatre, which had been operating for two years under the inspired leadership of Micheál Mac Liammóir and Hilton Edwards, was facing bankruptcy in 1930, Longford rescued it by buying £1200-worth of the company's shares.[8] He became chairman that year, and he and his wife Christine supported the theatre financially for the next thirty years, much to the detriment of the family fortune.[9] Longford also wrote a number of plays put on at the Gate, including one about Jonathan Swift entitled *Yahoo*, and staged versions in Irish of plays by Aeschylus, Sophocles and Euripides. When he fell out with Mac Liammóir and

Edwards in 1936, he formed his own company, Longford Productions, which put on plays at the Gate and at various venues around the country. When he died in 1961, the occasion was marked by a minute's silence in all of Dublin's theatres.[10]

Longford's three collections of translations from Irish bardic poetry were very much inspired by his nationalist views, a fair measure of which can be taken from the preface that he wrote to one of the volumes, in which he argued that the sources of his translations belonged to a native culture 'wiped out by the devastating wars of Elizabeth's and Cromwell's days', and adding: 'If we remember that the systematic annihilation of Irish culture was in full swing before Shakespeare and Spenser began to write, there is not reason to believe that Ireland, had circumstances been favourable, might not have achieved as much in literature as the larger island.'[11] But *Cúirt an Mheán Oíche* is far less overtly political than is much of the verse that Longford had translated earlier, and Longford seems to have seen in Merriman's poem less an occasion for lamenting the decline of Ireland's native culture, or for critiquing the state of Irish affairs in the 1940s, than a text organized around dramatic speeches that appealed to his theatrical side.[12]

The desire to translate *Cúirt an Mheán Oíche* into a poem particularly sensitive to the dramatic qualities of the original may account for Longford's decision to replace Merriman's irregular four-stress line with regular heroic couplets, a form that Longford associated with dramatic verse; he had translated Molière's *Tartuffe* in 1938 into couplets very like those he used for his translation of Merriman's poem.[13] Also, the speeches in Longford's translation are marked off with dramatic headings – 'The Girl's Speech', 'The Old Man's Speech', 'The Girl's Reply', and 'The Judgment' – and Longford introduces verse paragraphs at many points where none is indicated in the original; like an on-stage pause, these usually mark a shift in the argument or organization of a speech.

Longford's translation achieves its most dramatic effects by means of a diction and syntax that, at their best, render Merriman's relatively complex Irish into an English that has the immediate accessibility of writing for the stage, although usually at a fairly high price in terms of fidelity. For example, in the old man's account of being presented with a newborn child that he strongly suspects is not his, Merriman has:

> Mo scannradh scéil gan féith dhem chroidhe air –
> Clann dá dtéadhamh dam tar éis no hoidhche!

Cullóid anfadhach ainigidhe scólta, –
Bunóc ceangailte is bean an tighe breóidhte,
Pusóid leagaithe ar smeachaidí teó aca,
Cuinneóg bhainne dhá greadadh le fórsa,
Is mullach ar lánmhias bánbhiadh is siúicre
Ag Muirinn Ní Cháimliath báinliaigh an chrúca.[14]

(My surprise event, without the blood from my heart in him –
A child of passion for me after the evening!
A tempestuous, peevish, fretful commotion, –
An infant swaddled and the woman of the house sick,
A medicinal draught laid on the warm live coals for them,
A churn of milk being whipped with force,
And a heap on a platter of beautiful food and sugar
For Muirinn Ní Cháimliath, lady physician of the hand.)

Longford's translation, although a lot less rich poetically than the original, begins with a new paragraph, marking a shift in the old man's narrative, and then moves rapidly and clearly, with no syntactical confusion or delay:

> I woke next morning with a fearful start.
> A baby born to warm its father's heart!
> A storm of noise enough to wake the dead,
> A swaddled infant and my wife in bed!
> A posset boiled upon embers hot,
> A creamy pail a powerful stirring got,
> While milk and sugar in the midwife's claw
> O'erflowed the biggest dish you ever saw.[15]

Although Longford's English here simplifies, perhaps oversimplifies, Merriman's diction and syntax, the passage is alert in at least one place to the nuances of Merriman's Irish, 'claw' remembering various alternate meanings for 'crúca', all of them more or less appropriate to the work of a midwife, such as 'a hook', 'a crook', and, according to Dinneen, 'a human hand (said of grasping persons)'.

Later, in her reply to the old man's speech, when the young woman asks him why he should worry if his wife shares her sexual favours with other men, Merriman's Irish is particularly resistant to transparent literal translation:

Ca bhfuil do dhíth ag suidhe chum béile?
Ar caitheadh le mí aici a dtigheas 'n-a féile!
An luigide an chúil nó an lughade an láithreach
Fiche milliún má shiubhail le ráithe ann? (733–6)

(Where is your loss sitting for a meal
If she spent a month in a house of plenty!
Is the corner smaller or is the place smaller
If twenty million walked for three months there?)

Denis Woulfe's translation of this passage, aiming to be faithful to the prosodic qualities of the original, falls into awkwardness, if not confusion, in the first two lines:

Your loss recount at sitting meal
Should guests in crowds themselves regale.
Or will your store be dozed or wasted
If thousands more your titbits tasted?[16]

While Longford's version ignores Merriman's prosody, and takes considerable liberties with the meaning of the original, it is relatively straightforward and perfectly comprehensible on a first reading, or first listening:

If others feasted here, what's that to you?
You've got your dinner and that ought to do.
Is not your house as fine as 'twas before,
Tho' millions may have entered thro' the door? (p. 23)

Longford also occasionally relies on repetition to translate Merriman's Irish into relatively stage-conscious English. In her lament for her unmarried condition, Merriman's young woman says in her first speech:

'S é chráidh mo chroidhe is do scaoil gan chéill me
'S d'fhág mo smaointe is m'intinn traochta
Tráighte tinn mar taoim, go tréithlag,
Cráidhte claoidhte ag caoidh 's ag géarghol. (207–11)

(It tormented my heart and left me without sense
And left my thoughts and my mind exhausted

Dried up, sick as I am, weakly feeble,
Tormented, subdued, lamenting and keenly weeping.)

Longford's version replaces Merriman's characteristic sequence of phrases with one repeating phrase:

This broke my heart, 'tis this has made me mad,
'Tis this has robbed me of the wits I had,
'Tis this has left me languishing in tears,
Broken and weak and sick, a prey to fears! (p. 10)

Merriman's poem itself often achieves dramatic effects through the use of repetition, as when, for example, a few lines later, the young woman counts the costs of her failure to find a husband:

Chaitheas mo chiall le fiadhach gan éifeacht,
Dhalladar riamh me, d'iadhdar m'ae ionnam.
Tar éis mo chumainn, mo thurraing, mo ghrádh dhóibh,
Tar éis ar fhulaing me d'iomada crádhnuis,
Tar éis ar chailleas le caitheamh na scálaí,
Béithe balbha is cailleacha cártaí. (281–6)

(I lost my reason in a hunt without effect,
They always deceived me, they stopped my heart in me.
After my devising, my pushing, my love for them,
After what I suffered from too much vexation,
After what I lost on the cup-tossing,
Stammering women and hags of the cards.)

This kind of writing plays directly into Longford's theatrical hands, and he cheerfully extends Merriman's repeating phrase:

Vain were my plans, in vain I hunting went;
They put me down and baffled my intent.
In vain were love's assaults and adorations,
In vain my sufferings and my vexations,
In vain the hags that ate my fortune up
With telling fortunes, reading cards or cup. (p. 12)

Despite such moments of theatrical vigour, much of Longford's translation is marred by hackneyed diction and stale imagery, and bogged down as
well by his five-stress line, which is badly out of tune with Merriman's prosody.
O'Connor's translation, although less motivated by theatrical ambitions, is
in fact far more dramatically effective than Longford's, largely because of
O'Connor's ability to translate Merriman into vital spoken English. When the
young woman movingly expresses her fears of growing old and dying without
a family – 'Táim in achrann dhaingean na mbliadhnta, / Ag tarraing go tréan
ar laethibh liaithe / Is eagal liom éag gan éinne 'om iarraidh' (310–12) ('I am in
the firm fastness of the years, / Approaching rapidly the grey days / And I fear
a death without anyone asking for me') – O'Connor, as argued in the previous
chapter, finds a striking image to convey those feelings, and in a colloquial voice:
'Fast in the rope of the rushing years / With age and want in lessening span /
And death at the end and no hopes of a man'.[17] Longford's version is relatively
lifeless, and undermined by an inappropriate double rhyme as well: 'I'm in grave
danger now of growing old. / The days draw on; not long shall grey hairs tarry; /
I greatly fear I'll die before I marry' (p. 13).

Longford's translation also occasionally slips into clichés and phrases associated more with the culture of the Anglo-Irish big house than with Merriman's
rural, Irish-speaking Ireland. Something of this shows up in Arland Ussher's
translation – not surprisingly, since Ussher shares Longford's Anglo-Irish
background – but there's nothing in Ussher's version quite so wrong-footed as
Longford's translation of 'óigbhean scoththa chomh toghta 's is féidir' (246)
('an excellent young woman as choice as is possible') into 'just the nicest girl that
you could find' (p. 11), or of the sexually suggestive description of a young man as
'Cruaidhcheart ceanusach ceapaithe córach' (216) ('Rightly hardy, commanding,
determined, shapely') into 'An honest fellow and a charmer too' (p. 11), or of 'Do
dhallais an saoghal go léir let thaidhbhse, / 'S is aithnid dam féin tu i dtaobh
le coife' (389–390) ('You deceived all the world with your vanity, / And I myself
knew you having only a small cap') into 'You've dazzled all the world, but I'm a
chap / To know the head beneath the fancy cap' (p. 15).

Longford's tendency to reach for the general and unoriginal also has the
effect of toning down many of the sexually explicit passages in *Cúirt an Mheán
Oíche*. John Cowell, the author of a study of Longford's relationship with the
Gate Theatre, said of Longford's translation of Merriman's poem, apparently
intending the comment as praise: 'It is highly entertaining, there is no bawdiness

and it isn't even risqué'.[18] When the young woman, for example, describes her
sexual frustration by saying she spends her nights 'Ar leabain leamhfhuar dár
suathadh ag smaointe' (190) ('On an impotent cold bed disturbed by thoughts'),
Longford dodges any sexual implications: 'Tired with long thinking, chilled
beneath the clothes' (p. 10). And when the young woman describes the kind of
man she's not interested in as 'seanduine seanda crannda créimtheach, / Feamaire
fann is feam gan féile' (755–6) ('an aged, withered, decayed old person, / An
infirm, weak-loined person and a stalk without pleasure'), Longford translates
in language that is both evasive and inappropriately redolent of the drawing-
room: 'But this old, knotted ancient, why's he jealous? / I cannot stand these
disappointing fellows' (p. 23).

Longford also apparently permitted three substantial cuts to be made to
his translation, the effect of which was to eliminate the young woman's argument for abandoning celibacy, including her deliberately shocking references to
the sexual attractiveness of the clergy. The translation was published in an issue
of *Poetry Ireland*, and the editor attached a note to it saying that the cuts 'were
made solely at the printer's request'.[19] The elisions are all the more puzzling
when it is remembered that the editor of *Poetry Ireland* at the time was David
Marcus, who was hardly known for dodging controversy, and who, four years
later, published his own translation of *Cúirt an Mheán Oíche* in which the
passages cut from Longford's version are translated.

The old man tells the court at one point about the comfortable and pros-
perous life he led before he married:

> Is feasach dhon taobh so 'en tsaoghal mar bhí me
> Sealadh dem réim 's dem laethibh roimhe seo,
> Leitheadach láidir lán de shaidhbhreas,
> Eisteas le fághail is fáilte im theaghlach,
> Caraid i gcúirt is congnadh dlighe agam,
> Ceannus is clú agus comhar na saoithe,
> Tathac im chaínt is suim is éifeacht,
> Talamh is maoin ag suidheamh mo chéille! (477–84)

> (It is known to this side of the world how I was
> A period of my life and of my days before this,
> Proud, strong, full of riches,
> Accommodation available and a welcome in my household,

Friends in court and legal help for me,
Authority and fame and the companionship of the learned,
Substance in my speech and interest and importance,
Land and wealth confirming my prudence!)

Longford's translation of this passage might well be read as resonating with his own marginalized class in modern Ireland, nostalgically evoking life as it once was lived in Pakenham Hall:

Well do they know in all this countryside
The times I spent before I took a bride,
Lord of my own and rich and stout and tall,
With hospitality on tap for all;
With friends in Court the law I did not fear,
I'd stout supporters in the gentry here.
My speech was free, my talking took effect,
I'd land and means to win my word respect. (p. 17)

But when one considers Merriman's poem in dramatic terms, as Longford asks the reader to do, and so remembers that the character speaking these lines is hardly a sympathetic figure, the comfort and power that the old man laments having lost can be seen in the quite different light of Longford's nationalist convictions. From this point of view, this 'rich' man with 'supporters in the gentry' and 'means to win my word respect' is part of the unhappy history of Anglo-Irish governance. In a moment such as this, Longford's sensitivity to the theatrical nature of Merriman's poem, however much it tends to oversimplify the original from line to line, pays interpretive dividends, encouraging a relatively complex understanding of what Merriman was up to.

David Marcus: Marginality
and Sexuality

*L*ike Frank O'Connor, David Marcus (1924–2009) saw *Cúirt an Mheán Oíche* as remarkably relevant to the Ireland in which he was living, and for many of the same reasons, most of them having to do with an uneasiness with the cultural power of the Irish Catholic Church, and its attitudes toward sexuality.[1] And Marcus was, as O'Connor said every good Irish writer should be, in an adversarial relationship with Irish society. As a Jew – he was the grandson of Jewish immigrants from Lithuania – Marcus found himself very much on the edge of the mainstream Irish community in Cork City, where he grew up in the 1920s and 1930s,[2] and it was no doubt Marcus' sense of himself as a cultural and religious outsider that enabled him to see so clearly and to rail so forcefully against the Catholic Church and its influence on modern Irish life.

Given his background, Marcus' commitment to the translation of poetry from the Irish might be understood as an effort to offset his sense of marginalization by engaging with a tradition that was considered by many to be an essential bedrock of what it meant to be Irish. The question of Marcus' relationship to the Irish-language tradition is, however, more complicated than that. For one thing, Marcus was never fluent in the language – when Dolmen Press launched his translation of *Cúirt an Mheán Oíche*, he stayed away because he feared that he'd be called on to converse in Irish[3] – and so his work with Irish inevitably compounded his sense of being on the outside of native Irish culture. As he says in his autobiography, 'Although my love of Irish poetry led me to continue translating it for some years after I left school, not having any need or opportunity to speak the language, I never tried to, and so have always had to regard myself as an Irishman who did not speak his own language.'[4] Even had he been more fluent in Irish, the project of translating from it could be seen as more marginalizing than assimilating in mid-twentieth-century Irish society, in which, whatever lip service was paid to the language as a necessary part of Irish identity, it had in fact a functionally subsidiary status. Marcus would have been particularly aware of that secondary standing because of his distinguished career as a literary editor working, for the most part, with Irish literature written in English. He founded *Poetry Ireland* in 1948, and later created the 'New Irish Writing' page in the *Irish Press*, which he oversaw from 1967 to 1986; he also co-founded Poolbeg Press in 1976.

Marcus' sense of marginality is hardly unique among the translators of Merriman's poem who came before him; indeed, there seems to be something in *Cúirt an Mheán Oíche* that attracts translators living on one edge of Irish society or another. That there isn't enough known about Denis Woulfe to describe with any certainty his status in the Irish literary society of his day suggests that he was hardly a central figure in it. Michael C. O'Shea was an Irish-American living in Boston when he published his translation of *Cúirt an Mheán Oíche* in 1897. Both Arland Ussher and Lord Longford were of Anglo-Irish Ascendancy background, and O'Connor, although born into the Catholic majority, saw himself very much as a cultural outlaw in the provincial, church-dominated Ireland of the 1930s and 1940s.

Marcus was aware of at least three of Merriman's earlier translators. He read Ussher's version of 1926 in the Cork County Public Library when he was a young man, and found it, he said, a 'somewhat restrained rendition'.[5] When Lord Longford's version was published in *Poetry Ireland* in 1949, Marcus was the editor of the journal. Longford's translation appeared with three severe cuts that eliminated the original's highly provocative comments about celibacy, including the sexual attractiveness of Irish Catholic priests, but Marcus' translation, published four years later by the fearless Liam Miller, included the passages cut by Longford. But it was O'Connor's translation, and indeed O'Connor himself, that had by far the greatest influence on Marcus' work in translation from the Irish, and especially on his translation of *Cúirt an Mheán Oíche*.

Marcus was introduced to O'Connor in 1945, after O'Connor had read Marcus' first poetic translation from the Irish, a version of Cathal Buí Mac Giolla Ghunna's eighteenth-century poem 'An Bonnán Buí' ('The Yellow Bittern'), and had recommended it strongly to Jack White, the literary editor of the *Irish Times*, who published it.[6] The following year the Censorship Appeal Board turned down a petition by O'Connor's publisher to revoke the banning of O'Connor's translation. Noting that O'Connor's version, which he described as a 'superb rendition', was banned while the original was not, Marcus says in his autobiography, 'More or less as a one-man protest I decided to thumb my nose at the crass ukase of the establishment and frustrate it with an act of auto-pollution. I sought out the original and read it … I hadn't got very far beyond the opening twenty-two lines when I knew what I wanted to do'[7] – that is, translate the entire poem.

The translation that resulted bears some similarities to O'Connor's, particularly in its enthusiastic engagement with and many elaborations of Merriman's advocacy of sexual freedom and pleasure. For example, in her speech early in the poem describing the suffering that Ireland has endured, the bailiff says at one point: 'An cogadh is an bás gan spás dá ndíogadh, / Uabhar na righthe is ar imigh tar sáile, / An uair ná deineann sibh tuille ina n-áit díobh'[8] ('War and death without reprieve draining them, / The pride of kings that went over the sea, / When you are not making any more in their place'). The notion expressed in 'Uabhar na righthe is ar imigh tar sáile' is found in much Irish-language political poetry of the seventeenth and eighteenth centuries, but except for a reference to Oliver Goldsmith's 'The Deserted Village', a poem about the demise of rural life, Marcus seems less interested in the political implications of the bailiff's comments than in underscoring and intensifying the sexual reference in the final line of the passage: 'The land is like a deserted village; / Our best are banished, but you, you slob, / Have you ever hammered a single job?'[9]

Marcus' preoccupation with sexuality causes him more than once to under-play some of the social and political themes in *Cúirt an Mheán Oíche*, including those that, as O'Connor saw, resonated with post-independence Irish life. Earlier in her speech, the bailiff says:

Do scriosadh an tír is níl 'na ndiaidh
In ionad na luíbheanna acht flíoch is fiadhaile,
An uaisle b'fhearr chun fáin mar leaghadar,

Is uachtar-lámh ag fáslaigh shaidhbhre,
Fealladh le fonn, is foghail gan féachaint
D'fheannadh na lobhar, is an lom dá léirscrios. (79–84)

(The land destroyed and nothing after it
In place of the herbs but chickweed and weeds,
The best nobility wandering as they faded away to nothing
And rich upstarts have the upper hand,
Deceiving with inclination and pillaging without regard
Skinning the lepers and the naked in their devastation.)

O'Connor's version of this passage asks to be read with one eye on what he saw as the cultural and political devastation of Ireland in the 1930s and 1940s:

The country waste and nothing behind
Where the flowers were plucked but the weeds and wild;
The best of your breed in foreign places,
And upstart rogues with impudent faces
Planning with all their guile and spleen
To pick the bones of the Irish clean.[10]

When Marcus comes to this passage, he invents a sexual metaphor for the political loss lamented in the original, and then turns the bulk of his attention to the metaphor, allowing the issues with which the original is concerned more or less to disappear:

Our country's raped and Luck, the coward,
Shuns a virgin that's deflowered –
Far afield our men are shipped
While by grabbing hands she's stripped
And as, powerless, we watch,
All her beauty they debauch. (p. 11)

Not surprisingly, given the appeal that this side of Merriman's poem held for Marcus, his translation is at its best when dealing with passages in *Cúirt an Mheán Oíche* that have to do with matters of sexuality. When, for example, Aoibheall prophesies, near the end of the poem, that the clergy one day will be permitted to marry, and that Ireland's young women will profit greatly from this change, Merriman has her say:

Tiocfaidh an lá le lán-chéad Comhairle
Is cuirfuidh an Pápa lámh na comhachta air,
Suidhfe an chuideachta ar thubaist na tíre
Is scaoilfear chugaibh fá urchall cuibhrigh
Fiadhantas fola agus fothram na feóla
Is mian bhur dtoile, na tollairí teó so. (909–14)

(The day will come with full permission of a Council
And the Pope will put the hand of authority on it,
The assembly will meet on the misfortunes of the country,
And released to you under shackles will be
Wildness of blood and lustiness of the flesh
And desire of your will, these warm piercers.)

Marcus translates:

And then they'll live life to the full
Encouraged by a Papal Bull.
They have the best material
For such pursuits venereal,
And indeed the merest prick
Is all they need to do the trick. (pp. 40–1)

'Papal Bull', which is Marcus' invention, is suggestive enough, and the rhyming of 'prick' and 'trick', as well as the play on 'prick' itself, is alert to the sexual innuendo in 'tollaraí', meaning, according to Dinneen, 'robust fellows' but also 'piercers or borers'.

Marcus' eager engagement with the sexual dimension of Merriman's poem is perhaps at its keenest in his version of the young woman's comments on the sexual inclinations and attractions of Catholic priests, a passage cut from Lord Longford's earlier translation under Marcus' editorship. At one point in the passage, Merriman has the young woman say:

Is minic a buadhtar buaibh is gréithe
Cuigeann is cruach de chuaird na cléire;
Is minic lem chuimhne maoidheadh a dtréithe
Is iomad dá ngníomhradh fír-ghlic féithe;
Is minic do chuala ar fuaid na tíre

Siosarnach luath dá luadh go líonmhar,
Is chonnaic me taidhbhseach roinnt dá ramsa
Is uimhir dá gclainn ar shloinnte fallsa. (795–802)

(Often have cattle and gifts been gained
The contents of a churn and a rick from a visit of the clergy;
Often in my memory their qualities were praised
And a great number of their always-clever deeds of lust;
Often I heard throughout the land
A frenzied whispering being stirred up abundantly,
And I saw plainly some of their romping
And a number of their children with false surnames.)

Marcus' version is positively gleeful in its suggestiveness:

There's many a house that didn't begin
To prosper and smile till the priest dropped in,
And many a woman could toss her head
And boast of the time he blessed her bed;
Throughout the land there's ample proof
The Church is anything but aloof,
And many a man doesn't know that he
Has a son with a clerical pedigree. (p. 35)

Especially in the ironic line 'The Church is anything but aloof', the translation also expresses Marcus' scepticism about the force of the Catholic Church in modern Ireland.

In the preface to his translation, Marcus says, 'Just as Merriman used the spoken language of 1750 I have used the spoken language of 1950.'[11] The ambition to build his translation around contemporary dialogue was no doubt inspired by O'Connor's version of Merriman's poem. But whereas O'Connor's translation manages to address twentieth-century concerns without violating the cultural context of the original, Marcus' efforts to render Merriman in the English of mid-twentieth-century Ireland very often carry his translation far away from Merriman's linguistic and cultural orbit. Also, Marcus' view of Merriman's poem as relentlessly comic – he says in his preface that one reason he undertook the translation was that he was taken with 'the hilarity of its scenes' and 'wished to share the joke with others'[12] – underestimates the full range and achievement of Merriman's poem.

Comparison with O'Connor's translation reveals the limitations of Marcus' frequent use of anachronism to achieve comic effects: the narrator's description of his forced march with the bailiff, 'Is gluais chun siubhail go lúbach láidir, / Sciob léi síos me thríd na gleannta' (136–7) ('And set me moving to walk vigorously, firmly, / She swept me with her down through the glens'), is translated by O'Connor as 'And away we went at a terrible rate / Off through the glens in one wild rush' (p. 18) and by Marcus as 'She lofted me like a sack of spuds / And over the hills I was jet-propelled' (p. 13); the old man's description of a wedding, 'Clagarnach cheóil is ól gan choimse / Is chaitheadar cóisir mhórdach mhaoidhteach' (509–10) ('[There was] a storm of music and drink without moderation / And they enjoyed an undoubtedly grand feast'), is rendered by O'Connor as 'The supper was ready; the beer was plied; / The fiddles were flayed and the night advancing' (p. 30) and by Marcus as 'And the drink it took to stock the bar / Was enough to float a man-o'-war!' (p. 25); the old man's admiring words about the newborn baby his young wife presents to him, 'Chruadhadar a uilleanna, a chruibh's a chnámha' (578) ('His elbows, his fists, and his bones hardened'), is translated by O'Connor as 'His hands and wrists and elbows strong' (p. 33) and by Marcus as 'And his biceps bulging like King Kong!' (p. 27); the young woman's description of the material comforts with which the old man seduced his wife, 'Teallaighe teó agus móin a daoithin, / Ballaí fód gan leoithne gaoithe' (671–2) ('Warm hearths and turf in plenty, / Walls of sod without a breath of wind'), is rendered by O'Connor as 'The stack of turf, the lamp to light, / The sodded wall of a winter's night' (p. 36) and by Marcus as 'A separate banking account of her own, / A butler, a car, and a telephone' (p. 32); and, finally, the young woman's account of the old man's sexual inadequacies, 'Is an feóidhteach fuar so suas léi sínte / Dreoighte duairic, gan bhuadh gan bhíogadh' (689–90), ('And this cold, withered old man stretched out by her / Putrefied, surly, without virtue, without vigour'), is translated by O'Connor as 'Like a wintry wind to a woman in bed!' (p. 36) and by Marcus as 'Who, lure as she might, would never mate her / But lay like a human refrigerator' (p. 32).

Even in those moments in which Merriman's voice shifts away from the comic, which O'Connor effectively translates by altering his tone, Marcus remains stuck in a one-dimensional comic mode. For example, when the young woman expresses her fears of growing old alone, there is no trace of the comic in Merriman's text:

Táim in achrann daingean na mblianta,
Ag tarraint go tréan ar laethibh liaithe,
Is eagal liom éag gan éinne 'om iarraidh.
A Phéarla ó Pharrthas, screadaim is glaedhim ort,
Éiric m'anma ort! aitchim thu is éighim ort,
Seachain ná scaoil me im shraighill gan áird,
Ná im chailligh gan chrích gan bhrigh gan bhláth,
Gan charaid gan chlainn gan choim gan cháirde
Ar theallachaibh draighin gan feidhm gan fáilte. (310–18)

(I am in the firm fastness of the years,
Approaching rapidly the grey days,
And I fear a death without anyone asking for me.
Pearl from Paradise, I implore and I call on you,
Ransom my soul, I beseech you and I appeal to you,
Take care, don't dismiss me as a useless slattern,
Or as a hag unmarried, without virtue, without bloom,
Without friends, without children, without protection, without credit
At inhospitable firesides without use, without welcome.)

As was argued in the chapter on O'Connor, this is one of those moments in which O'Connor exhibits his short-story writer's sensitivity to the complexities of human character, and he does so in part by following Merriman in eschewing the comic voice:

For here I am at the place I started,
And that is the cause of all my tears,
Fast in the rope of the rushing years
With age and want in lessening span
And death at the end and no hopes of a man.
But whatever misfortunes God may send,
Spare me at least that lonesome end!
Do not leave me to cross alone
Without chick nor child when my beauty's gone
An old maid counting the things I lack
Scowling thresholds that hurl me back. (pp. 23–4)

Marcus, on the other hand, fails to register the fears of the young woman with conviction largely because he's unwilling, or unable, to set aside the comic voice that dominates his translation; in his version of this passage, the woman's speech includes an inappropriate double end-rhyme, as well as a supposedly comic image of herself as 'a gibbering goat':

> And what's worse – I haven't that youthful vigour
> And soon I'll be losing my girlish figure;
> The years won't wait, and I'm afraid
> I'll die a miserable old maid.
> Whatever else may be my lot
> I'd suffer – anything but that;
> Don't turn me loose at the end of my days
> Like a gibbering goat with a vacant gaze
> Who, having no family or friend,
> On cast-out leavings must depend. (p. 18)

Marcus says in the preface to his translation, 'I have striven to make it a translation in both senses: a version that would be as true as possible to the spirit of the original, and also an attempt at presenting the poem as Merriman might have written it were he alive now and composing in English.'[13] It is, of course, impossible to say how Merriman would have written *Cúirt an Mheán Oíche* had he been composing it in English in the 1950s. But for all its empathy with Merriman's advocacy of sexual freedom, and for all its attempts to translate that empathy into a poem that speaks against the Catholic Church's puritanical teachings in the middle decades of the twentieth century, Marcus' translation, veering too far and too often toward the contemporary, is not, in the end, true to 'the spirit of the original'.

Patrick C. Power: Scholarship and Poetic Translation

atrick C. Power (1928–2008) came to *Cúirt an Mheán Oíche* from a background more scholarly than poetic. By the time his translation appeared, in 1971, he had published two academic studies – *The Story of Anglo-Irish Poetry (1800–1922)* (1967), essentially an evaluation of the effect of the Irish-language tradition on Irish poetry written in English, and *A Literary History of Ireland* (1969) – and he earned his Ph.D. from University College Galway the same year. The first (and last) academically trained scholar to produce a poetic translation of *Cúirt an Mheán Oíche*, Power was a product of an Irish academy that was expanding steadily through the middle decades of the twentieth century; indeed, Power's translation of Merriman's poem reflects the growth of third-level education in those years just as Lord Lordford's theatrically-conscious translation speaks to the rise of the Irish theatre in the first decades of the century. Not surprisingly, Power believed that translation needed to be grounded in scholarly knowledge; in *The Story of Anglo-Irish Poetry*, he says:

> It might be said with much truth that translation from one language into another is virtually impossible to do in a perfect manner. Something is nearly always lost in the process. But it seems to be true that a sound scholarly

knowledge of both languages is essential and a deep understanding of the mental habits of the people whose poetry is being translated.[1]

Power published his translation of Merriman's poem side by side with a version of the original. He says in his introduction that the dual nature of his text reflects a desire to bring *Cúirt an Mheán Oíche,* 'in its original form and its English version', to the attention of a wider range of readers than it had previously enjoyed.[2] Behind this desire lies a view of the importance and fragility of Ireland's Gaelic past. In *A Literary History of Ireland,* Power warns that the disappearance from Irish culture of the Irish-language tradition, 'the accumulated experience of our people over one and half millennia at least,' would be 'a great catastrophe to the separate identity of the Irish people'.[3] Power was not, however, of Daniel Corkery's persuasion, as his notion of 'separate identity' recognizes both of Ireland's major traditions: 'The heritage of the Irish people, then, is both the Gaelic and Anglo-Irish literatures. Both enshrine the consciousness of the whole Irish nation and he who cuts himself off from any one of these two deprives himself of a significant portion of his literary heritage.'[4] Thus for Power, translation from the Irish is crucial to fostering an understanding not just of the threatened Irish-language tradition, but also of the dual nature of Irish culture.

Power's scholarly background also stands behind his understanding of the central concerns of Merriman's poem, and of the relevance of those concerns to modern Ireland. Like O'Connor, Power was sceptical, to say the least, of attempts to construct a modern Irish identity that would fuse the conservative and puritanical attitudes of the Irish Catholic Church with the Gaelic tradition. But whereas O'Connor measured the failings of modern Ireland against the ideals of the revolution that brought it about, Power took a longer, more scholarly view. In his book *Sex and Marriage in Ancient Ireland,* published five years after his translation of *Cúirt an Mheán Oíche* appeared, Power argues that the Brehon Laws, under which Gaelic Ireland was governed until the Norman invasion in the twelfth century, were markedly liberal regarding sexual mores and marriage:

> These are a revelation for anyone thinking that our modern Irish attitudes to sexual and marital affairs are somehow that of our ancestors. Nothing could be further from the truth. In sober legal language the brehon laws legislated for Irish society in a manner which puts the most indulgent and humane legal system to shame.[5]

Ireland's Gaelic past also has particular relevance, Power argues, for the rise of feminist consciousness in modern Ireland. The Brehon Laws were based, Power says, on the principle that 'women were not mere chattels but had a framework within which they could carve out much freedom for themselves'.[6] By contrast, he says, 'The modern Irish state ... turned out to be a poor version of the most narrow-minded Victorian attitudes imaginable.'[7]

These views very much inform Power's translation of *Cúirt an Mheán Oíche*; in his introduction, Power identifies as the poem's central concern 'the celebration of the right of woman to sex and marriage'.[8] Unfortunately, Power's commitment to scholarly accuracy, along with his lack of experience in writing poetry, all too often interferes with his ability to translate Merriman's central themes, as he sees them, into fluent English verse.

In *Sex and Marriage in Ancient Ireland*, Power argues that in a society in which human rights are under pressure, it is women 'who have suffered the most and been deprived of redress',[9] Yet when he comes to the passage in *Cúirt an Mheán Oíche* in which the suffering of the young woman, and especially her fears of growing old without children or husband, are expressed with passion and gravity – a moment that, as has been argued in earlier chapters, provides a kind of litmus test for Merriman's translators – Power's shortcomings as a poet are unhappily in evidence. In Merriman's text, the young woman says:

> Fáth mo sheanchais fhada, mo phianchreach!
> Táim in achrann daingean i mblianta,
> Ag tarraing go tréan ar laethe liatha;
> Is eagal dom éag 'is gan aon dom' iarraidh.
> A phéarla ó Pharthas! screadaim 'is éim ort,
> Eiric m'anama ort, aichím is glaoim tú!
> Seachain! ná scaoil mé im straoil gan áird
> Ná im chailleach gan chríoch, gan bhrí, gan bhláth,
> Gan chara, gan chlann, gan choim, gan chairde,
> Ar theallach an draighin gan feidhm, gan fáilte.[10]

> (The reason of my long story-telling, woe is me!
> I am in the firm fastness of the years,
> Approaching rapidly the grey days;
> And I fear a death without anyone asking for me.
> Pearl of Paradise, I implore and I call on you,

Ransom my soul, I beseech you and I appeal to you,
Take care! don't leave me as a useless slattern
Or as a hag unmarried, without virtue, without bloom,
Without friends, without children, without protection, without credit
At inhospitable firesides without use, without welcome.)

Power translates:

The cause of all this talk is, oh dear!
That I'm fighting strongly against the years,
Approaching the days of greyness fast;
I fear to die by a man unasked!
Oh Pearl of Paradise! I scream and invoke you,
Ransom my spirit, I beg and implore you!
Take care! don't dismiss me as a streel that's useless,
Or a hag unmarried, powerless, bloomless,
Friendless, childless, without guts or credit,
At firesides a scold without use or welcome. (309–18)

'Oh dear!' is an astonishingly inept translation of the passionate 'mo phian-chreach', and the awkwardness of 'I fear to die of a man unasked' results from following too closely the syntax of the original. 'I scream', although a literal translation of 'screadaim', is not true to spoken English, and 'without guts' falls far short of Merriman's sexually suggestive 'gan choim', where 'choim' means 'covering' as well as 'protection'. Power's representation of this deeply felt speech collapses entirely a few lines later when he renders "Is mise mar táim gan tál gan tsíolrach' (330) ('And myself as I am without issue, without progeny') as 'While I remain as I am with no children or kiddies' (330).

Power's translation demonstrates in general the inevitable difficulties that arise in translating a poem written in one language into a poem written in another when the translator, especially one with more scholarly than poetic credentials, tries to adhere too closely to the language and syntax of the original. When the narrator, for example, describes the building in which the court is seated as 'Taibhseach dathúil daingean dea-dhóirseach' (142) ('Magnificent, substantial, solid, easily accessible'), Power translates, 'Lovely, strong, well-doored, substantial'; 'well-doored' is a more-or-less literal translation of 'dea-dhóirseach', but it is awkward and untrue to spoken English. And Power's version of the bailiff's comment that 'Is docharach dubhach mar d'fhúig gach daoirse / Go doilbhir dúr i ndubhcheart dlithe' (85–6) ('It's distressing and sorrowful that, like the worst case of every oppression / A hard affliction in the dark denial of the law') tries too hard to reproduce in English the complex syntax of Merriman's Irish: 'It's sad and grievous that each bondage left, / In sad affliction without law to protect' (85–6). Frank O'Connor's translation of these two lines is, by contrast, the work of a poet with sufficient confidence to move far enough away from the literal meaning and syntax of the original to transform Merriman's Irish into two lines of sound English verse: 'But the worst of all these bad reports / Was that truth was darkened in their courts.'[11]

Power's scholarly approach to *Cúirt an Mheán Oíche* does, however, have its compensations, the most significant of which stem from Power's decision to imitate Merriman's use of terminal assonance, something that no other translator of Merriman has attempted.[12] Although Power's commitment to this practice can undermine fluency –for example, the old man's comments about the young woman's clothes, 'I ndatha, i gcóir, is i gclóca síoda. / Faire go deo arú! Sceol cár fríth é' (417–18) ('In colours, in fittings, and in a silken cloak. / Alas, alas! Relate where was it got'), become in Power's translation 'In colours, correct and in silken cloak; / But wait! where 'twas got is an anecdote!' (417–18) – Power's echoing of Merriman's terminal assonance does at times bring his translation admirably close to the prosody of the original. Power is often at his best in translating Merriman's lists of related words and phrases running over several lines – a practice that Power says testifies 'to the love of word-music and pure sound which was the delight of eighteenth-century poets'[13] – in part because his terminal assonance avoids the artificial quality of terminal rhyme. In her description of what an attractive man would look like, for example, Merriman's young woman runs off an extensive series of descriptive adjectives:

Mo chumha! mo chrá! ba bhreá sin éad bheith
Ar lonnaire láidir, lánmhear, léadmhar,
Shantach, sháiteach, shásta, sheasmhach,
Ramsach, ráflach, rábach, rabairneach;
Lascaire luaimneach, luascach, líofa;
Balcaire buan nó buailteoir bríomhar;
Faraire suairc nó cuairteoir cumasach;
Scafaire suthain nó cluantóir cuisleannach. (817–24)

(My sorrow! my torment! that would be fine to be jealous
In a bright, strong, brave, agile man,
Fierce, thrusting, pleasing, firm,
Romping, given to raillery, vigorous, prodigal;
Rollicking, nimble, moving, fluent;
A long-lived strong person, or an effective thresher,
A brave, affable fellow or a powerful visitor;
A sharp idler or a strong-armed flatterer.)

There is far too much sexual wordplay in these lines for any translator to accommodate fully, but Power's translation, although inevitably thinning out the sexual richness of the original, does manage to imitate effectively the movement of Merriman's lines:

My sorrow! my hurt! jealousy is fine
In a hero who's strong and brave and wild,
Greedy, gushing, willing and resolute,
Romping, railling, rapid and generous:
A rollicker, sprightly, volatile, flattering,
A steady tough or a lively hammerer;
A merry companion or effective visitor;
A straying type or a muscular trickster. (817–24)

Power's translation is also sensitive to the practice, common in Irish-language poetry, of assonantal links falling off as well as on the final syllable in a line: 'lighten' and 'horizon' (6–7), 'magnificent' and 'amazon' (47–8), 'great ones' and 'favour' (89–90), 'distracted' and 'unsubstantial' (271–2), 'choose them' and 'useless hunt' (280–1), 'luxuriantly' and 'seducing' (759–60), and (a double assonance) 'limbs here' and 'thin feet' (1039–40).

Power's scholarly allegiance to Merriman's text also at times enables him to bring over effectively into English verse Merriman's devotion to detail, a quality that frequently escapes some of Merriman's earlier translators. The old man's description of the cabin that he says the young woman grew up in – 'Lag ina dhrom 'is gabhla ar lúbadh / Agus clagarnach dhonn go drom ag túirling' (413–14) ('Weak at its top and props bending / And a heavy brown rain heavily pouring down') – provides an example. Arland Ussher's translation of these two lines loses the arresting image of the rain's colour: 'And crazy roof and couples bending / And rain in fearful floods descending'.[14] Lord Longford's version isn't any more attentive to the specifics of Merriman's description: 'The ruined roof hangs weakly over all, / And sagging rafters let the torrents fall!'.[15] Power's version, on the other hand, staying relatively close to Merriman's text, misses none of its details: 'Weak is the roof-ridge, the gables are bending; / A down-pour heavily, brownly descending' (413–14).

The version of Merriman's text that Power includes with his translation differs considerably from editions published earlier.[16] In his introduction, Power defends his editorial choices, saying that he wanted to provide 'an interesting text, based on unused sources, rather than slavishly following what is often regarded as the established writ'.[17] One passage from Power's edition that doesn't appear in earlier published versions of Merriman's poem amplifies, with quite graphic detail, the young woman's description of the difficulties her friend had in arousing her elderly husband:

> Is minic a ghlac sí a shalt neamhbhríomhar,
> 'Is chuimil dá clais a chab 'na síoghinneach,
> Chuireadh go fras é ar faid 'na mínchrobh
> Agus ní phriocadh an spreas chun bail' ná bíogadh. (767–70)
>
> (Often she took his un-vigorous rod,
> And rubbed its head on her groove in her bewitching stamina,
> Put it nimbly lengthwise in her smooth hand
> And did not goad the dry twig to success or rousing.)

Power translates:

> It's often she grasped his lifeless sceptre
> And rubbed its mouth to her groin with frenzy,
> Took it within her soft hand nimbly
> And roused not the wretch to excitement or business. (767–70)

A passage such as this reveals the poetic as well as scholarly contribution that Power's version makes to the translation history of *Cúirt an Mheán Oíche*: it's based on a passage that doesn't appear in earlier versions of the poem; it's faithful to the original's tendency not to turn a blind eye to anything, especially anything having to do with sexuality; and its use of terminal assonance imitates with consider-able effectiveness one of the key elements in the metrical make-up of Merriman's poem. Not bad for someone who was not, by profession anyway, a poet.

Cosslett Ó Cuinn: The Footprint of Sectarianism

osslett Ó Cuinn, a Church of Ireland rector born in Co. Antrim in 1907, worked on behalf of ecumenism in Ireland, and devoted much of his considerable literary energy to writing in Irish and advocating the language's cultural importance, undertakings that no doubt were viewed with some scepticism by many of his background and religion. But despite his ecumenical leanings, Ó Cuinn had reservations about some aspects of the Irish Catholic Church, and when he came to translate *Cúirt an Mheán Oíche* late in his life – he completed it in 1979, when he was seventy-two, and it was published three years later[1] – some of those reservations found their way into his translation. The anti-Catholicism surfaces only in traces – it doesn't dominate the translation nearly to the extent to which Michael C. O'Shea's romantic nationalism colours his version, published nearly a century earlier – but its presence underscores the force of sectarian difference in Irish culture, especially in the North, and especially in the 1970s.

Ó Cuinn first became acquainted with the Irish language while a student at St Columba's College in Rathfarnham and, later, at Campbell College in Belfast.[2] He read classical languages at Trinity College Dublin, where he also later studied for the ministry, and had a considerable gift for languages, at one point reportedly being conversant in Latin, Greek, Hebrew, Aramaic, Italian, German, French, Spanish and Irish; as the *Irish Times* commented at his death in 1995, Ó Cuinn 'collected languages as other people collected pictures, ceramics, and other works of art'.[3] While at Trinity, Ó Cuinn became friends with Seoirse Mac Canna, from Lurgan, Co. Armagh, who was also studying for the ministry, and who was fluent in Irish. (Mac Canna's father had been an official in Conradh na Gaeilge.) During his years at Trinity, Ó Cuinn also spent some time on the Great Blasket, and met George Thompson, who, at Trinity on a scholarship from Cambridge, had learned Irish while visiting the island a number of times in the early 1920s. In the 1930s, Ó Cuinn became increasingly focused on Ulster Irish, as he began visiting Gabhla off the coast of Co. Donegal and, later, Tory Island and Árainn Mhór, collecting local songs and stories in the language.

Throughout his many years as a Church of Ireland rector (he was ordained in 1931), working in various parishes on both sides of the border, Ó Cuinn never lost his dedication to Irish. Indeed, in the face of the effort, especially strong in the decades immediately following the establishment of the Irish Free State in 1923, to link Gaelic culture to Irish Catholicism as a basis for a distinctively Irish identity, Ó Cuinn argued that the language was particularly essential for Irish Protestants precisely because they were being marginalized; in a lecture given in the summer of 1931, he said that Irish was 'a subject of importance if we are to understand the past of our Church and country: and ... if we neglect it, we may prevent ourselves and our Church from making any contribution to our country's future'.[4]

The year before Ó Cuinn finished his translation of *Cúirt an Mheán Oíche*, he published a long satirical poem in Irish entitled *Slánú an tSalachair* (*Redeeming the Dirt*) that gave vent to some of his scepticism about the Catholic clergy and certain doctrines of the church. As Ó Cuinn's biographer says, no one who reads the poem can be blind 'ar a mhíshásamh leis an Eaglais Chaitliceach Rómhánach' ('to his dissatisfaction with the Roman Catholic Church').[5] Although the poem condemns Protestants for tending to be anti-Catholic, as well as Catholics for tending to be anti-Protestant, it contains a sharply satirical portrait of the Catholic clergy:

Tá do cheist agus a freagra san pennycatechism acu,
Míneoid siad á nÚdarás
lena dtuigtear do choir's do chás

...

Glac lena rá mar bhriathar Dé,
nó beidh siad ina dhéidh
ort, is gheo' tú buille baichle
(ó stadadh den choinneal-bháthadh)
is cuirfidh siad a ndroim leatsa,
a ghiolla na ceiste a d'iarr freagra
is croithfidh siad uisce coiscreactha
ar scabaill ar chaith máthair ab í
nó ar sheanbhó naofa bheannaithe aimrid,
a bheaireas broimeannaí in ionad bainne.[6]

(They have your question and its answer in the penny catechism.
They will expound their Authority
so that your sin and your case is understood

...

Take what they say as the word of God,
or they will be after
you, and you will get a blow from the gang
(since refraining from excommunication)
and they will put their backs to you,
you fellow of the question who wanted an answer,
and they will shake consecrated water
on a scapular that a mother wore
or on a saintly, blessed, barren old cow,
who gives farts instead of milk.)

Although Ó Cuinn's dissatisfaction with some aspects of Catholicism is by no means the driving force of his translation of Merriman's poem, it leaves an unmistakable footprint. When, for example, the young woman, in her first speech, describes various folk superstitions that she followed to attract a husband, Ó Cuinn's translation suggests a link between Catholic ritual and superstition, a common enough view of Catholicism among some Protestants. In Merriman, the young woman says:

Níl cleas dá mbéidir léamh ná trácht air
Le teacht na ré nó tréis bheith lán di,

Um Inid, um Shamhain, ná ar shiúl na bliana
Ná tuigim gur leamhas bheith ag súil le ciall as!

···

Is deimhin nárbh obair liom troscadh le cráifeacht,
Is greim ná blogam ní sholgainn trí trátha.[7]

(There isn't a trick that it would it be possible to read of or mention
With the coming of the moon or after its being full,
Around Shrovetide, around Hallowe'en, or throughout the year
That I understand that it's folly to be looking for sense out of it!

···

It's a certainty that it was not work for me to fast with piety,
And a bit or a sup I would not swallow for days.)

Ó Cuinn inserts into his version of this passage specific references to the church and Lent:

I tried all tricks, I played all tunes
By waxing or by waning moons
At Shrove and at All Hallows' tide.
At feasts such as our holy guide,
The Church, does through the year provide
My many games I vainly tried.

···

All Lent I fasted piously
And slimmed myself industriously.[8]

In translating an earlier passage in the young woman's speech, describing the many Irish women left without fulfilment or protection, Ó Cuinn converts the frustrated women into nuns, and uses the occasion to represent in satirical terms the church's teachings about the value of rejecting the physical, natural, and material world. In Merriman, the young woman says: 'Na sluaite imíonn gan chríoch, gan chaomhnadh, / Ar fuaid an tsaoil seo d'fhíorscoith béithe / 'Na gcailleacha dubha gan cumhdach céile' (177–9) ('The crowds that go without fulfilment, without protection, / For the very best women throughout this world / To be sad, celibate women without protection of a spouse').

Ó Cuinn translates:

Young women flee from worldliness
With such unlimited excess,
And all the finest girls I know
Out of this world aspire to go,
Renouncing hope of spouse or son
Each wears black clothes and knows no one
And for no crime thought of, or done,
Condemns herself to be a nun. (p. 17)

Later, in her second speech, the young woman says that she's opposed to celibacy because it takes young, sexually attractive priests out of the marriage market:

Cumha ní ghlacfainn le cafairí coillte,
Snamhairí galair ná searraigh gan soilse,
Acht márlaigh bhodacha, tollairí tréana
I dtámhaíl chodlata is obair gan déanamh…! (779–82)

(I would not regret gelded praters,
Diseased cringers or young things without brightness,
But lusty youths, virile piercers
In the lethargy of sleep and work not being done…!)

Ó Cuinn expands these four lines into eight, managing in the process to slip in some mocking comments about the papacy:

Some I'd spare gladly, who'd require
Castrati from the papal choir,
Insects whose business is to ail
Colts that know only how to stale.
But how can those whose manliest part
Could drive a nail straight in with art
Go idling off in dreams to Roam
With so much work to do at home? (p. 65)

Ó Cuinn also translates Aoibheall's prophesy, pronounced near the end of the poem, that celibacy will eventually disappear – 'Seachain go fóill na comhachtaigh íogmhar' / Is caithfidh siad pósadh fós, pé chífeas!' (907–8) ('Shun awhile the cruel, powerful persons / And they will have to marry still, whatever will happen!') – with more anti-clerical venom:

[73]

Don't contradict the hierarchy.
Leave them, since they're so sensitive,
In that long past age in which they live.
Yet married men they yet shall be
Whoever lives long enough to see. (p. 78)

Ó Cuinn's translation met with a decidedly mixed reception. When he submitted it to Seán Feehan, the founder of Mercier Press, which had published Patrick C. Power's version in 1971, Feehan was sufficiently impressed to assemble a group of actors – Joe Dowling, Fidelma Murphy, Eamonn Kelly and Máire Ní Dhomhnaill – to produce a recording of it, and in the liner notes, Feehan says that Ó Cuinn 'has achieved a deeper identification with Merriman than any of his predecessors'.[9] But Máirtín Ó Cadhain, several of whose stories Ó Cuinn had translated, apparently objected to parts of it,[10] and Ó Cuinn himself seems to have had his doubts; his biographer says that Ó Cuinn's wife told him that Ó Cuinn was unhappy 'faoi ghairbe nithe áirithe' ('about a roughness of certain things') in the translation.[11]

Although he had done a fair amount of writing in Irish, including poetry, Ó Cuinn, like Power, had few if any credentials as a writer of English verse, and his translation bears the marks of the amateur. For one thing, although O'Cuinn's version is much longer than the original – 1639 lines compared to Merriman's 1026 – it fails to translate effectively much of Merriman's most striking imagery. In the opening of the poem, for example, Merriman's narrator describes the effect of seeing a range of mountains in these terms: 'Taitneamhach aoibhinn suíomh na sléibhte / Ag bagairt a gcinn thar droim a chéile' (7–8) ('Pleasing, delightful the situation of the mountains / Brandishing their heads over each other's backs'). Most of Merriman's earlier translators try to bring over into their versions the image in the second line here: Arland Ussher has 'The hills that rear their heads on high / Over each other's backs to spy'[12]; Frank O'Connor 'Mountains in ranks with crimson borders / Peering above their neighbours' shoulders'[13]; Lord Longford 'Each dear, delightful form of cliff and boulder, / Each peak that nodded on another's shoulder'[14]; and David Marcus 'How silently the mountains rest / Their heads upon each other's breast'.[15] Ó Cuinn, however, retreats into generalities, and the image is lost: 'The mountain ranges row on row / A formidable beauty show' (p. 1).

Ó Cuinn renders a six-line passage in the young woman's first speech lamenting the marriage of sexually attractive men to older women into eight limp lines that overlook most if not all of the rich sexual suggestiveness of the original. In Merriman, the young woman says:

An uair chím preabaire calma croíúil
Fuadrach fearamhail barramhail bríomhar
Stuama feasamhach seasamhach saoithiúil
Gruaidhdheas greannamhar geanamhail gnaíúil
Nó buachaill bastalach beachanta brógdheas
Cruacheart ceannasach ceaptha córach. (211–16)

(When I see a dashing, brave, cordial man
Bustling, manly, funny, vigorous
Sensible, knowing, steadfast, accomplished
Pleasant-cheeked, humorous, loving, comely
Or a boy showy, vigorous, with a nicely shaped boot
Rightly hardy, commanding, determined, shapely.)

The sexual innuendo here comes fast and furious, in, for example, 'seasamhach', which means 'standing' and 'firm' as well as 'steadfast', and 'beachanta', which means 'waspish' or 'stinging' as well as 'vigorous'; also, behind the suggestive 'chruacheart' is the verb 'cruaim', which means 'I harden' or 'I stiffen'. O'Cuinn's version washes out virtually all the sexual playfulness of the original:

I see the sturdy, healthy blade,
Young, manly, handsome and well-made,
The gay, the gentle and the kind,
The men of sense, the wise of mind,
Those who know how and when to act
Who show unerring grace and tact,
The men determined and efficient
In all things formidably proficient. (p. 19)

The inadequacies of this kind of evasive translation are all the more evident when read alongside John Verling's quite graphic illustrations that accompany Ó Cuinn's text in the Mercier edition.

That said, there are a handful of exceptions to Ó Cuinn's general insensitivity to the vigour of Merriman's poem. Ó Cuinn's rendering of the old man's description of how the child that his wife presents to him was conceived – not by him – is pointed, compressed, and in tune with the unrestrained spirit of the original. In Merriman, the old man says:

> Ní deacair a mheas nach spreas gan bhrí
> Bhí ceangailte ar nasc ar teasc ag mnaoi,
> Gan chnámh gan chumas gan chuma gan chom
> Gan ghrá gan chumann gan fuinneamh gan fonn,
> Do scaipfeadh i mbroinn aon mhaighre mná
> Le catachas dradhain an groidhire breá,
> Mar chuireann sé i bhfeidhm gan mhoill gan bhréig
> Le cumas a bhaill is le loigheamh a ghéag
> Gur crobhaire crothadh go cothrom gan cháim é
> Le fonn na fola is le forthram na sláinte. (619–28)

> (It's not difficult to think that is not a dry branch without force
> Who would be tied on a chain for a task by a woman,
> Without a bone, without ability, without a figure, without a waist
> Without love, without friendship, without vigour, without desire,
> Who would beget in the womb of any healthy woman
> With passionate concupiscence the fine hearty fellow,
> As he demonstrates at once, without falsehood
> With the power of his member and with the cut of his limbs
> That he is a strong, able person created justly without fault
> With desire of the blood and with the lustiness of health.)

Ó Cuinn translates:

> 'Twas no toneless, boneless, stoneless waster
> With no wish for a woman or power to taste her
> Who filled with tomcat lust gone mad
> Some woman's womb with this fine lad
> Whose young limbs' energy and grace
> Suffice to prove that in his case
> This merry little get was got
> Mid healthy sounds when blood was hot. (p. 50)

But if one remembers that Thomas Kinsella was working on his translation of *Cúirt an Mheán Oíche* about the same time that Ó Cuinn was composing his –

Kinsella published part of his version in 1981 and a complete translation in 1986 – one cannot fail to see, as the next chapter will argue, how important a poetic sensibility is to the practice of verse translation. But there is another difference between these two translators. An Irish poet of Catholic background living in Dublin, Kinsella was concerned chiefly in his translation of Merriman's poem with building solid bridges between Ireland's Irish- and English-language traditions, and his translation pays little or no attention to the question of sectarian difference, even though the North was, at the time, in violent turmoil. A Church of Ireland rector born and reared in Northern Ireland did not, it seems, have that option.

Thomas Kinsella: 'A Dual Approach'

homas Kinsella is the first of Merriman's translators who is a poet by profession, someone, as Kinsella himself said of Aodhgán Ó Rathaille, 'whose life can be seen as a true poetic career'.[1] Denis Woulfe was a schoolmaster, Michael C. O'Shea a journalist whose main concern seemed to be Irish nationalism, Arland Ussher an essayist and philosopher, Frank O'Connor chiefly a short-story writer, Lord Longford a dramatist and man of the theatre, David Marcus a literary editor, Patrick C. Power a scholar and teacher and Cosslett Ó Cuinn a Church of Ireland rector. As a professional poet, Kinsella brings to his translation of *Cúirt an Mheán Oíche* essentially aesthetic concerns about the relationship between the modern Irish poet writing in English and the Irish-language tradition. Especially at the start of his career, Kinsella saw that tradition as necessary but existing at a distressing remove, and he has spent a considerable part of his career trying to bring it closer. Translation from the Irish has proved particularly important to this enterprise, not just in making, as Kinsella once said, 'an offering to the past from which I feel separated',[2] but also in constructing a meaningful relationship between Ireland's Irish- and English-language traditions, and so in arguing for the dual nature of Irish writing and Irish culture.

Kinsella has been translating from the Irish from the beginning of his 'true poetic career'. In the 1950s, when he was just starting to write, he translated several Irish-language poems from early periods, publishing them in his collection *Poems & Translations* in 1961. Not long after this, he took on the substantial project of translating into English the epic *Táin Bó Cuailnge*, an enterprise that occupied him through the 1960s. (The translation was published in 1969.) In the 1970s, he worked on *An Duanaire: 1600–1900: Poems of the Dispossessed*, a collection, published in 1981, of a hundred poems in Irish accompanied by Kinsella's translations of them into English verse, including a version of about a third of *Cúirt an Mheán Oíche*. Five years later, *The New Oxford Book of Irish Verse*, edited by Kinsella, appeared, containing more than 125 of Kinsella's translations, including a version of *Cúirt an Mheán Oíche* in its entirety. To all this work, Kinsella brought what he once described as 'a missionary zeal',[3] and it certainly can be argued that with the possible exception of Michael Hartnett, no other contemporary Irish poet has made such a substantial and wide-ranging contribution to poetic translation from the Irish.

Kinsella's work also marks a turning point in the importance of poetic translation within the canon of Irish writing. In the nineteenth century, only James Clarence Mangan and Samuel Ferguson devoted significant parts of their careers to translation, and although a number of twentieth-century writers before Kinsella produced a fair amount of accomplished translation – James Stephens, Frank O'Connor and Austin Clarke, for example – they were exceptions. But since Kinsella's considerable forays into translation, it has become the order of the day for Irish poets, even for those with little Irish. Moreover, many translators after Kinsella have taken contemporary poetry in Irish as their province, effectively insisting on the dual nature of contemporary Irish writing and culture. Following the publication of *An Duanaire* in 1981, a number of dual-language anthologies of contemporary Irish-language poetry, with translations by various hands, began to appear: *The Bright Wave / An Tonn Gheal: Poetry in Irish Now* (1986), *An Crann Faoi Bhláth: The Flowering Tree: Contemporary Irish Poetry with Verse Translations* (1991) and *Irish Poetry Now: Other Voices* (1993). The poems in Nuala Ní Dhomhnaill's collection *Pharaoh's Daughter*, published in 1990, were accompanied by verse translations from no fewer than thirteen different contemporary Irish poets.

In an oft-cited essay based on a talk that he gave at the Modern Language Association meeting in 1966, Kinsella says that an Irish poet of his generation, looking back over the Irish poetic tradition for inspiration and models, finds, beyond Yeats and the 'almost total poetic silence' of the nineteenth century, 'a great cultural blur: I must exchange one language for another, my native English for eighteenth-century Irish'.[4] This fractured tradition, he says, has destabilized his own poetic identity: 'I recognize that I stand on one side of a great rift, and can feel the discontinuity in myself.'[5] In his preface to *The New Oxford Book of Irish Verse*, Kinsella argues for the importance of translation in healing that discontinuity. Noting that the previous edition of the anthology, edited by Donagh MacDonagh and Lennox Robinson, contained only 'a tiny handful of translations from the Irish', Kinsella says that 'Irish poetry is important in both languages', and that the primary aim of his anthology is to 'present an idea of these two bodies of poetry and of the relationship between them'.[6]

The importance of that relationship extends, for Kinsella, to the broadest reaches of Irish culture and literary history. As he says in *The Dual Tradition: An Essay on Poetry and Politics in Ireland*, published in 1995: 'The Irish tradition exists as a dual entity. It was composed in two languages. The changing emphases between one language and another reflect changing circumstances through the centuries … A dual approach is … essential if the literature of the Irish tradition is to be fully understood.'[7] In light of this view, it's significant that both versions of Kinsella's translation of *Cúirt an Mheán Oíche* – the shorter one in *An Duanaire* and the complete one in *The New Oxford Book of Irish Verse* – were published as parts of anthologies, thereby defining the appropriate context for his translation as the entire tradition of Irish writing, in both languages.

Perhaps more than anything else, Kinsella's handling of what he refers to as 'images and ideas' enables him to negotiate effectively between Merriman's tradition and his own, affirming the value of each and the vital connection between them. In the introduction to *An Duanaire*, Kinsella says that his translations are not 'free versions', and that 'all images and ideas occurring in the Irish are conveyed in translation and images or ideas not occurring in the Irish are not employed'.[8] This does not at all mean that Kinsella's translations aspire to the literal, but rather that Kinsella seeks to translate by finding 'images and ideas' in English that are anchored firmly in the Irish, but also poetically effective in their own right.

Comparing Kinsella's translation of *Cúirt an Mheán Oíche* to the work of earlier translators reveals how much Kinsella gains in this process in terms of constructing bonds between Merriman's language and tradition and his own. When, for example, the old man rises to respond to the young girl's first speech, Merriman's narrator describes him in these terms:

Preabann anuas go fuadrach fíochmhar
Seanduine suarach is fuadach nimhe fé,
A bhaill ar luascadh is luas anáile air,
Dradhain is duais ar fuaid a chnámha.[9]

(Up jumps with a furious motion
A dirty old man and a poisonous violence about him,
His limbs shaking and a shortness of breath on him,
Displeasure and distress throughout his bones.)

Denis Woulfe's translation of these lines is governed by his desire to adhere as closely as possible to Merriman's prosody, even at the cost of rendering the images of the original into quite other images:

A Grey old man of feeble frame
With hasty steps straight forward came
His palsied limbs emaciated
His pallid phiz quite desolated.[10]

'Grey' for 'suarach' seriously dilutes Merriman's characterization of the old man, and there's no evidence in the original that he is 'of feeble frame'; indeed Merriman's narrator says that the old man jumped up 'go fuadrach fíochmhar'. Nor is there any mention in the original that the old man's 'phiz' is 'pallid'. Arland Ussher sees the old man as aggressive rather than feeble, but he lapses into the kind of cliché and generalization that at times give his translation the unfortunate ring of inept Victorian verse:

Scarce ended was the maid's harangue
When a gruff old warrior upsprang
Of rugged build and rude attire
And trembling less with age than ire.[11]

As one might expect, Frank O'Connor's version is considerably more adept than are Woulfe's or Ussher's at using concrete imagery to get to the bottom of the old man's character, although much of it is only loosely tied to the original:

Then up there jumps from a neighbouring chair
A little old man with a spiteful air,
Staggering legs and sobbing breath
And a look in his eye like poison and death.[12]

The 'neighbouring chair' and the notion that the man is 'little' are O'Connor's inventions, and 'spiteful air' represents quite a liberal interpretation of 'go fuadrach fíochmhar'. But Merriman's 'nimhe' finds its way into O'Connor's fine image of 'an eye like poison and death', and 'A bhaill ar luascadh' is spiritedly – and accurately enough – rendered as 'Staggering legs'. Lord Longford's translation of the passage, with the exception of his final image, is thoroughly predictable and conventional, and his five-stress line dissipates much of the rhythmic energy of the original:

> Then up there sprang, all venomous with rage,
> A vile old man who shook with spite and age.
> His limbs were feeble and his breath was short.
> With sourness in each bone he faced the Court.[13]

David Marcus characteristically wanders far, far from the original:

> Then up there sprung, as if he'd been stung,
> A wizened old josser, and down he flung
> His cap in rage, and danced on it,
> Till people thought he'd thrown a fit.[14]

Kinsella brings to this passage a loyalty to the original, as well as a finely tuned poetic sensibility that recreates, without betraying, Merriman's imagery:

> Then up there leaped a mangy elder
> in venomous haste, all fire and fuss
> with shivering limbs and palpitations
> with fury and frenzy in all his bones.[15]

Part of the success of Kinsella's translation in general depends on its ability to compress rather than depart from phrases and images in the original, as in 'venomous haste', which neatly combines the sense of Merriman's 'fíochmhar' and 'fuadach nimhe'. Also, 'luas anáíle air' is compressed effectively into 'palpitations', and 'Mangy elder', although not a literal translation of 'seanduine suarach', is true to its general meaning at the same time that it constitutes an effective image in English. Finally, 'frenzy in all his bones' provides a striking poetic equivalent for 'duais ar fuaid a chnámha'.

Kinsella's handling of prosody provides another indicator of how his translation of Merriman works to promote a meaningful relationship between

Ireland's two traditions. Traces of Merriman's prosody are everywhere to be found in Kinsella's translation, but at the same time the translation is thoroughly grounded in the forms of English verse and the rhythms of English speech. In his introduction to *An Duanaire*, Kinsella describes his approach to prosody when translating from the Irish:

> With a great deal of the [Irish-language] poetry of the period the effects are bound up with prosody and technique: the syllabic or accentual rhythms, devices of rhyme, assonance and so on. All of this is untranslatable. The occasional alliterations in the English, the ghosts of metrical procedures, give only a hint of the easeful elaborateness and linguistic elegance of many of the best poems in the book.[16]

In Kinsella's translation of *Cúirt an Mheán Oíche*, those 'ghosts of metrical procedures' remind the reader of the translation's origins in the Irish-language tradition without undermining the integrity of the translation as an English-language poem. This is evident in the first two lines of the translation: 'By the brink of the river I'd often walk, / on a meadow fresh, in the heavy dew' (p. 222). The two pairs of assonantal links in the first line and the triple link in the second do not – and are not meant to – echo precisely the abbc/abbc pattern of assonance in the original: 'Ba ghnáth mé ag siúl le ciumhais na habhann / Ar bháinseach úr's an drúcht go trom' (1–2) ('It was usual for me to be walking along the edge of the river / On a fresh green and the dew heavy'). The flexible imitation of Merriman's prosody is not allowed to interfere with either the rhythm or the sense of Kinsella's lines in English.[17]

Kinsella also relies on neither rhyme nor assonance to represent the effects of the terminal assonance in the original. All of Merriman's earlier translators rely on terminal rhyme for this, with the exception of Power, who does use terminal assonance. In his introduction to *An Duanaire*, Kinsella explains his decision not to use terminal rhyme in any of his translations from the Irish: 'Accepting that there must be losses in translation, it seemed to us that the loss involved in opting for rhyme could be too heavy, especially if the rhymes in English were still to remain an inadequate reflection of the prosodic qualities of the original poems.'[18] The avoidance of terminal rhyme or assonance also points Kinsella's translation of Merriman's poem toward the practice of much modern poetry in English, including his own, as does his decision not to begin each line with a capital letter.

There are, however, occasions in which Kinsella's 'ghosts of metrical procedures' take the form of terminal assonance over an extended number of lines – there is a calculated irregularity about all prosodic aspects of his translation – echoing Merriman's tendency to group his couplets. In the young woman's first speech, for example, when she sets out her own attractive qualities, Merriman has her say:

> Créad é an t-abhar ná tabharfaí grá dhom
> Is mé comh leabhair, comh modhamhail, chomh breá so?
> Is deas mo bhéal, mo dhéad's mo gháire,
> Is deas mo ghné, is tá m'éadan tláth tais,
> Is glas mo shúil, tá m'úrla scáinneach
> Bachallach búclach cúplach fáinneach,
> Mo leaca is mo ghnúis gan smúid gan smáchaill,
> Tarraingthe cúmtha lonrach scáfar. (227–34)

> (What is the reason that I would not be given love
> And I as slender, as modest, as fine as this?
> Nice is my mouth, my teeth and my laugh,
> Nice is my appearance, and my forehead is mild, gentle,
> Green are my eyes, my hair is in locks,
> Curled, ringleted, double-plaited, beautiful,
> My cheeks and my face without defect, without blemish,
> Attractive, shapely, luminous, comely.)

Kinsella's translation definitely sets up echoes with Merriman's use of terminal assonance, but at the same time his young woman speaks an English free from artificiality or awkwardness:

> Where is the cause I remain unloved
> and I so slender, fine and shy?
> My mouth so good, and my teeth and smile?
> I've a glowing complexion, a tender brow.
> I have delicate eyes and a forelock fine,
> curled and plaited and looped and twined.
> My features, free from dirt or grime,
> are fine-drawn, shapely, timid and bright. (p. 227)

[84]

This kind of careful poetic translation, sensitive to the original but conscious as well of the translator's responsibility to the poetic tradition in which he is writing, is everywhere to be found in Kinsella's version of *Cúirt an Mheán Oíche*. The young woman, in her first speech, says that the few young men in Ireland willing to wed are marrying the wrong kind of women, such as 'Caile-na-gcos-is-folt-gan-réiteach' (224) ('A girl of the feet and hair untidy); this becomes, in Kinsella's translation, 'some trollop all feet, with her hair unfixed' (p. 227). The old man's statement that the young woman who married his neighbour was famous throughout Ireland for her sexual infidelities, including 'Ag consaigh ainigí Thradraí an phónra' (455) ('By the peevish, uncouth people of Tradraí of the beans') is rendered as 'with the baleful bean-growing brutes of Tradraí' (p. 233); the old man's description of himself before he married as 'Leitheadach láidir, lán de shaidhbhreas' (479) ('Proud, strong, full of riches') is translated into 'a powerful swaggerer flush with cash' (p. 233); the old man's lament that '... iarr mé / Síneadh ar leabain le hainnir do liath mé' (512–13) ('... I tried / Stretching on a bed with a girl who turned me grey') becomes '... I lusted / to bed with that woman who turned me grey' (p. 234); the old man's account of reports about his young wife – 'Ar lár 'na lóiste ag pósta is aonta. / B'fhada á mheilt a teist 's a tuairisc' (517–18) ('On the floor a drone for married and single. / It was long that her reputation and her character were discussed') – is rendered as 'and relax on her back for married or single. / Her name and fame were long chewed over' (p. 234); and the young woman's admiring description of the sexual attractiveness of the clergy – 'Coirp is coim is toill ar táimhchrith' (768) ('Bodies and waist and buttocks in a swooning trembling') – becomes 'bums, bellies, and bodies a-tremble softly' (p. 240).

There is real scholarship at work in Kinsella's poetic translation of *Cúirt an Mheán Oíche*; Kinsella is in fact far more alert to the nuances and multiple meanings of Merriman's Irish than are any of Merriman's earlier translators. For example, at one point, the young woman characterizes the ordinary Irish woman as 'na spaid gan fear gan pháiste' (184) ('a barren person without a man, without a child'); Kinsella's translation describes these women as being 'sunk like sods without child or man' (p. 226), combining the sense of 'spaid' as 'a barren person' with its more literal meaning of 'clod' or 'wet turf or earth'. By contrast, Ussher takes nearly three lines to translate this one line, without capturing any of the senses of 'spaid' suggested in Kinsella's translation; in his version, Ireland's women 'mope in the maiden state, / Without husband heaping the golden store /

Or children creeping on hearth and floor' (p. 22). Woulfe and O'Connor don't get any closer to representing the various meanings of 'spaid'; Woulfe translates the line as 'And I for one do sorely cry / No husbands care nor heir have I' (183–4), and O'Connor has 'Bitter old maids without house or home' (p. 19). Even Patrick C. Power, whose scholarly expertise might be expected to come into play here, fails to get beyond the surface meaning of 'spaid': 'I without husband or baby am barren.'[19]

In her second speech, the young woman says there's no need for sexual jealousy in 'Feamaire fann is feam gan féile' (756) ('An infirm, weak-loined person and a stalk without pleasure'); Kinsella translates, 'a feeble stud with an empty stick' (p. 240), where 'stick' is alert to several meanings of 'feam', which means 'tail' or 'rubber-like stump' as well as 'stalk', 'stem', or 'rod'. In the old man's defence-of-bastards passage, Kinsella translates 'Créim ní fheicim ná daille ná caoiche / I léim-ar-leithre dár hoileadh ó mhnaoi ar bith' (603–4) ('A blemish I do not see or dimness or blindness / In an illegitimate child given for rearing by any woman') as 'and I see no blemish or blink or blindness / in these jump-the-guns brought up by women' (p. 236). Citing *Cúirt an Mheán Oíche*, Dinneen gives 'an illegitimate offspring' as a figurative meaning for 'léim-ar-leithre', but Kinsella works the literal meaning of the phrase, 'a leap to one side' into his phrase 'jump-the-guns'. In her speech near the end of the poem, Aoibheall attacks men who ruin girls' reputations without having natural desires of their own, men who do not take 'Taitneamh don ghníomh ná fíoch na féithe' (935) ('Pleasure in the act or fury of the vein'); Kinsella translates, 'delight in the act or the organ's itch' (p. 244). Ó Dónaill gives 'the heyday in the blood' for 'fíoch na féithe', but 'féith' can mean 'sinew' or 'muscle' as well as 'vein', 'blood', or 'lust', all of which are reflected perfectly in Kinsella's 'organ's itch'.

A particularly striking example of the fusion of Kinsella's scholarly understanding of Merriman's Irish with his own finely tuned poetic sensibility is his translation of the passage in which the young woman lists the various herbs that, following the practices of folklore, she used to help her find a husband. Many translators have had trouble with this passage, and Liam P. Ó Murchú concedes that it's difficult to establish with certainty the names of the herbs listed in the original.[20] Kinsella, ever alert to the multiple meanings in Merriman's Irish, makes sexual or bodily jokes out of the names. The first herbs mentioned by the young woman, for example, are 'Magairlín meidhreach, meill na mbualtaibh, / Taithigín taibhseach, toill na tuairte' (341–2) ('Early purple orchid, cowslip, /

Great figwort, shepherd's purse'). Kinsella translates: '—little Balls-of-Joy or Lumps-of-Dung, / the Shining Splicer, or Hammer-the-Hole' (p. 230). Dinneen gives 'early purple orchid' as the primary meaning of 'magairlín meidhreach', but Kinsella's rendering of it as 'little Balls-of-Joy' remembers that 'magairlí' means 'testicles' and 'meidhreach' means 'merry' or 'frisky'. In his 1949 edition of Merriman's poem, Risteárd Ó Foghludha glosses 'meill na mbualtaibh' as the equivalent of 'bainne bó bleacht', the Irish for 'cowslip'. Remembering that 'meill' is the genitive form of 'meall', meaning 'ball' or 'globe', and relying on the 'cow-dung' meaning of 'bualtach', Kinsella translates the phrase as 'Lumps-of-Dung'. Ó Foghludha says that 'taithigín taibhseach' is the equivalent of 'lus na gcnapán', the Irish for 'lesser celandine', while Dinneen glosses it as 'great fig-wort' or 'wild rocket'. But 'taibhseach' literally means 'visible' or 'striking in appearance', and seeing 'taithigh', meaning 'to consort with', behind 'taithigín', Kinsella translates the phrase as 'the Shining Splicer'. Citing *Cúirt an Mheán Oíche*, Dinneen says 'toill na tuairte' refers to 'a plant, used as a love-charm', while Ó Foghludha glosses it as the equivalent of 'bolgán béice', which he describes as 'plannda i bhfoirm sparáin, a dhéineann fothram nuair luightar cos air' ('a plant in the form of a purse that makes a great noise when it is stepped on'). Kinsella, remembering that 'toll' means 'hole' or 'cavity', and 'tuairt' a 'heavy blow', translates the phrase as 'Hammer-the-Hole'.

Because of his loyalty to Merriman's text, and because he has no overt political, social or philosophical agenda, Kinsella avoids bending his translation to accommodate one set of issues or another, as most of Merriman's earlier translators do. The effect of this can be measured by comparing with earlier translations Kinsella's version of a passage that is part of the old man's comments in support of bastards. In Merriman, the old man says:

> Scaoil a chodladh gan chochall gan chuíbhreach
> Síol an bhodaigh 's an mhogalfhuil mhaíteach,
> Scaoil fá chéile do réir nádúra
> An síolbhach séad is an braon lábúrtha. (631–4)

> (Make free to sleep without a cloak, without fetters
> The seed of the churl and of the boastful noble blood,
> Make free together according to nature
> The seed of the precious ones and the base drop.)

No doubt motivated by his liberal humanism, Ussher turns a blind eye to the uncomfortable social and political implications of 'bodaigh' and 'lábúrtha, and translates Merriman's text into a straightforward argument for social equality:

> But let simple nature and noble blood
> Mix and make a godlike brood;
> Let high and low in love unite
> Like the birds and beasts by nature's right. (p. 42)

Marcus, working out of his own vision of social equality, converts the passage into a plea for justice in the modern world:

> Let the proletariat
> Mate with the aristocrat,
> Proclaim the news throughout the land
> That love is free and no longer banned. (p. 29)

Kinsella, on the other hand, doesn't blink at the less-than-flattering words used by Merriman's old man to describe the poor, words that are, after all, true to the old man's character:

> Set loose in bed, without shackle or tie,
> seed of the lout and the brazen noble;
> release together, as Nature bids,
> the seed supreme and the vulgar drop. (p. 237)

The view, held by a number of critics, that Kinsella's translations from the Irish are intended chiefly to carry the reader back to the Irish-language original seriously underestimates Kinsella's accomplishments as a poetic translator. To say, as Maurice Harmon has done, that Kinsella's work in translation 'throws light upon the Irish poems, rather than upon the English translations',[21] or, to go further, as Donatella Abbate Badid has done, and say that Kinsella's translations from the Irish avoid 'creating English analogues – poems that will stand by themselves',[22] is to fail to see not just the poet behind the translations, but, more specifically, a poet whose 'true poetic career' has been thoroughly committed to giving poetry written in Irish an authentic poetic life in English, and so to recognizing the inherently dual nature of Irish poetry and Irish culture. As Kinsella himself once said: 'We have a dead language with a powerful literature and a colonial language with a powerful literature. The combination is an extremely rich one.'[23]

Seamus Heaney: Ovid, Feminism and the North

S eamus Heaney's poetic translation of *Cúirt an Mheán Oíche* is, unfortunately, only partial. Of the 1026 lines in the standard version of Merriman's poem, Heaney's translation, published in 1993, accounts for just 320, less than a third of the original; it includes the opening description of nature, the narrator's abduction by the bailiff, the bailiff's speech about the ills of Ireland, the opening twenty-seven lines of the young woman's first speech, and then Aoibheall's speech near the end of the poem, followed by the young woman's threatening remarks about the narrator's sexual shortcomings, and, finally, by the narrator's timely awakening.

Despite its frustrating brevity, Heaney's incomplete translation is of considerable interest, not just for its unquestioned poetic merit, but also for the various effects that Heaney achieves by juxtaposing Merriman's poem with Ovid's account, in *The Metamorphoses*, of Orpheus and Eurydice; in his text, entitled *The Midnight Verdict*, Heaney places his version of Merriman between his translation of Ovid's story of the poet Orpheus's loss of Eurydice, taken from Book X of *The Metamorphoses*, and that of the death of Orpheus, taken from Book XI. This framing places *Cúirt an Mheán Oíche* in the broad context of the European tradition, but not in the specific context of medieval European literature usually associated with the poem.[1] More important, it enables Heaney to read Merriman's poem in the context of various feminist concerns that were emerging in Irish culture in the 1980s and early 1990s. As Heaney himself once said, *Cúirt an Mheán Oíche* can be interpreted as 'a paradigm of the war initi- ated by the women's movement for women's empowerment, their restoration to the centre of language and consciousness and thereby also to the centre of all institutions and functionings of society'.[2] The importance of imaginative freedom, a central concern of much of Heaney's own poetry, also surfaces as a theme in Heaney's translation of Merriman, largely in the difference between the ending of Merriman's poem, in which the narrator escapes punishment, and Ovid's account of the death of Orpheus. Finally, given Heaney's northern background, and the profound engagement in his poetry of the 1970s and 1980s with the sectarian violence in the North, it's hardly surprising to find that his partial translation of Merriman's poem also can be seen as recommending alter- natives to the exclusivist cultural, political and religious attitudes lying behind the Troubles.

In his essay 'Orpheus in Ireland: On Brian Merriman's *The Midnight Court*', published two years after *The Midnight Verdict* appeared, Heaney argues that Frank O'Connor's translation of 1945 was so shaped by O'Connor's 'own provoc- ative anti-puritanical agenda' that it was not as sensitive as it might have been to 'the under-music of the women's voices'.[3] Since then, interest in Merriman's poem has shifted, Heaney says, away from seeing it as a means of promoting a liber- tarian stance against a repressive religious and social atmosphere, and toward a view of the poem as arguing for the empowerment of women – something evident in Patrick C. Power's translation of 1971. Although Heaney concedes that Merriman's poem embodies attitudes likely to offend contemporary femi- nists, such as 'the normative status which the poem ... grants to the state of marriage', Merriman also gave his women, Heaney says, 'bodies and brains and let them speak as if they lived by them', and in particular he endowed the young woman in the witness box with 'a transfusion of emotional and rhetorical energy long denied to women by poets who had preceded him'.[4]

Oddly enough, given this final point, Heaney translates only twenty-seven lines from the young woman's first speech, and nothing from her second. Still, his translation of the opening of her first speech is calculated to represent as fully as possible that 'emotional and rhetorical energy long denied to women'. At one point in the speech, she details all that she suffers as a single woman:

Mo dhochar, mo dhó, my bhrón mar bhíom
Gan sochar gan seoid gan só gan síth
Go doilbhir duaiseach duamhar díoch
Gan codladh gan suan gan suairceas oíche,
Acht maslaithe i mbuairt gan suaimhneas sínte
Ar leabain leamh fhuar dár suaitheadh ag smaointe.[5]

(My harm, my scorching, my sorrow that I am
Without profit, without jewels, without comfort, without rest
Gloomy, cheerless, toilsome, destitute
Without sleep, without rest, without a night's mirth,
Save only insults in sorrow, without peace stretched
On an impotent cold bed disturbed by thoughts.)

In Heaney's translation, this speech is delivered in particularly unrestrained language that emphasizes both the young woman's sexual frustrations and her right to speak freely about them:

I'm scorched and tossed, a sorry case
Of nerves and drives and neediness,
Depressed, obsessed, awake at night,
Unused, unsoothed, disconsolate,
A throbbing ache, a dumb discord,
My mind and bed like a kneading board.[6]

In the second line, Heaney converts the material losses that Merriman's young woman laments into specifically sexual ones. Also, rendering 'Gan codladh' as 'Unused', 'gan suan' as 'unsoothed', and 'gan suaimhneas' as 'A throbbing ache' considerably drives up the sexual temperature of the speech. Finally, Heaney's young woman suffers both in 'mind and bed', the phrasing insisting on the need for intellectual as well as sexual freedom for women.

Heaney's reading of *Cúirt an Mheán Oíche* in a feminist light is also evident in the emphasis that his translation places on Merriman's bailiff as a character who challenges conventional idealized views of maidenhood, attitudes embodied for Merriman's audience in the figure of the beautiful, fairy-like *spéirbhean* in the Irish-language *aisling* tradition who predicts the end of English rule in Ireland, and for Heaney's audience in disempowering idealizations of female innocence.[7] In Heaney's translation, the bailiff speaks in language that is not only sexually suggestive but also obsessed with the body. In Merriman, she describes at one point the unsatisfied girls and women of Ireland as:

> Consaigh chorpartha is borrcaigh óga
> Is bunsaigh bhrothallach fola agus feola,
> Lóistigh liosta agus ligthigh shásta
> Is mórgaigh shioscaithe d'imigh i bhásta.
> Is trua gan toircheas tollairí 'on tsórt so,
> Is trua gan tormach brollaigh is bóta iad. (105–10)

> (Large, manly women and well-developed young maidens
> And warm-blooded and warm-fleshed slips of girls,
> Lingering idlers and lithe, satisfied [ones]
> And select, dignified maidens who went to waste.
> It's a pity not to have strapping offspring from this sort,
> It's a pity that they are without swelling of breast and mound.)

Heaney translates:

> Think of the way they're made and moulded,
> The flush and zest in their flesh and blood –
> Those easy ladies half on offer
> And the big strait-laced ones, all ignored.
> Why aren't they all consoled and gravid,
> In full proud sail with their breasts in bud? (p. 26)

The framing of *Cúirt an Mheán Oíche* by Ovid's *Metamorphoses* also provides Heaney with a means of defending Merriman against the view that a considerable strain of sexism runs through his poem. For Heaney, the ending of Merriman's poem, often seen as somewhat abrupt and unsatisfying, deflects 'a mythic potency', the myth being that of the death of Orpheus 'at the hands of frenzied maenads'.[8] Heaney specifically associates the frustrated women of Ireland with 'maenads' earlier in his translation; when the young woman pleads for help from Aoibheall, saying that her sexual frustration is driving her mad – 'Bhain dom threoir me is sheoil gan chiall me, / Chaith mar cheo me dóite pianta –' (175–6) ('[That] took me from my way and drove me senseless, / Consumed me like a fog, burned with pains –') – Heaney translates, 'Until I'm raving and round the twist / Like a maenad whirled in a swirl of mist –' (p. 29). The sudden waking of

Merriman's narrator before the punishment laid out for him can be exacted puts off, Heaney says in his essay on *Cúirt an Mheán Oíche*, the 'archaic beast' that has 'stirred under the poem's surface', and that the reader desires to see 'unleashed into action'.[9] Specifically, Merriman turns away at the last minute from a scene in which women kill a male poet, precisely the scene enacted at the end of the Orpheus story. Thus, while affirming the empowerment of women in general, as Heaney reads the poem, *Cúirt an Mheán Oíche* does not represent that empowerment as necessarily at odds with male freedom or creativity itself.

At the very end of the poem, in which Merriman's narrator describes the moment of his waking – 'Scaras lem néall, do réidheas mo shúile / Is phreabas, do léim, ón bpéin im dhúiseacht' (1025–6) ('I started from my sleep, I cleared my eyes / And I jumped with a bound from the pain upon my awaking'), Heaney translates: '... Then my dreaming ceased / And I started up, awake, released' (p. 34). That final 'released' calls attention to the narrator having escaped the 'archaic beast' unleashed against Orpheus at the end of Ovid's poem. Also, because Merriman's narrator is, presumably at least, a version of Merriman himself, his being 'released' at the end reminds the reader that he is able, as the author of the poem, to free himself through the power of his creative imagination.[10]

The interweaving of Merriman and Ovid has political as well as feminist implications. Like much of Heaney's work in translation, his version of *Cúirt an Mheán Oíche*, and in particular the links that it establishes between Merriman and Ovid, promote a liberation from the kind of narrow constructions of Irish identity that Heaney sees as enabling the sectarian conflict in Northern Ireland.[11] *The Midnight Verdict*, which was published a year before the IRA ceasefire, might be seen as particularly effective in promoting cultural diversity over cultural duality as it presents the reader with two texts – one from ancient Rome and originally written in Latin, and one from eighteenth-century Ireland and originally written in Irish – both translated into contemporary English. To read the book is, as Eugene O'Brien has said, 'to submerge oneself in the cultural hybridity that has become contemporary Ireland'.[12] Also, the English into which Heaney translates Merriman's Irish is marked by occasional traces of Ulster-Scots, suggesting common ground between Merriman's native territory and Heaney's, and implicitly arguing for all-Ireland notions of Irish identity that embrace hybridity. These linguistic points of contact also allow Heaney to suggest implicit parallels between Merriman's scepticism about the idealization of Irish identity for nationalist ends, embodied most notably in his parodic figure of the bailiff, and Heaney's scepticism about the unyielding dualistic constructions of Irish identity that have fuelled much of the violence in the North.

In an interview, Heaney referred to the dialect that he heard as a boy growing up in Co. Derry in the 1940s as his 'Scullionspeak register',[13] and it can be found in a number of places in Heaney's translation of *Cúirt an Mheán Oíche*. Merriman's description of the bailiff's mouth, for example, as 'A draid is a drandal mantach méirsceach' (56) ('Her mouth and her fissured toothless gums') becomes, in Heaney's translation, 'With her ganting gums and her mouth in a twist' (p. 25), where 'ganting' is Ulster-Scots for 'yawning'.[14] The young woman's flattering remark addressed to Aoibheall early in her first speech – 'B'easnamh cruaidh thu i dTuamhain 's i dTír Luirc' (172) ('You were greatly wanted in Thomond and in Tír Luirc') – is translated by Heaney as 'Thomond can thole no more! Assist us!' (p. 28), where 'thole', Ulster-Scots for 'suffer', is a word that Heaney says he frequently heard growing up.[15] When Aoibheall says, late in the poem, 'Ní chuirimse i bhfáth 'o bharr mo chainte / An foirfeach fálta cáslag cloíte' (891–2) ('I consider of no importance as a point of my talk / The feeble, spent, exhausted old men'), Heaney translates, 'Yet who gives a damn in the end of all / For them and their dribbling stroup and fall?' (p. 31), where 'stroup' can mean in Ulster-Scots 'spout' or 'hosepipe'. And when the young woman addresses the narrator as 'a chroí gan daonnacht' (961) ('heart without humanity'), Heaney translates it as 'you cold-rifed blirt' (p. 32), where 'rife' is an intensifying suffix in Ulster-Scots, and 'blirt' refers to female genitals.

As might be expected of a poet gifted with so fine an ear, Heaney's translation is remarkably sensitive to the music of *Cúirt an Mheán Oíche*. In trying to bring that distinctive music in Irish over into English verse, most of Merriman's translators before Heaney, with the important exception of Thomas Kinsella and the less important one of Patrick C. Power, rely on regular terminal rhyme with some attention – quite a bit in Denis Woulfe's translation, very little in Lord Longford's – paid to internal assonance. Along with occasional but irregular internal assonance, Heaney employs a variety of terminal links, most frequently half-rhyme, which, in conjunction with regular rhyme and assonance, enables him to vary the pitch of his couplets to reflect the wide range of effects achieved by Merriman's terminal assonance.

The advantages to be gained from this strategy can be seen in the opening lines of Heaney's translation; in Merriman's Irish, the poem famously begins:

Ba gnáth me ag siúl le ciumhais na habhann
Ar bháinseach úr's an drúcht go trom,
In aice na gcoillte i gcoim an tsléibhe
Gan mhairg gan mhoill ar shoilse an lae.
Do ghealadh mo chroí an uair chínn Loch Gréine,
An talamh's an tír is íor na spéire,
Taitneamhact aoibhinn suíomh na sléibhte
Ag bagairt a gcinn thar dhroim a chéile.
Do ghealfadh an croí bheadh críon le cianta
Caite gan bhrí nó líonta'o phianta,
An séithleach searbh gan sealbh gan saibhreas
D'fhéacfadh tamall thar bharra na gcoillte
Ar lachain'na scuainte ar chuan gan ceo
Is an eala ar a bhfuaid's í ag gluaiseacht leo. (1–14)

(It was usual for me to be walking along the edge of the river
On a fresh green and the dew heavy,
Beside the woods in the middle of the mountain
Without oppression, without hindrance at daylight.
My heart lightened when I would see Loch Gréine,
The ground, the country and the horizon,
Pleasing, delightful the situation of the mountains
Brandishing their heads over each other's backs.
The heart would lighten that would be worn-out for ages
Spent without strength or filled with pains,
The bitter, emaciated person without property, without riches
Would look a while beyond the tops of the woods
At ducks in their clutches in a harbour without fog
And the swan among them and she moving with them.)

Heaney translates:

I used to wade through heavy dews
On the riverbank, in the grassy meadows,
Beside the woods, in a glen apart
As the morning light lit sky and heart
And sky and heart kept growing lighter

At the sight of Graney's clear lough water.
The lift of the mountains there! Their brows
Shining and stern in serried rows!
My withered heart would start to quicken,
Everything small in me, hardbitten,
Everything hurt and needy and shrewd
Lifted its eyes to the top of the wood
Past flocks of ducks on a glassy bay
And a swan there too in all her glory. (p. 23)

Heaney's mastery of imagery and diction is certainly on display here: 'I used to wade (rather than 'walk') through heavy dews', 'the morning light lit sky and heart', 'lift of the mountains', 'My withered heart would start to quicken', and 'Everything hurt and needy and shrewd'.[16] But the passage demonstrates as well how much prosodic diversity and nuance Heaney's use of a variety of terminal echoes achieves. The first couplet is constructed around double terminal links, the assonantal echo between 'heavy' and 'meadows' and the half-rhyme between 'dews' and 'meadows'. This is followed by a couplet joined by regular rhyme, then one using half-rhyme, in turn followed by the visual rhyme between 'brows' and 'rows', a couplet constructed on terminal assonance, and then half-rhyme in the last two couplets, with the final half-rhyme falling on the weak, almost throwaway, final syllable of 'glory'.

In his essay 'Orpheus in Ireland', Heaney argues vehemently against reading *Cúirt an Mheán Oíche* in strictly sociological or historical terms. Although the poem does, he says, 'constitute a definite, exhilarated retort to economic conditions and matrimonial patterns in East Clare in the late eighteenth century', only the most insensitive reader could settle for interpreting the poem as 'an act of civic concern on the poet's part'.[17] Indeed for Heaney, the poem has very much to do with the power of the creative imagination, set free by the courtroom setting. 'For Merriman,' Heaney says, 'the courtroom was not a method, but a stroke of genius; its real virtue lay in the way it released the flood of the poet's inventiveness.'[18] That courtroom, Heaney adds, is essentially a carnivalesque space 'where Merriman's imagination runs riot'.[19]

Heaney's translation undoubtedly contains moments in which the spirit of carnival, with its strong, shocking whiff of rebellion against convention, comes through, perhaps most notably in his rendering of the beginning of the young woman's speech in which she complains to Aoibheall about the desperate state of Irish women in these terms: 'Mná na Banba in anacra suíte, / Ar nós má leanaid na fearaibh dá bhfuadar / Ó, mo lagar, acht caithfeamna a bhfuadach' (192–4) ('The women of Ireland in affliction fixed, / So that if the men follow their inclination / Oh, alas, but we will have to abduct them'). Heaney translates: 'Observe the plight of Ireland's women, / For if things go on like this, then fuck it! / The men will have to be abducted!' (p. 29). Although one might argue that with 'fuck it' Heaney has ventured a bit beyond the world and language of the original, the phrase certainly translates the sense of freewheeling and rebellious speech that Heaney finds so central to Merriman's poem. Unfortunately for Heaney's readers, most of that sense of freedom and rebellion is located in the young woman's two lengthy speeches and the old man's equally lengthy rejoinder, and, with the exception of the opening few lines of the young woman's first address to the court, the language of these speeches is, in Heaney's translation, the language of silence.

Ciaran Carson: 'Wavering between Languages'

C iaran Carson brought to his translation of *Cúirt an Mheán Oíche*, published in 2005, not just considerable experience in translating, but also a postmodern awareness of the impossibility of doing it. That scepticism is itself grounded in a sense, also postmodern, of the inherent instability of language and meaning, something that Carson's own poetry often exults in. His translation of Merriman's poem, which he said appealed to him in part because in it 'the language itself is continually interrogated',[1] relishes the complexities of Merriman's language and poetic strategies, and works to maintain their presence within the translation. In this regard, Carson's translation might be said to belong to the category of what Neal Alexander has called 'foreignizing translations' – translations that, far from trying to create a transparent window onto the original text, illuminate the inevitably incomplete and troubled relationship between original and translation.[2]

For Carson, translation is always problematic; talking about his version of Seán Ó Ríordáin's preface to his collection *Eireaball Spideoige*, he says: 'bringing one language to bear on another is like going through a forest at night, where there are many forking paths, and each route is fraught with its own pitfalls ... I know now that if I were called on to translate that passage again, I would do it differently, because I would have changed my mind by then.'[3] And in the fore-word to his translation of *Cúirt an Mheán Oíche*, conceding that it's impossible to reproduce in English Merriman's prosody and meanings, Carson says the most that any translator can hope for is to produce a work that bears 'a sidelong, metaphorical relation to the original'.[4]

Translation from the Irish has figured in Carson's work throughout his career, including a version of the *Táin Bó Cuailnge* done in the wake of Thomas Kinsella's translation of it, as well as translations of modern and contemporary poets like Seán Ó Ríordáin, Nuala Ní Dhomhnaill, and the Belfast poet Gearóid Mac Lochlainn. Even his earliest forays into the field are characterized by a self-conscious representation of the translator at work. His first collection of poems, *The New Estate* (1976), includes adaptations of several early Irish lyrics, and in his version of one of the best-known of these, 'M'airiuclán hi Túaim Inbir,' attributed to *Buile Suibhne* (*Mad Sweeney*), Carson posits a link between the hermit-as-poet (Suibhne) and the poet-as-translator (Carson). In the first stanza of the original, the hermit-monk describes his abode in these terms:

M'airiuclán hi Túaim Inbir
ni lántechdais bes sestu
cona retglannaib a réir
cona gréin cona escu.[5]

(My little oratory in Túaim Inbir
a full house is not more delightful
with its stars in attendance
with its sun, with its moon.)

Carson's translation of this stanza ends with an image, not in the original, that reminds the reader of the poet at work, be he hermit or translator:

More ingenious than a mansion,
My little house is lit
By trickeries of sun and moon.
The stars are all in scansion.[6]

Carson grew up in a bilingual environment in Belfast, English being spoken on the streets, Irish in the house. The experience made him, he says, 'deeply suspicious of language in general ... suspicious, but not averse to the pleasure to be had from words'.[7] In his memoir *The Star Factory*, Carson recalls experiencing this kind of bilingual gratification as a child:

> I used to lull myself to sleep with language, mentally repeating, for example, the word *capall*, the Irish for horse, which seemed to be more onomatopoetically equine than its English counterpart; gradually, its trochaic foot would summon up a ghostly echo of "cobble", till, wavering between languages, I would allow my disembodied self to drift out the window and glide through the silent dark gas-lit streets above the mussel-coloured cobblestones.[8]

The 'pleasure to be had from words', so clearly on display in the passage itself – and in much of Carson's own poetry, especially in collections like *The Irish for No* (1987) and *Belfast Confetti* (1990) – often takes a particular form when the words are Irish. In an essay on Seamus Heaney's translation of *Buile Suibhne*, Carson argues that one of the primary traits of the original is its exploitation of various layers of meaning in specific words and phrases, 'the words themselves generating lines of implicit enquiry' – a multiplicity that, he says, is part of 'the deep structure' of the language.[9] And in *The Star Factory*, citing numerous examples from Dinneen's dictionary, Carson notes how many different meanings can be held in some kind of relationship in a single word or phrase in Irish.[10] As Frank Sewell has argued, comparing Carson with Seán Ó Ríordáin, whereas Ó Ríordáin felt torn between Irish and English, Carson's imagination 'is only increased and multiplied by his bilingualism, enriched (not confused or diminished) by cross-fertilization.'[11]

Especially for a poet who grew up in Belfast, and still lives there, the notion of 'cross-fertilization' inevitably carries political, religious and social implications. Carson's translation of *Cúirt an Mheán Oíche* is, however, far less overtly invested than is Heaney's in using Merriman to call into question the exclusivist attitudes and values driving much of the violence in Northern Ireland, although one can argue that Carson's willingness to push against the conventional boundaries of language, in his own poetry as well as in his translations, in effect resists the narrow, formulaic notions and discourses of Irish identity that lay behind the Troubles.[12]

In the foreword to his translation of *Cúirt an Mheán Oíche*, Carson remarks: 'Marcel Proust says somewhere that a writer inhabits his native language as if it were a foreign country. For me, both languages—so familiar yet so foreign – became strange, as I wandered the borders between them.'[13]

It is those borders that Carson's translation of Merriman's poem self-consciously patrols, and if it is less faithful to the original than Kinsella's version, it is remarkably sensitive to how Merriman's Irish works and specifically to how the poem draws on and illuminates what Carson calls the 'deep structure' of the language, the ability to express a wide range of meanings in a single word or phrase. Merriman, Carson says, 'is the great illusionist, continually spiriting words into another dimension',[14] and Carson's translation often works to 'spirit' Merriman's words into the other dimension of English, spinning out lines of meanings and suggestions in a process that strives to keep Merriman's linguistic and poetic strategies alive inside the translation. When the young woman, for example, complains in her first speech about the kind of women that young Irish men marry, if they marry at all, Merriman has her say:

> Dá dtuiteadh amach le teas na hóige
> Duine fán seacht ar theact féasóige
> Cheangal le mnaoi, ní míntais thoghfaidh,
> Thaitneamhach shuíte 'o shíol ná d'fhoghlaim,
> Clódheas chaoin ná míonla mhánla
> A mb'eol di suí nó tíocht do láthair,
> Acht doineantach odhar nó donn doilíosach
> Chruinnigh le doghrainn cabhair nách cuí dho.[15]

> (If it happened, with the heat of youth,
> That one person in seven on coming to a beard
> Marrying a woman, not a delicate wraith will he take,
> Pleasing, proud of race or of learning,
> Nicely formed, refined or gentle, gracious
> Who would know whether to sit or come in to your presence,
> But a cheerless, dull person or melancholy, swarthy [woman]
> Who gathered with difficulty help that was not proper for her.)

Carson's translation constructs its own 'lines of implicit enquiry' that depart energetically but not at all recklessly from Merriman's lines:

> And even if Richard or Ricky or Dick,
> Some fine strapping youngster with plenty of kick,
> Ties up with a woman, she won't be a lass

Full of vigour and wit, or a lady with class,
Or a beauty endowed with an hourglass physique,
Or a budding young scribe of poetic mystique,
But a mangey old bag or a hatchet-faced bitch,
Who'll go to her grave undeservedly rich.[16]

Carson gives a name to the 'duine' in Merriman's second line, and then runs a series of changes on it, imitating a technique often found in Merriman's poem. Similarly, the young woman's complaint that young men wouldn't marry a young woman 'd'fhoghlaim' is expanded into 'a budding young scribe of poetic mystic'. At the same time, Carson translates 'clódheas' into the contemporary 'hourglass physique', a reminder of the English side of the border. His 'mangey old bag' for 'doineantach odhar' has much the same effect, but is also sensitive to several meanings of 'odhar', including 'weather-beaten' and 'sallow'.

Comparing Carson's rendering of these lines with Thomas Kinsella's and Frank O'Connor's versions reveals how alert Carson's translation is to the workings of Merriman's Irish. Kinsella's translation is more faithful to Merriman's text than Carson's, but less interested in foregrounding Merriman's poetic and linguistic strategies:

If it happens at all, in the heat of youth,
that a man out of seven, on feeling his beard,
goes out with a girl, it's never some mild one
nicely settled in seed and breed,
well-mannered, gentle, soft, and shapely,
who can seat herself or make an entrance,
but an icy dullard or woeful ghost
with an ill-fitting dowry gathered in pain.[17]

O'Connor's version departs quite freely from the literal meaning and linguistic nuances of Merriman's text in an effort to create a credible character speaking colloquial English:

And if one of them weds in the heat of youth
When the first down is on his mouth
It isn't some woman of his own sort,
Well-shaped, well-mannered or well-taught,

Some mettlesome girl that studied behaviour,
To sit and stand and amuse a neighbour,
But some pious old prude or sour defamer
Who sweated the couple of pounds that shame her.[18]

Later, when the young woman boasts about her physical attributes – 'Féach mo chom, nách leabhair mo chnámha, / Níl me lom ná crom ná stágach' (237–8) ('Look on my waist, are my bones not slender, / I'm not bold or bent or stiff') – Carson translates: 'And look at my waist and my elegant frame! / I'm not clumsy, or frumpy, or hunchbacked, or lame' (p. 26). The phrase 'elegant frame' bears what Carson calls 'a sidelong, metaphorical relation' to the literal meaning of 'leabhair mo chnámha', while being sensitive as well to a number of other meanings embedded in 'leabhair', including 'limber', 'svelte' and 'long and graceful'. Also, in his second line, Carson spins four adjectives out of Merriman's three, all of them alert to a range of related meanings in the original, especially 'bowed', 'curved', 'crouching', and 'drooping' for 'crom', and 'lumbersome', 'clumsy', 'halting' and 'rickety' for 'stágach'.

At times, Carson generates a list of overlapping adjectives, a technique found frequently in Merriman's poem, even where there are none in the original. When the old man questions the young woman as to how she acquired the clothes she's wearing, Merriman has him say: 'Faire go deo arú! fóill cár fríodh é? / Aithris cá bhfaigheann tú an radharc so mhaíonn tú / Is aithris cár thuill tú an leadhb gan bhrí seo?' (418–20) ('Alas, alas! wait, where was it got? / Relate where you get this appearance you boasted of / And relate how you earned this rag without substance?'[19]). Carson's version of this passage looks more like Merriman than Merriman: 'But tell me! What paid for those elegant clothes? / The ribbons, the chiffon, the frills and fandangles? / The spangles, the sequins, the bracelets and bangles?' (p. 34).

As has often been noted, the Irish language is particularly given to the concrete rather than the abstract,[20] and Carson's own poetry is very much committed to representing the specific; he once said that he admired Joyce 'for his delight in the particular' and that Joyce's writing inspired 'many of my own attempts to render the actuality of things'.[21] As one way of keeping Merriman's Irish present in his translation, Carson foregrounds this characteristic of the diction and imagery in *Cúirt an Mheán Oíche*, at times indeed going beyond the specificity of Merriman's Irish. The effect of this can be seen in Carson's version of the first two lines of the poem, which renders Merriman's' Ba gnáth me ag siúl le ciumhais na habhann / Ar bháinseach úr's an drúcht go trom' (1–2) ('It was usual for me to be walking along the edge of the river / On a fresh green and the dew heavy') as '"Twas my custom to stroll by a clear winding stream, / With my boots full of dew and the lush meadow green' (p. 19). Not only is Merriman's 'abhann' converted into the more detailed 'clear winding stream', but also those boots, not in the original, make the action of 'ag siúl' highly specific and personal, as does the image of their being 'full of dew'.[22] A few lines later, Carson freely translates Merriman's description of the kind of person likely to benefit from the beauties of Loch Gréine – 'Do ghealfadh an croí bheadh críon le cianta / Caite gan bhrí nó líonta 'o phianta' (9–10) ('The heart would lighten that would be worn-out for ages / Spent without strength or filled with pains') – into 'It would lighten the heart, be it listless with age, / Enfeebled by folly, or cardiac rage –' (p. 19), where 'cardiac rage' is more specific than Merriman's 'líonta 'o phianta' and glances back as well to 'an croí' in the previous line.[23]

An even more striking instance of this kind of over-translation of Merriman's concrete language is Carson's rendering of the old man's description of the young woman's living quarters. In Merriman, the old man says the shack has nothing in it but:

> ... mata 'na smuirt gan chuilt gan chlúdadh,
> Dealamh gan luid gan phluid gan tsúsa,
> I gcomhar bhotháin gan áit chum suí ann,
> Sú sileáin is fáscadh aníos ann. (407–10)

> (... a dirty mat without a quilt, without a cover,
> Bare without a stitch, without a blanket, without a rug,
> In a communal shack without a place in it for sitting,
> Soot shedding and pressing down on it.)

Carson translates:

> ... a dirty old floor-rug not fit for a horse,
> With no mattress or bedclothes, or counterpane spread,
> And no pillow to cradle the filth of your head,
> In a festering cabin with nowhere to sit,
> With swill underfoot and the air thick with soot. (p. 34)

The extra line 'And no pillow to cradle the filth of your head' adds in a notably personal image. Much the same effect is achieved by 'swill underfoot', a phrase that is also alert to additional meanings of 'sileáin', including 'rivulet', 'drain', and 'channel'.

Carson's sensitivity to the concreteness of Merriman's Irish is particularly forceful in his versions of the many passages in the poem having to do with sexuality. When, for example, the old man claims that the young woman grew up poor – 'Is fada do dhrom gan cabhair ón léine, / Is togha drochduine do thuigfeadh 'na gá thu' (392–3) ('Your back is long without help from a shirt, / It's a very bad person who would realize you to be in need of it') – Carson characteristically ups the sexual ante with specific images not found in the original: 'That for knickers and shift you've got nothing in place, / As a pimp might discover, likewise a good breeze' (p. 34). Although 'shift' is one possible meaning for 'léine', the jump to 'knickers and shift' is considerable, and very much in keeping with the old man's venomous obsession with female sexuality. And 'pimp' for 'drochdhuine' speaks for itself.

Carson's version of the young woman's comments about the sexual meanderings of the clergy bristles with specific sexual imagery, a good deal of it of Carson's invention. At one point, for example, Merriman has the young woman say:

> Is minic a buaitear buaibh is gréithe
> Cuigeann is cruach do chuaird na cléire,
> Is minic lem chuimhne maíodh a dtréithe
> Is iomad a ngníomhartha fíorghlic féithe. (795–8)

> (Often have cattle and gifts been gained
> The contents of a churn and a rick from a visit of the clergy,
> Often in my memory their qualities were praised
> And a great number of their always-clever deeds of lust.)

Carson loads his version with sexual suggestiveness:

> And many's the girl who had set out her stall
> Found it heaving with goods, from a clerical call.
> It's well I remember their members being praised
> For the wonderful families their efforts have raised. (p. 49)

Cúirt an Mheán Oíche no doubt also appealed to Carson because of the ways in which, as Declan Kiberd has argued, it 'reconciles the structures of poetry with ... the cadences of everyday speech'.[24] Carson spent much of the ten years and more between the publication of his first book of poems, *The New Estate* (1976), and his second, *The Irish for No* (1987), working in traditional Irish music, and, as he once said, 'that experience did, in whatever underground way, make me think of the possibility of getting orality into the poetry'.[25] Like O'Connor's version of Merriman's poem, Carson's translation is very much at ease with the everyday speech of the Ireland of his time. But Carson's version differs from O'Connor's in its sensitivity to the multiplicity of meanings to be found in various Irish words and phrases, thus allowing Merriman's eighteenth-century Irish a strong presence in his translation.

This strategy can be seen in comparing O'Connor's and Carson's renderings of the young woman's account, in her first speech, of her social life. Merriman has her say:

> Ní feacathas fós me i gcóngar daoine
> Ag faire ná ag tórramh óig ná chríonna,
> Ar mhachaire an bháire, an ráis ná an rince,
> I bhfarradh na dtáinte, ar bhántaibh líonta
> Acht gofa go sámh gan cháim ar domhan
> I gculaithe shásta ó bharr go bonn.
> Beidh a cheart im chúl do phúdar fillte,
> *Starch* is stiúir i gcúl my chaidhpe,
> Húda geal gan ceal ribíní,
> Gúna breac's a cheart rufaí leis. (251–60)

> (I have not yet been seen in the vicinity of people
> Watching or paying attention to young or old,
> On a field of the match, the race or the dance,
> In the company of the multitudes, on crowded grasslands
> But was dressed pleasantly without a fault in the world
> In agreeable clothes from head to sole.
> The right amount of closely applied powder will be in my hair,
> Starch and a rakish angle in the back of my coif,
> A bright hood with no lack of ribbons,
> A speckled gown and the right amount of ruffs with it.)

O'Connor translates this passage quite freely, rendering it fluidly into colloquial English:

> But ask the first you meet by chance,
> Hurling match or race or dance,
> Pattern or party, market or fair,
> Whatever it was, was I not there?
> Didn't I make a good impression,
> Turning up in the height of fashion,
> My hair was washed and combed and powdered,
> My coif like snow and stiffly laundered;
> I'd a little white hood with ribbon and ruff
> On a spotty dress of the finest stuff. (p. 22)

Carson's version, while certainly at home with colloquial English, also carries specific traces of Merriman's Irish:

> But at any reception, or party or spree,
> At wedding or wake, of whatever degree,
> At sports-field, or race-course, or on the fair green,
> Where step-dancing punters in dozens are seen,
> I'd be nicely turned out in an eye-catching kit,
> From shoulder to hem of superlative fit,
> My poll lightly powdered (too much is *de trop*),
> My bonnet well starched, and adjusted just so,
> The hood *à la mode*, trailing ribbons galore;
> My gown of shot silk (that stuff I adore)
> And its bodice befitting a well-made young maid. (p. 26)

Among the many echoes of Irish, 'spree' in the first line remembers the Irish 'spraoi', meaning 'fun' or 'sport', and in the fourth, 'step-dancing punters', although a contemporary phrase, is alert to various suggestive meanings in 'táinte', such as 'raids' or 'pursuits'. Also, 'galore', paired by rhyme with the contemporary 'that stuff I adore', carries an echo of the Irish 'go leor', meaning 'plenty of'. The final, extra line in the passage is Carson's invention, and adds specificity and sexual suggestiveness, particularly in the phrase 'well-made young maid'.

Even the rhythms of Carson's translation of *Cúirt an Mheán Oíche* waver self-consciously between Merriman's Irish-language poetry and English verse, more specifically the tradition of Irish folk songs in English. In the foreword to his translation, Carson says that he'd been struck while reading Merriman's poem by 'a strangely familiar rhythm', that of a jig tune, 'Paddy's Panacea', that he says he'd heard from a Co. Clare singer. Perceiving a relationship between the rhythm of the jig and Merriman's 'internal rhymes and four strong beats to the line', he decided, he says, to adopt 'Paddy's Panacea' as a basis for his translation of Merriman.[26]

In metrical terms, Carson's line is essentially anapaestic tetrameter, but, like Merriman's four-stress line, frequently irregular. Carson's line is also marked by assonantal and consonantal links that in a loose but usually quite calculated way imitate Merriman's prosody. For example, when Merriman's narrator describes the building in which the court is sitting as 'Soilseach seasmhach lannamhail lómrach' (141) ('Luminous, steadfast, spacious, bright'), Carson translates, 'Stately, capacious, ornate, chandeliered (p. 23), starting the line uncharacteristically, as does Merriman, with a stressed syllable, and linking three syllables by assonance, echoing quite closely Merriman's line, which, in addition to the usual abbc pattern of assonance on the four stressed syllables, contains an extra link between the unstressed syllable in 'Soilseach' and the stressed syllable in 'seasmhach'. The narrator's description of the bailiff – 'A draid is a drandal mantach méirscheach' (56) ('Her mouth and her fissured, toothless gums') – is rendered by Carson as 'Purple-gummed, ulcered, with no teeth within' (p. 20), where the first syllable of 'Purple' carries a stress, producing a line of five rather than the usual four beats, and where the awkward clash of 'gummed' and 'ulcered' is heightened by the assonantal echo. It is a line as metrically repugnant as the bailiff's mouth is ugly.

Umberto Eco has said that translators inevitably have to negotiate with a number of ghosts and presences – 'with the ghost of a distant author, with the disturbing presence of a foreign text, with the phantom of the reader they are translating for'.[27] Carson reported that while working on his translation of *Cúirt an Mheán Oíche*, he dreamt about Merriman, on the morning of New Year's Day in 2005 – the year of the two-hundredth anniversary of Merriman's death:

> I was wandering on a dark hillside when I saw a light in the distance. I followed it, and came to a little house. The door was ajar; timidly, I pushed it open. Merriman was sitting by the hearth, wearing a greatcoat. He gestured at me to sit down. I did so, and we conversed. True, he did most of the talking, but I was fully able to follow the flow of his intricate Irish. I cannot remember what was said. When I awoke, I was disappointed to find my Irish restored to its former poverty. But I felt that I had been touched, just a little, by the hand of the Master.[28]

Robert Welch has argued that this dream represents an important and revealing sign of an extraordinary closeness between Merriman the Co. Clare poet and Carson the Belfast poet-translator. 'Serious poets, serious translators are inescapably involved in these conversations with their dead forebears,' Welch says, because 'there is some kind of connection that goes on, in really major translation, between the dead poet's spirit and the vital shifting intelligence and nervous system of the translator'.[29]

Perhaps the same cannot quite be said for all of Merriman's translators, but it's worth remembering that Carson's version of Merriman's poem belongs to a long tradition of poetic translations of *Cúirt an Mheán Oíche*, stretching back to Denis Woulfe's version done roughly two centuries earlier. It's a tradition that not only offers ways of charting changes in Irish culture in the years between 1780 and 2005, but also opportunities for understanding the nature and value of poetic translation from the Irish, a practice that has been going on regularly since Jonathan Swift first put his hand, in 1720, to translating Aodh Mac Gabhráin's 'Pléaráca na Ruarcach'. And whatever the quality of the various translations that have been made of *Cúirt an Mheán Oíche* over the years, all of Merriman's translators have, in one way or another, encountered Merriman's ghost, all have been touched, as have their readers, by the hand of the Master.

Appendix:
Text of *Cúirt an Mheán Oíche*
with literal translation

This text is based on Risteárd Ó Foghludha's edition of 1912. Three of the eleven translators considered in this study worked from this text, and one from the revised edition of it published in 1949. See the Bibliography for a complete listing of published editions of the poem.

The term 'literal translation' is, of course, highly suspect, as there can be no literally accurate translation of any text from one language into another. This might be said to be especially true when the original is a poem as deeply grounded in the Irish-language tradition as is Cúirt an Mheán Oíche. That said, I've tried to provide a translation that comes as close as is possible to a word-for-word and line-for-line version of Merriman's poem, even if the result at times may be more awkward than fluent. I'm indebted to the many glosses and prose translations of difficult passages provided by Liam P. Ó Murchú in his 1982 edition of the poem, and to all of Merriman's many translators, including, of course, the eleven considered in this study. However, the responsibility for this translation, and for its inevitable shortcomings, is mine alone.

Ba ghnáth me ag siubhal le ciumhuis na habhann
Ar bháinseach úr's an drúcht go trom,
In aice na gcoillte i gcoim an tsléibhe,
Gan mhairg gan mhoill ar shoillse an lae.
Do ghealadh mo croidhe nuair chínn Loch Gréine,
An talamh, an tír, is íoghar na spéire,
Taitneamhacht aoibhinn suidheamh na sléibhte
Ag bagairt a gcinn tar druim a chéile.
Ghealfadh an croidhe bheadh críon le cianta –
Caithte gan bhrígh nó líonta'e phianta –   10
I séithleach searbh gan sealbh gan saidhbhreas
D'fhéachfadh tamall tar barra na gcoillte
Ar lachain'n-a scuainte ar chuan gan cheo,
An eala ar a bhfuaid's í ag gluaiseacht leó,
Na héisc le meidhir ag éirghe in áirde
Péirse im radhairc go taidhbhseach tárrbhreac,
Dath an locha agus gorm na dtonn
Ag teacht go tolgach torannach trom,
Bhíodh éanlaith i gcrainn go meidhrach módhmhar,
Léimneach eilte i gcoillte im chómhgar,   20
Géimneach adharc is radharc ar shlóighte,
Tréanrith gadhar is *Reynard* rómpa.

Ar maidin indé bhí an spéir gan cheó,
Bhí *Cancer*, ón ngréin,'n-a caorthaibh teó
Is í gabhtha chum saothair tar éis na hoidhche
Is obair an lae sin réimpi sínte.
Bhí duilleabhar craobh ar ghéaga im thimcheall,
Fiorthann is féar'n-a slaoda taoibh liom,
Glasradh fáis is bláth is luíbhna
Scaipfeadh le fán dá chráidhteacht smaointe.   30
Do bhí mé cortha is an codladh dhom thraochadh,
Do shíneas thorm ar cothrom sa bhféar ghlas
In aice na gcrann i dteannta trínse,
Taca lem cheann's mo hannlaí sínte.
Ar cheangal mo shúl go dlúth le chéile,

It was usual for me to be walking along the edge of the river
On a fresh green and the dew heavy,
Beside the woods in the middle of the mountain,
Without oppression, without hindrance at daylight.
My heart lightened when I would see Loch Gréine,
The ground, the country and the horizon,
Pleasing, delightful the situation of the mountains
Brandishing their heads over each other's backs.
The heart would lighten that would be worn-out for ages –
Spent without strength or filled with pains –   10
In a bitter, emaciated person without property, without riches
Who would look a while beyond the tops of the woods
At ducks in their clutches in a harbour without fog,
The swan among them and she moving with them,
The fish with friskiness rising up
Perch in my view, striking, speckle-bellied,
The colour of the lake and the blue of the waves
Coming violently, noisily, heavily,
Birds are in trees, joyous, graceful
And leaping does in woods near me,   20
A sounding horn and a sight of crowds,
Dogs running hard and *Reynard* in front of them.

Yesterday morning the sky was without fog,
Cancer, of the sun, was a warm glowing mass
And it harnessed for work after the night
And the work of that day stretched before it.
The leaves of the branches were on limbs around me,
Wheat grass and grass in swaths beside me,
Luxuriant greens and flowers and herbs
Would scatter astray thoughts however troubled.   30
I was exhausted and sleep was wearing me out,
I stretched across on a level in the green grass
Beside the trees near a trench,
A prop for my head and my limbs stretched.
On fastening my eyes tightly together,

Greamuighthe dúnta i ndúbhghlas néallta,
Is m'aghaidh agam foilighthe ó chuilibh go sásta
I dtaidhbhreamh d'fhuiling me an cuilithe cráidhte
Do chorruigh do lom do pholl go hae me
Im chodladh go trom gan mheabhair gan éirim.   40

Ba ghairid mo shuan 'nuair chuala, shaoil me,
An talamh magcuairt ar luascadh im thimcheall,
Anfadh a dtuaidh is fuadach fíochmhar
Is calaidh an chuain ag tuargain teinte;
Siolladh dhem shúil dar shamhluigheas uaim
Do chonnarcas chugham le ciumhuis an chuain
An mhásach bholgach tholgach thaidhbhseach
Chnámhach cholgach ghoirgeach ghaibhdeach;
A haeirde ceart, má mheas me díreach,
Sé nó seacht de shlata is fuidhlach,
Péirse beacht dá brat ag sraoilleadh
Léi san tslab le drab is ríoball.   50
Ba mhuar ba mhéadhar ba fiadhain le féachaint
Suas 'n-a héadan créachtach créimeach,
Ba anfadh ceanntair, scannradh saoghalta,
A draid's a drandal mantach méirscreach.
A rí gach mádh! ba láidir líomhtha
A bíoma láimhe agus lánstaf innti,
Comhartha práis 'n-a bharr ar spíce
Is comhachta báille in áirde air scríobhtha.   60

Adubhairt go dorrdhach d'fhoclaibh dána: –
'Múscail! corruigh! a chodlataigh ghránna;
Is dubhach do shlighe bheith sínte it shliasta
Is cúirt 'n-a suidhe is na mílte ag triall ann;
Ní cúirt gan acht gan reacht gan riaghail
Ná cúirt na gcreach mar chleacht tu riamh
An cúirt seo ghluais ó shluaighte séimhe –
Cúirt na dtruagh na mbuadh is na mbéithe.
Is muar le maoidheamh ar shíolrach Éibhir

Fixed shut in a firm lock of sleep,
And my face hidden from flies satisfactorily
In a dream I suffered tormented eddies
That moved me to distress, that pierced me to the heart
In a heavy sleep without consciousness, without desire.   40

My rest was not long when I heard, I thought,
The surrounding ground rocking around me,
A storm from the north and a fierce squall,
And the jetty hammering fusillades;
With a glance from my eye I imagined
That I saw coming toward me at the edge of the harbour
A big-thighed person, stout-bellied, violent, of striking appearance
Big-boned, wrathful, surly, stout-calved;
Her correct height, if I judged exactly,
Six or seven yards and a surplus,   50
A particular perch of her cloak trailing
With her in the mud with mire and moisture.
It was unusual, it was august, it was wild to be looking
Up into her gashed, corroded face,
They were a terror of the district, a real fright
Her mouth and her fissured, toothless gums.
King of every fate! strong and smooth was
Her beam of a hand and a great staff in it,
An emblem of brass at the top of the spike
And a bailiff's authority written upon it.   60

She spoke harshly with bold words: –
'Awake! move! ugly sleeper;
It's sad your way to be stretched on your side
And a court sitting and the thousands travelling there;
Not a court without decree, without law, without rule,
Or a court of the plunderers as you are ever accustomed to
This court sprang from gentle crowds –
A court of mercy, of virtue, and of women.
And great with boasting of the seed of Éibhir

Uaisle sídhe mar shuidhdar d'aonghuth   70
Dhá lá is oidhche ar bhinn an tsléibhe
I bpálás bhuidhnmhar Bhruighean Mhaighe Gréine.
Is daingean do ghoill sé ar shoillse an ríogh
'S ar mhaithibh a theaghlaigh thaidhbhsigh sídhe,
'S ar uimhir na buidhne bhí 'n-a ndáil
Mar d'imthigh gach díth ar chríochaibh Fáil –
Gan sealbh gan saoirse ag síolrach seanda,
Cheannus a ndlíghe ná cíos ná cheannphoirt,
Scriosadh an tír is ní'l n-a ndiadh
In inad na luíbhna acht flígheach is fiadhail;   80
An uaisle b'fhearr chum fáin mar leaghdar
Is uachtar láimhe ag fáslaigh shaidhbhre,
Ag fealladh le fonn is foghail gan féachaint
D'fheannadh na lobhar 's an lom dá léirscrios.
Is dochrach dúbhach mar dhiugha gach daoirse
Doilbhe dúr i ndúbhcheilt dlighthe
An fann gan feidhm ná faghaidh ó éinne
Acht clampar doimhin is luighe chum léirscrios,
Fallsacht fear dlighe is fachtnaidhe árdnirt,
Cam is calghais faillighe is fábhar,   90
Scamal an dlighe agus fíordhath fannchirt,
Dalladh le bríb, le *fee* 's le fallsacht.

Farra gach fíor, is fuidheall níor fágadh,
Dearbhadh díble ar Bhíobla an lá san
Cúis dar ndóigh ná geobhairse saor tríd, –
Cnú na hóige dhá feóidh le faolrus
Is easnamh daoine suidhte ar Éire –
Do mheath let chuimhne an síolrach daonna;
Is folamh 's is tráighte fágadh tíortha,
An cogadh is an bás gan spás dá ndíogadh,   100
Uabhar na righthe 's ar imthigh tar sáile
'Nuair ná deineann sibh tuilleadh 'n-a n-áit díobh.
Is nár d'bhur n-iomad gan siorraigh gan síolrach
Is mná 'n-a muirear ar muir 's ar tíorthaibh,

[Were] the noble fairies as they spoke with one voice   70
Two days and an evening on a mountain peak
In a palace fond of company, the Fairy Dwelling of the Plain of Gréine.
Intensely it distressed the excellency the king
And the goodness of his proud fairy followers
And a number of the company that was gathered
How every deprivation befell the territories of Ireland –
Without property, without freedom for an ancient race,
Sovereignty in law or rent or rulers,
The land destroyed and nothing after it
In place of the herbs but chickweed and weeds;   80
The best nobility wandering as they faded away to nothing
And rich upstarts have the upper hand,
Deceiving with inclination and pillaging without regard
Skinning the lepers and the naked in their devastation.
It's distressing and sorrowful, like the worst case of every oppression,
A hard affliction in the dark denial of the law
The weak without influence who get nothing from anyone
But great deceit and submitting to destruction,
Falseness from the man of law and derision from high power,
Crookedness and fraud, neglect and favouritism,   90
The law [is] a darkness with nothing of [even] weak justice,
Blinding with bribe, with fee, and with falseness.

Along with every truth and judgment that was not abandoned,
Public evidence was sworn on the Bible that day
A matter indeed that you will not get free from, –
The fruit of youth withering with want of cultivation
And a deficiency of settled people in Ireland –
In your memory, human begetting failed;
Empty and exhausted the lands were left,
War and death without reprieve draining them,   100
The pride of kings that went over the sea
When you are not making any more in their place.
It's shameful great numbers of you without offspring, without progeny
And women in throngs on sea and on land,

Connsaigh chorpordha is borracaigh óga,
Is bonnsaigh bhrothallach fola agus feóla,
Lóistigh liosta agus leigithigh shásta
Is mórdhaigh shioscaithe d'imthigh i bhásta;
Is truagh gan toirrcheas tollairí 'en tsórt so,
Is truagh gan tormach brollaigh is bóta iad,   110
Is minic iad ullamh an focal dá bhfaghdís
Ag tuitim dá mogaill is molaimse a bhfoidhnne.

'Sé cinneadh le saoithe i gcrích na comhairle
In inad na daoirse dh'innsin dóibh sin: –
Duine den bhuidhin seo, líon a gcomhachta,
Ar thuitim don dísle, suidheamh i bhFódla.

Tairgeann Aoibheal, croidhe gan chlaonbheart,
Cara na Muimhneach, sídhbhean Léithchraig,
Scaradh le saoithibh sídhe na sluagh so
Scathamh do scaoileadh daoirse i dTuadhmhain.   120
Gheall an mhíonla chaointais chóir seo
Fallsacht dlighe do chlaoidhe go cómhachtach,
Seasamh i dteannta fann is fánlag
Is caithfidh an teann bheith ceannsa tláth libh,
Caithfidh an neart gan cheart so stríocadh
Is caithfidh an ceart 'n-a cheart bheith suidhte;
Geallaimse anois nách clis ná comhachta,
Caradus *Miss* ná *Pimp* 'n-a comhdhalta
Shiubhalfas tríd an dlighe seo ghnáith
'S a gcúirt 'n-a suidhe ag an síolrach neamhdha;   130
Tá an chúirt seo seasmhach feasta 'san bhFiacail,
Suibhailse, is freagair í, caithfe tu triall ann,
Siubhail gan tafann go tapa ar do phriacail,
Siubhail! nó stracfad san lathaigh im dhiaidh thu!'
Do bhuail sí crúca im chúl 'san chába
Is ghluais chum siubhail go lúbach láidir,
Scuab léi síos me trí sna gleannta,
Cnoc Mhánmhaighe is go binn an teampaill.

Large, manly women and well-developed young maidens,
And warm-blooded and warm-fleshed slips of girls,
Lingering idlers and lithe, satisfied [ones]
And select, dignified maidens who went to waste;
It's a pity not to have strapping offspring from this sort,
It's a pity that they are without swelling of breast and mound,   110
Often they are ready, if they would get the word,
To fall from their clusters and I praise their patience.

It's the decision of the wise ones at the end of the council
In place of this oppression of which they were told: –
[That] a person of this company, endowed with their authority,
By a throw of the dice, establish a session in Ireland.

Aoibheall, her heart without blemish,
A friend of the Munsterman, a fairy-woman of Léithchraig,
Offers to part from the fairy-sages of this hosting
For a while to redeem the oppression in Thomond.   120
This plaintive, honest, gentle maiden promised
To defeat legal falsehood commandingly,
To stand with the weak and the feeble
And the strong must be gentle and tender with you [women],
The strong without this correct manner must yield
And right as right must be established;
I promise now that neither tricks nor influence,
The friendship of *Miss* nor *Pimp* nor companion
Will march through this law as usual,
In their court in which the heavenly tribe is seated;   130
This court is established henceforth in Feakle,
Walk, and attend it, you must travel there,
Walk quickly at your peril without complaining,
Walk! or I will pull you in the mud after me!'
She stuck a crook in my back and in the cape
And set me moving to walk vigorously, firmly,
She swept me with her down through the glens
Of Cnoc Mánmhaigh and to the gable of the church.

Is deimhin go bhfeaca me ar lasadh le tóirsibh
An teaghlach taitneamhach maiseamhach mórtach   140
Soillseach seasmhach lannmhail lómrach
Taidhbhseach tathacach daingean deaghdhóirseach,
Chonnairc me an tsídhbhean mhíonla bhéasach
Chumuis 'n-a suidhe ar bhínse an tsaorchirt,
Chonnairc me gárda láidir luaimneach
Iomadach árrthach tárraingthe suas léi,
Chonnairc me láithreach lánteach líonta
Ó mhullach go lár de mhná is de dhaoine,
Chonnairc me spéirbhean mhaordha mhallruisc
Mhilisbhog bhéaltais mhéarlag mhealltach   150
Thaitneamhach shásta tháclach fhionn
'N-a seasamh in áirde ar chlár na mionn.
Bhí a gruaig léi scaoilte síos go slaodach
Is buaireamh suidhte fíor 'n-a féachaint,
Fuinneamh 'n-a radharc is faghairt 'n-a súile
Is fiuchadh le draghan uile aighnis fútha;
A caínt dá cosc le loscadh a cléibhe,
Gan gíog 'n-a tost acht tocht dá traochadh,
Do b'fhuiris a rádh gur bás badh rogha léi
Is tuile gan tlás ag tál go trom léi, –   160
'N-a seasamh ar lár an chláir 'n-a saighead
'S í ag greadadh na lámh 's ag fáscadh a laghar.

An uair do ghoil sí go folcaí fíochmhar
Is d'fhuascail osnaí gothaí caínte
D'imthigh an smúit is d'iompuigh snódh uirthi,
Thiormuigh a gnúis is dubhairt mar 'neósad: –
'Míle fáilte is gárdus cléibh romhat,
A Aoibheall, a fháidhbhean ársa on Léithchraig,
A shoillse an lae is a rae gan choimse,
A shaidhbhreas shaoghalta i ngéibhinn daoirse,   170
A cheanusach bhuadhach ó shluaighte an aoibhnis,
Ba easnamh cruaidh thu i dTuadhmhain 's i dTír Luirc;

And indeed I saw ablaze with torches
The pleasing, elegant, august household,   140
Luminous, steadfast, spacious, bright
Magnificent, substantial, solid, easily accessible,
I saw the gentle, well-mannered fairy-woman
Capable in her sitting on the bench of noble justice,
I saw the strong, nimble guard
Numerous, powerful drawn up around her,
I saw immediately a full house filled
From top to floor by ladies and by people,
I saw a proud, languid-eyed sky-woman
Sweet, soft-lipped, tender-fingered, beguiling   150
Pleasing, satisfying, fair hair falling in tresses
Standing up at the witness-table.
Her hair was unbound down in layers
And true vexation settled in her look,
Energy in her vision and fire in her eyes
And boiling with every anger and contention;
Her talk being hindered by her burning bosom,
Silent without a peep but a fit of grief exhausting her,
It would be easy to say that death would be her choice
And a flood without surcease pouring heavily from her, –   160
Standing at the centre of the table like an arrow
And she beating her hands and squeezing her fingers.

When she wept furious floods
And sighs released vowels of speech
The gloom departed and her complexion changed,
She dried her face and said as I will tell: –
'A thousand welcomes and heart's joy to you,
Aoibheall, ancient woman prophet from Léithchraig,
Light of the day and moon without limit,
Treasure long-lived in distress and bondage,   170
Powerful, victorious from hosts of pleasure,
You were greatly wanted in Thomond and in Tír Luirc;

'S é túis mo cháis is fáth mo chaointe,
Cúis do chráidh me is d'fhág me claoidhte,
Bhain dem threoir me is do sheóil gan chiall me,
'S chaith mar cheó me dóighte i bpianta, –
Na sluaighte imthigheann gan chrích gan chaomhnadh
Ar fhuaid an tsaoighil seo d'fhíorscoith béithe
'N-a gcailleacha dubha gan cumhdach céile,
Caithte gan clú gan cionnta claonbheart.   180
Is aithnid dam féin san méid seo shiúbhlas
Bean agus céad nár mhéin leó a dhiúltadh,
Is mise in a measc mo chreach mar táimse
D'imthigh im spaid gan fear gan pháiste.
Mo dhochar mo dhóghadh mo bhrón mar bhíom
Gan sochar gan sógh gan seóid gan síth,
Go doilbhir duaibhseach duadhmhar dítheach,
Gan codladh gan suan gan suairceas oidhche,
Acht maslaithe i mbuairt gan suaimhneas sínte
Ar leabain leamhfhuair dár suathadh ag smaointe.   190
A Cháidh na Carraige breathain go bíodhgach
Mná na Banba in anacra suidhte,
Ar nós má leanaid na fearaibh dá bhfuadar
Óch, mo lagar! acht gcaithfamna a bhfuadach.
'S é am nur mhéin leó céile phósadh
An t-am nur dhéirc le héinne góbhail leó!
An t-am nár bh'fhiú bheith fútha sínte –
An seandaigh thonnda shúighte chlaoidhte.
Dá dtuiteadh amach le teas na hóige
Duine fén seacht ar theacht féasóige   200
Ceangal le mnaoi, ní míntais thogfidh –
Thaitneamhach shuidhte 'e shíol ná d'fhoghluim,
Clódheas chaoin ná míonla mhánla
A mb'eól di suidhe ná tigheacht do láthair,
Acht doineanntach odhar nó donn doilgheasach
Do chruinnigh le doghraing cabhair nách cuibhe dhi!
'S é chráidh mo chroidhe is do scaoil gan chéill me
'S d'fhág mo smaointe is m'intinn traochta

It is the origin of my concern and the reason for my lament,

The cause that vexed me and left me exhausted,

That took me from my way and drove me senseless,

And consumed me like a fog, burned in pains, –

The crowds that go without fulfilment, without protection

For the very best women throughout this world

To be sad, celibate women without protection of a spouse,

Worn out without reputation, without fault of evil behaviour.   180

I myself know, wherever I have walked,

A hundred and one women who wouldn't want to refuse,

And myself among them, woe is me as I am,

I am left as a barren person without a man, without a child.

My harm, my scorching, my sorrow as I am

Without profit, without comfort, without jewels, without rest,

Gloomy, cheerless, toilsome, destitute,

Without sleep, without rest, without a night's mirth,

Save only insults in sorrow, without peace stretched

On an impotent cold bed disturbed by thoughts.   190

Cáidh of Carraig, look with interest on

The women of Ireland in affliction fixed,

So that if the men follow their inclination

Oh, alas, but we will have to abduct them.

The time when they desire to marry a wife is

The time it would not be enough for anyone to go with them!

The time it would not be worth it to be stretched under them –

The lethargic, fixed, exhausted antiquities.

If it happened, with the heat of youth,

That one person in seven on coming to a beard   200

Marrying a woman, not a delicate wraith will he take –

Pleasing, proud of race or of learning,

Nicely formed, refined or gentle, gracious

Who would know whether to sit or come in to your presence,

But a cheerless, dull person or a melancholy, swarthy [woman]

Who gathered with difficulty help that was not proper for her!

It tormented my heart and left me without sense

And left my thoughts and my mind exhausted

Tráighte tinn mar taoim, go tréithlag,
Cráidhte claoidhte ag caoidh's ag géarghol, –   210
Nuair chím preabaire calma croidhmhail
Fuadrach fearmhail barrmhail bríoghmhar
Stuamdha feasmhach seasmhach saoithmhail
Gruaidhdheas greannamhar geanmhail gnaoidhmhail,
Nó buachaill bastallach beachanta bróigdheas
Cruaidhcheart ceanusach ceapaithe córach
Buaidhte ceannuighthe ceangailte pósta
Ag fuaid ag cailligh ag aimid nó ag óinmhid,
Nó ag suairle salach de chaile gan tionnscal,
Stuaiceach stailiceach aithiseach stanncach   220
Suaidhteach sodalach foclach fáidhmhail
Cuardach codlatach goirgeach gráinmhail.
Mo chreach is mo lot! tá molt míbhéasach,
Caile na gcos is folt gan réidhteach,
Dá ceangal anocht's é loisc go léir me,
Is cá bhfuil mo locht ná toghfaidhe réimpi?
Créad é an t-adhbhar ná tabharfaidhe grádh dham
Is me chomh leabhair, chomh modhmhail chomh breagh so?
Is deas mo bhéal, mo dhéid's mo gháire,
Is geal mo ghné, is tá m'éadan tláth tais,   230
Is glas mo shúil, tá m'úrla scáinneach
Bachallach búclach cúplach fáinneach,
Mo leaca is mo ghnúis gan smúit gan smáchall
Tarringthe cumtha lonnrach scáthmhar,
Mo phíop, mo bhrághaid, mo lámha, mo mhéara,
Ag síorbhreith barr na háilne ó chéile.
Féach mo chom! nach leabhair mo chnámha,
N'íl me lom ná crom ná stágach,
Seo toll is cosa is colann nach nár liom,
'S an togha an socair fé *chover* ná tráchtaim.   240
Ní suairle caile ná sreangaire mná me
Acht stuaire cailce tá taitneamhach breagh deas,
Ní sraoill ná sluid ná luid gan fáscadh,
Ná smíste duirc gan sult gan sásamh,

Dried up, sick as I am, weakly feeble,
Tormented, subdued, lamenting and keenly weeping, –   210
When I see a dashing, brave, cordial man
Bustling, manly, funny, vigorous
Sensible, knowing, steadfast, accomplished,
Pleasant-cheeked, humorous, loving, comely,
Or a boy showy, vigorous, with a nicely shaped boot,
Rightly hardy, commanding, determined, shapely
Defeated, bought, bound, married
To a witch, to a hag, to a foolish woman, or to a simpleton,
Or to a dirty whelp of a girl without industry,
Obstinate, starchy, shameful, self-willed   220
Haughty, arrogant, verbose, gossiping
Acquisitive, sleepy, irritable, hateful.
My ruin and my destruction! there is an ill-mannered sulky person,
A girl of legs and hair untidy,
Being married tonight and it scalding me entirely,
And where is my fault that I would not be chosen before her?
What is the reason that I would not be given love
And I as slender, as modest, as fine as this?
Nice is my mouth, my teeth and my laugh,
And bright my appearance, and my forehead is mild, gentle,   230
Green are my eyes, my hair is in locks
Curled, ringleted, double-plaited, beautiful,
My cheeks and my face without defect, without blemish
Attractive, shapely, luminous, comely,
My throat, my bosom, my hands, my fingers,
Forever vying with one another for the height of beauty.
Look on my waist, are my bones not slender,
I am not bald or bent or stiff,
Of these buttocks and legs and body I am not ashamed,
And the best at rest under cover I don't mention.   240
I am not a slattern of a girl or an ungainly woman
But a handsome, chalk-white woman who is pleasing, fine, nice,
Not a slattern, nor a bad woman, nor a slut without tidiness,
Nor a boorish female without enjoyment, without satisfaction,

Lóiste lobhtha ná toice gan éifeacht,
Acht óigbhean scoththa chomh toghtha's is féidir.
Da mbeinnse silte mar tuilleadh dhem chomhursain,
Leadhbach liosta gan tuigsin gan eólus,
Gan radharc, gan ghliocus in imirt mo chórach,
Mo threighid! cár mhisde me rith in éadóchus?   250
Ní feacathas fós me i gcomhgar daoine,
Ag faire ná ag tórramh óg ná críona,
Ar mhachaire an bháire an ráis ná an rinnce,
I bhfarradh na dtáinte ar bánta líonta,
Acht gabhtha go sámh gan cháim ar domhan
I gculaithe shásta ó bharr go bonn.
Beidh a cheart im chúl de phúdar fillte,
Starch is stiúir i gcúl mo choife,
Húda geal gan ceal ribíní,
Gúna breac's a cheart ruffaí leis;   260
Is annamh go brách gan fásáil aerach
Thaitneamhach bhreágh lem cheárdán craorag,
Is aniomdha luíbhna craoibha is éanlaith
Ar m'aprún síogach ríoghdhach *cambric*;
Sála cumtha cumhanga córach
Árda sleamhaine ar *screw* fém bhróga,
Búclaí is fáinní is láimhne síoda,
Fonsaí práislí is lásaí daoira.
Seachain, na saoil gur sceinnteach scáthmhar,
Aimid gan ghaois ná naoindach náireach   270
Eaglach uaigneach uallach fhiadhain me,
Gealthach gan ghuais gan stuaim gan téagar;
I bhfalach ní raghainnse ó radharc na gcéadta,
Is ceannusach taidhbhseach m'aghaidh agus m'éadan,
Is dearbhtha bhím dom shíorthesbeánadh
Ar mhachaire mhín gach fíoriomána,
Ag rinnce, ar báire, rás is radaireacht,
Teinte cnámh is ráfla is ragairne,
Ag aonach margadh is Aifreann Domhnaigh,
Ag éileamh breathnuighthe, ag amharc gach togha fir.   280

A rotten sluggard nor a hussy without sense,
But an excellent young woman as choice as is possible.
If I were lazy like many of my neighbours,
Silly, tedious, without understanding, without knowledge,
Without vision, without cleverness in playing for what is my due,
My bitter grief! what would be the harm for me to run into despair?   250
I have not yet been seen in the vicinity of people,
Watching or paying attention to young or old,
On a field of the match, the race or the dance,
In the company of the multitudes, on crowded grasslands,
But was dressed pleasantly without a fault in the world
In agreeable clothes from head to sole.
The right amount of closely applied powder will be in my hair,
Starch and a rakish angle in the back of my coif,
A bright hood with no lack of ribbons,
A speckled gown and the right amount of ruffs with it;   260
It's very seldom that without an airy floral design
Pleasing and fine is my crimson cloak,
And a great many herbs, branches and birds
On my striped, regal apron of cambric;
Heels shapely, slender, comely
Sleek heights on a screw under my shoes,
Buckles and rings and gloves of silk,
Hoops, bracelets and high-priced laces.
Beware, don't suppose that I am a timid, skinny girl,
A simpleton without intelligence or modest innocence   270
Fearful, lonely, scatter-brained, uncultivated,
Wild without enterprise, without good sense, without substance;
In hiding I would not go from the view of the hundreds,
Commanding and proud are my face and my brow,
It's certain that I'm always displaying myself
On the smooth field of every true hurling,
At dance, at match, race and courting,
Bonfires and gossiping and revelling,
At fair, market and Sunday Mass,
Courting observation, looking at every choice man.   280

Chaitheas my chiall le fiadhach gan éifeacht,
Dhalladar riamh me, d'iadhdar m'ae ionnam.
Tar éis mo chumainn, mo thurraing, mo ghrádh dhóibh,
Tar éis ar fhulaing me d'iomada crádhnuis,
Tar éis ar chailleas le caitheamh na scálaí,
Béithe balbha is cailleacha cártaí.
Ní'l cleas dá mb'fhéidir léaghamh ná trácht air
Le teacht na rae nó tar éis bheith lán di,
Um Inid ná um Shamhain ná ar shiubhal na bliadhna
Ná tuigim gur leamhus bheith ag súil le ciall as.   290
Níor bh'áil liom codladh go socair éanuair díobh
Gan lán mo stoca de thorthaibh fém chluasa,
Is deimhin nár bh'obair liom troscadh le cráibhtheacht,
Is greim ná blogam ní shlogainn trí trátha,
In aghaidh an tsrotha do thomainn mo léine,
Ag súil trím chodladh le cogar óm chéile,
Is minic do chuaid me ag scuabadh an stáca,
Ingne is gruaig fén luaithghríos d'fhágainn,
Chuirinn an tsúist fé chúil na gaibhle,
Chuirinn an ramhan go ciún fén adhairt chugham,   300
Chuirinn an choigíol i gcillín na háithe,
Chuirinn mo cheirtlín i dteine aoil Mhic Rághnaill,
Chuirinn an ros ar chorp na sráide,
Chuirinn san tsop chugham tor gabáiste.
N'íl cleas aca súd dá ndubhras láithreach
Ná hagrainn congnadh an deamhain's a bhráthar,
'S é fáth mo scéil go léir's a bhrígh dhuit
Mar táim gan chéile tar éis mo dhíchill,
Fáth my sheanchus' fhada, mo phianchreach,
Táim in achrann dhaingean na mbliadhnta,   310
Ag tarraing go tréan ar laethibh liaithe
Is eagal liom éag gan éinne 'om iarraidh.
A Phéarla ó Pharrthas screadaim is glaedhim ort,
Éiric m'anma ort, aitchim thu is éighim ort,
Seachain ná scaoil me im shraoill gan áird
Ná im chailligh gan chrích gan bhrígh gan bhláith,

I lost my reason in a hunt without effect,
They always deceived me, they stopped my heart in me.
After my devising, my pushing, my love for them,
After what I suffered from too much vexation,
After what I lost on the cup-tossing,
Stammering women and hags of the cards.
There isn't a trick that it would be possible to read of or mention
With the coming of the moon or after its being full,
Around Shrovetide or around Hallowe'en or throughout the year
That I understand that it's folly to be looking for sense out of it.   290
I didn't wish to sleep quietly any of these times
Without my stocking full of fruit under my ears,
It's a certainty that it was not work for me to fast with piety,
And a bit or a sup I would not swallow for days,
Against the current I would immerse my shirt,
Hoping in my sleep for a whisper from my spouse,
It's often that I went sweeping the stack,
Nails and hair under the ashes I would leave,
I would put the flail in the corner of the hearth,
I would put the spade silently under my pillow,   300
I would put the distaff in the kiln near the ford,
I would put my ball of thread in the limekiln of Mac Rághnall,
I would put the flaxseed in the middle of the street,
I would put in my bedding a head of cabbage.
There isn't a trick of these that I spoke of a moment ago
That would not invoke the aid of the devil and his brother,
It's the reason of my entire story and its meaning for you
That I am without a spouse after doing my best,
The reason of my long story-telling, woe is me,
I am in the firm fastness of the years,   310
Approaching rapidly the grey days
And I fear a death without anyone asking for me.
Pearl of Paradise, I implore and I call on you,
Ransom my soul, I beseech you and I appeal to you,
Take care, don't dismiss me as a useless slattern
Or as a hag unmarried, without virtue, without bloom,

Gan charaid gan chloinn gan choim gan cháirde
Ar theallacha draghain gan feidhm gan fáilte.
Dar a fuil uimpe teinte is tóirneach!
Dalladh me suidhte maoidhte im óinmhid,   320
Sealbh gach sógha ag rógha gach diugha
'S ag ainnibh na Fódla os comhair mo shúl.
Tá sumac ag Saidhbh go saidhbhir sómhach,
Muirinn i meidhir's a haghaidh ar a nóchar,
Mór is Mairsile i macnus múchta,
Is mórchuid magaidh ortha ag fachnaid fúm-sa;
Is giodamach sámh í Sláínge, is Síle
Sisile is Áine is ál'n-a dtimcheall,
Tuilleadh mar táid de mhnáibh na tíre
Is mise mar táim gan tál gan tsíolrach.   330
Is fada gan feidhm is foidhnne dhamhsa é,
Lagar'om leaghadh's mo leigheas im chomhachta
Maille re luíbhna díble dreóighte
Is arthanna draoidheachta chlaoidhfeas fós dam
Buachaill deas nó gas galánta
Bhuaidhfeas ceart a shearc's a ghrádh dham.
Do chonnarch go leór den tsórt dá dhéanamh
Is chuirfinn i gcóir na comhgair chéadna:
Is daingean an congnadh ag dúbailt daoine
Greamanna d'úbhla is púdar luíbhna,   340
Magairlín meidhrach, meill na mbualtaibh,
Taithigín taidhbhseach, toill na tuairte,
Mealladh na minnseach, claidheamh na mbonnsach,
An cumainnín buidhe's an draoidheacht chum drúise,
Duilleabhar dóighte ar nós gur rún é,
Is tuilleadh dhen tsórt nach cóir a mhúineadh.
Do b'iongantus muar i dTuadhmain le chéile
An bhroingheal so thuas ag buadhchan céile;
Is d'innis sí damhsa, ar ndóigh, trí rún,
Um Inid's í pósta ó bhórd na Samhn'   350
Nár ibh is nár ól acht an reóithnach fionn
Is cuillibh na móna dóighte ar lionn.

Without friends, without children, without protection, without credit
At inhospitable firesides without use, without welcome.
By blood, prayer, fires and thunder!
I am blinded certainly, surely, a foolish woman,   320
Possession of every comfort by the very worst of the lot
And by the blighted ones of Ireland in front of my eyes.
Saidhbh, who is rich and comfortable, has a plump man,
Murinn in joy and her face toward her spouse,
Mór and Mairsile smothered in luxury,
Great mockery is on them jeering at me;
Airy and tranquil are Sláinge and Síle
Sisile and Áine and a brood of children around them,
More of the women of the country as they are
And myself as I am without offspring, without progeny.   330
It's long that I have been patient without action,
Weak from my wasting away and my cure in my power
By means of putrified common herbs
And magic charms that will win for me yet
A fine boy or an elegant young man
And will gain for me rightly his affection and his love.
I saw plenty of the kind being done
And I would apply the same means:
Strong help for coupling people are
Bits of apples and the powder of herbs,   340
The early purple orchid, cowslip,
Great figwort, shepherd's purse,
Kid's desire, ribwort,
Yellow cumin and love charm,
Leaves burned as if it is a secret,
And more of this kind that it's not right to teach.
A great wonder in all of Thomond was
This beautiful maiden above at gaining a spouse;
And she told me, of course, in secret,
Around Shrovetide, and she married since the verge of Hallowe'en   350
That there was neither eating nor drinking but the white withered grass
And a store of peat burned in ale.

Is fada me ag foidhnneadh, faghaimse fuascailt,
Seachain ar mhoill me, saighead chum luais é;
Muna bhfuil leigheas dom threighid it chuairt-se
Cuirfe me faghairt i bhfeidhm má's cruaidh dham.'

Preabann anuas go fuadrach fíochmhar
Seanduine suarach is fuadach nimhe fé,
A bhaill ar luascadh is luas anáile air,
Draghan is duais ar fuaid a chnámha.   360
Ba dhreóil an radharc go deimhin don chúirt é,
Ar bórd 'n-a thaidhbhse im éisteacht dubhairt sé: –
'Dochar is díoghbháil is síorchrádh cléibh ort
A thoice le místáid a shíol gábha is déarca,
Is dóth nach iongantus laigeacht na gréine
Is fós gach tuibaist dar imthigh ar Éire,
Mar mheath gach ceart gan reacht gan dlighe againn,
Ár mba bhí bleacht gan lacht gan laoigh aca,
Is dá dtagadh níos mó de mhorscrios tíortha
Is gach faision dá nódhacht ar Mhóir 's ar Shíle.   370
A thoice gan chrích nach chuimhin le táinte
Olcus an síolrach daoine ó dtángais,
Gan focal le maoidheamh ag do shinsear gránna
Acht lopaigh gan bhrígh, lucht míre is mála.
Is aithnid dúinne an snamhaire is athair duit,
Gan charaid gan chlú gan chúil gan airgead,
'N-a leibide liath gan chiall gan mhúineadh,
Gan mheidir gan mhias gan bhiadh gan anlann,
Gan faice ar a dhrom is a chabhail gan chóta,
Acht gad ar a chom is a bhonn gan bhróga.   380
Creididh a dhaoine, dhá ndíoltaidhe ar aonach
Eisean 's a bhuidhean tar éis íoc gach éileamh,
Dar colainn na naoimh badh dícheall muar do
Pota maith dighe len' fhuidhlach d'fhuascailt.
Nach muar an t-óbhacht 's an gleó i measc daoine
Truaghaire 'et shórt gan bhó gan chaoirigh,
Búclaí it bhróga is clóicín síoda ort,

It's long I have patience, may I get relief,
Guard me against delay, an arrow for my speed;
Unless there is a cure for my grief in your visit
I'll take extreme measures if it's hard for me.'

Up jumps with a furious motion
A dirty old man and a poisonous violence about him,
His limbs shaking and a shortness of breath on him,
Displeasure and distress throughout his bones.   360
Wretched was the sight indeed for the court,
At the [witness-] table in his vanity in my hearing he said:
'Harm and deprivation and eternal agony of the breast on you,
Infamous wench, offspring of want and alms,
It's likely that the weakness of the sun is not a surprise
And also every mischance that has come on Ireland,
As every right of ours has grown feeble without principle, without law,
Our cows that were milch cows without yield, without calves from them,
And if more of the great destruction of lands were to come
Every fashion, however new, is on Mór and on Síle.   370
Wench unmarried, do multitudes not remember
The evil of the breed of people you came from,
Not a word to boast of for your ugly ancestors
But louts without sense, tramps and bag people.
We know the serpent who is father to you,
Without a friend, without reputation, without shelter, without money,
A grey clown, without sense, without education,
Without a pail, without a dish, without food, without sauce,
Without anything on his back and his torso without a coat,
Except a cord around his waist and his soles without shoes.   380
Believe [it], people, if one sold at a fair
Himself and his crowd, after paying every debt,
By the body of the saints, it would be a great effort for him
A good pot of drink to redeem with the surplus.
Is there not great joking and clamour among people
[That] a miserable person of your kind, without a cow, without a sheep,
[Has] buckles on your shoes, a silk cloak on you,

[133]

Is ciarsúir póca ag góbhail na gaoithe ort!
Do dhallais an saoghal go léir let thaidhbhse,
'S is aithnid dam féin tu i dtaobh le coife.   390
Is deacair dham labhairt, do lom is léir dham,
Is fada do dhrom gan chabhair ón léine;
Is togha drochdhuine do thuigfeadh 'n-a gábha thu
Is feabhus do ruffa let mhuinchilte cáimric.
Tá canafas saor chum sraod go bhásta
Is cá bhfios don tsaoghal nach *stays* é 'ot fháscadh?
Feiceann an tír ort frínse is fáinne
Is ceileann do laímhne grís is gága.
Acht aithris ar bórd, nó inneósad féin é, –
An fada nár ól tu deóir let bhéile?   400
A chonartaigh bhoicht na gcos gan ionladh,
Dochar it chorp le *Bucks* gan anlann!
Is fuiris dar liúm dot chúl bheith taidhbhseach,
Do chonnarc lem shúile an chúil 'n-a luigheann tu;
Garbh ná mín ní shíntear fúth ann,
Barrach ná líon dár sníomhadh le túrna,
Acht mata 'n-a smuirt gan chuilt gan chlúdadh,
Dealbh gan luid gan phluid gan tsúsa,
I gcomhar bhótháin gan áit chum suidhe ann
Acht súgh sileáin is fáscadh aníos ann,   410
Fiadhaile ag teacht go fras gan choimse
Is rian na gcearc air treasna scríobtha,
Lag ina dhrom 's na gabhla ar lúbadh
Is clagarnach dhonn go trom ag túirlint.
A chumainn na bhfáidh! nach árd do labhair sí!
Gustalach gálbha gártha gabhann sí
I ndathaibh i gcóir 's i gclócaí síoda,
Faire go deó arú! fóill, cár fríoth é?
Aithris cá bhfaghair an radharc so mhaoidheann tu,
Is aithris cár thuill tu an leadhb gan bhrígh seo;   420
Is deacair a shuidheamh gur fríoth go cóir iad –
Is gairid ó bhís gan síol an órlaigh.
Aithris cá bhfuair tu luach an húda,

And a pocket handkerchief moving the wind on you!
You deceived all the world with your vanity,
And I myself knew you having only a small cap.   390
It's difficult for me to say, your poverty is clear to me,
Your back is long without help from a shirt;
It's a very bad person who would realize you to be in need of it
And an excellence of ruff on your sleeve of cambric.
There is cheap canvas for underclothing to the waist
And who in the world knows it is but stays confining you?
The country sees on you fringe and rings
And your gloves conceal blotches and cracks.
But relate to the [witness-] table or I myself will tell it, –
How long since you drank a drop with your meal?   400
Poor vulgar woman of the feet without washing,
Harm to your body from Bucks without sauce!
It's easy, it seems to me, your hair to be showy,
I saw with my eyes the nook in which you lie;
Neither rough nor smooth is stretched under you there,
Tow nor flax that was spun on a spinning wheel,
But a dirty mat without a quilt, without a cover,
Bare without a stitch, without a blanket, without a rug,
In a communal shack without a place for sitting in it,
But soot shedding and pressing down on it,   410
Weeds flourishing without moderation
And the track of the hens written across it,
Weak at its top and the props bending
And a heavy brown rain heavily pouring down.
Fellowship of the seers, is it not excellently that she spoke!
Wealthy, haughty, radiant she goes
In colours, in fittings, and in silken cloaks,
Alas, alas! wait, where was it got?
Relate where you get this appearance you boast of,
And relate how you earned this rag without substance;   420
It's difficult to establish that they were rightly got –
It isn't long since you were without enough seed for a square inch.
Relate where you got the price of the hood,

Is aithris cá bhfuair tú luach do ghúna,
Acht leagaimíd uainn car ghluais an cóta,
Is aithris cá bhfuair tu luach na mbróga.
A Aoibheal cheanusach charthannach chomhachtach,
Guidhim thu, gairim thu, freagair is fóir me,
Is fíor gur feasach me farairí Fodla
Suidhte greamuighthe ag sladaidhthe 'en tsórt so.   430
Dar láimh mo charad! is aithnid dam comhursa
Láimh le baile agam, gairid do chomhgar,
Buachaill soineannta sruimile sónntach
Ar buaileadh duine aca chuige mar nóchar.
Is searbh lem chroidhe nuair chím im radharc í –
A gradam, a críoch, a poimp 's a taidhbhse;
Sealbhach bó aici is eórna ag fás di,
Airgead póca is ór 'dir lámha aici.
Do chonnairc me indé í ar thaobh na sráide,
Is cumusach tréan an léire mná í,   440
Malfaire másach mágach magmhail,
Marbh le cámus lán do ladmhus,
Mar 'each gur claon liom éad do mhúscailt,
Scannal do scéidh ná scéalta scrúdadh,
Do b'fhuiris dam innsin cruinn mar chuala
An chuma n-a mbíodh sí sraoillte suaidhte,
Stracaithe ar lár is gáir 'n-a timcheall,
Sraithte ar an sráid nó i stábla sínte.
Mairfidh a tásc is tráchtfar choidhche
Ar mharthana ar cháil 's ar gháir a gníomhartha   450
In Uibh Bhreacáin an aráin 's an fhíona,
I dTír Mhachláin na mbánta míne,
Ag ísle is ársa Mháinse is Ínse,
Chill Bhreacáin, an Chláir is Chuince,
Ag connsaigh ainmhidhe Treadraighe an phónra
Is fonnsaigh falachaidhe Chreatlaighe an chórda.
Faire, ba chlaon í, tar éis a ndubhairt me
Glacfainn gur saor í fé n-a cionta,
Acht bheirim don phláigh í lá mar chím í

And relate where you got the price of your gown,
But we set aside where the coat sprang from,
And relate where you got the price of the shoes.
Commanding, charitable, powerful Aoibheall,
I pray to you, I call upon you, answer and save me,
It's true that I am aware that the warriors of Ireland
Are fixed, caught by rogues of this sort.   430
By the hand of my friend! I know a neighbour
Close by my town, near your vicinity,
A pleasant boy, an easy-going, spirited person
Who was taken by one of these as a spouse.
Bitterness is in my heart when I see her –
Her showiness, her married state, her pomp and her vanity;
She has a herd of cows and barley growing for her,
She has pocket silver and gold between her hands.
I saw her yesterday on the side of the street,
She's a vigorous, powerful, fine, tall woman,   440
A sturdy, strong, large-hipped, fleshly, mocking person,
Benumbed with fault-finding, full of sauciness.
Except that I'm not inclined to rousing up jealousy,
Putting forth scandal or spreading slander,
It would be easy for me to tell exactly as I heard it
The way she used to be plucked, kneaded
Dragged on the floor and laughter about her,
Spread out in the street or stretched in a stable.
Her reputation will live and will be mentioned forever
The existence, the fame, and the repute of her achievements   450
In Ibrickane of the bread and the wine,
In Tiermaclane of the fine pastures,
By the humble and the venerable of Máinse and Inse,
Kilbrickane, Clare and Quin,
By the wild, brutish men of Treadraighe of the beans
And the cowardly cut-throats of Creatlaighe of the corduroy.
Look, were she inclined according as I said,
I would accept that she was free from her sin,
But a plague on her the day that I saw her

Leagaithe láimh le Gárus sínte,   460
Caithte ar an ród gan órlach fúithi
Ag gramaisc na móna ar bhóithribh Dhubhdhoire.
M'iongantus ann os ceann mo chéille
Is crithim go fann le scannradh an scéil seo, –
Ise bheith seang nuair theann gach éinne í
Is druidim le clann nuair shanntuigh féin í.
Is mór n-a grása é ag rádh na mbriathar,
Nóimeant spás níor ghábha le hiarraidh
Ó léaghadh ar bórd os comhair na coinnle
An tÉgo Vos so d'órduigh Íosa   470
Gur réidh sí lacht go bleacht 'n-a cíocha
Acht naoi mí beacht is seachtmhain cinnte!

Breathain gur baoghal don té tá scaoilte
Ceangal go héag fé thaobh den chuing seo,
I sealbh gach saoth, is éad dá shuathadh –
In aisce, mo lean! mo léaghan ní bhfuaireas.
Is feasach dhon taobh so 'en tsaoghal mar bhí me
Sealad dem réim 's dem laethibh roimhe seo,
Leitheadach láidir lán de shaidhbhreas,
Eisteas le fághail is fáilte im theaghlach,   480
Caraid i gcúirt is congnadh dlighe agam,
Ceannus is clú agus comhar na saoithe,
Tathac im chaint is suim is éifeacht,
Talamh is maoin ag suidheamh mo chéille!
M'aigne síoch is m'intinn sásta –
Chailleas le mnaoi mo bhrígh 's mo shláinte!
Ba taitneamhach leabhair an crobhaire mná í,
Bhí seasamh is com is cabhail is chámha aici,
Casadh 'n-a cúl go búclach trilseach,
Lasadh 'n-a gnúis go lonnrach soillseach,   490
Cuma na hóighe uirthi is sógh 'n-a gáire,
Is cuireadh 'n-a cló chum póige is fáilte!
Acht chreathas le fonn gan chonn gan cháirde
Ó bhaitheas go bonn go tabhartha i ngrádh dhi.

Laid down close by Gárus, stretched,   460
Thrown on the road without an inch of anything under her
By the turf gang on the Doora road.
My wonder at this above my reason
And I tremble weakly with surprise at this story, –
She being slender when everyone squeezed her
And moving with a child when she strongly desired it.
Great is the grace to say the words,
A moment of respite there was no need to ask for
Since declaring at altar in front of the candles
The *I join you* that Jesus ordained   470
Until she emitted milk abundantly from her breasts
[Was] but an exact nine months and a week certainly!

Observe that a danger for the person who is free is
A tie until death under this bond,
In possession of every tribulation, and jealousy disturbing him –
In vain, alas, my lesson I did not learn.
It's known to this side of the world how I was
A period of my life and of my days before this,
Proud, strong, full of riches,
Accommodation available and a welcome in my household,   480
Friends in court and legal help for me,
Authority and fame and the companionship of the learned,
Substance in my speech and interest and importance,
Land and wealth confirming my prudence!
My spirit peaceful and my mind content –
I lost to a woman my strength and my health!
She was pleasing and slender, the strong, able woman,
She had poise and a waist and a body and bones,
A twist in her hair, ringleted, plaited,
A blush in her face, resplendent, luminous,   490
The appearance of youth on her and joy in her laugh,
And an invitation in her form for me of kisses and welcome!
But I shook with desire, without sense, without respite
From head to foot until taken in love by her.

Is dearbh gan dobhta ar domhan gur díoghaltus
Danardha donn dom thabhairt ar m'aimhleas
D'fhearthainn go trom ar bhonn mo ghníomhartha
Ó fhlaitheas le fonn do lom líon me.
Do snamnadh suidhte snaidhm na cléire,
Is ceangladh sinn i gcuing le chéile,   500
Ghlanas gan chinnteacht suim gach éileamh
Bhaineas le baois gan ghaois an lae sin.
Cothrom go leór, níor chóir me cháineadh –
Stopas an gleó bhí ag cóip na sráide,
Bacaigh go léir, bhí an cléireach sásta,
An sagart róbhuidheach is b'éidir fáth leis!
Lasamair tóirsí is comhursain cruinn ann,
Leagadh ar bórdaibh mórchuid bídh chughainn,
Clagarnach cheóil is ól gan choimse,
Is chaitheadar cóisir mhórtach mhaoidhteach.   510
Mo dhíth gan easbhaidh nár tachtadh le biadh me
An oidhche baisteadh nó ar san gur iarras
Síneadh ar leabain le haindeis do liath me
'S do scaoil le gealaigh gan charaid gan chiall me.
'S é tásc do gheóbhainn ag óg's ag aosta
Gur breallán spóirt ag ól's ag glaedhach í
I mbotháin ósta is bóird dá bpléascadh,
Ar lár 'n-a lóiste ag pósta is aonta.
Do b'fhada dá mheilt a teist's a tuairisc,
Do b'fhada gur chreid me a bheag ná a mhuar de,   520
Do b'eaglach le gach beirt dá gcuala é
Go rachainn im pheilt im gheilt gan tuairisc.
Fós ní ghéillfinn, caoch mar bhí me,
Do ghlór gan éifeacht éinne mhaoidh é;
Acht magadh nó greim gan feidhm gan chéill
Gur aithris a broinn dam deimhin gach scéil!
Níor chúrsaí leamhuis ná dúrdam bréige é,
Ná dubhairt bean liom go ndubhradh léithe é
Acht labhair an bheart i gceart's in éifeacht –
Do bhronn sí mac abhfad roimh ré dham!   530

It's certain without any doubt that it is a vengeance
Very cruel, bringing me to my loss,
That rained heavily because of my deeds,
From heaven with zeal, whose power wasted me.
We were knotted, settled by the joining of the clergy,
And we were bound in a yoke together, 500
I cleared without stinginess the amount of every claim
That related to the witless folly of that day.
It was fair enough, it was not right to blame me –
I stopped the fighting by a streetgang,
Beggars entirely, the clergy were satisfied,
The priest too thankful and perhaps with reason!
We lit torches and neighbours assembled there,
A great deal of food was laid out on tables for us,
[There was] a storm of music and drink without moderation,
And they enjoyed an undoubtedly grand feast. 510
My loss without lack that I was not strangled with food
The night I was baptized or that I tried
Stretching on a bed with a wretch who turned me grey
And let me go to madness without a friend, without sense.
I would get a report from young and from old
That she was a vessel for sport, drinking and shouting
In drinking shanties and tables for banging on,
On the floor a drone for married and single.
It was long that her reputation and character were discussed,
It was long before I believed little or much of it, 520
Fearful was every couple that heard it
That I would go mad in my pelt without a trace.
Still I would not yield, blind as I was,
To a voice without substance from anyone who declared it;
But [as] a mockery or a morsel without use, without sense
Until her womb told me the truth of every story!
It wasn't matters of fun or gossip,
Nor a woman told me that it was told to her,
But the deed spoke truly and effectively –
She presented a son to me long before time! 530

[141]

Mo scannradh scéil gan féith dhem chroidhe air –
Clann dá dtéadhamh dam tar éis na hoidhche!
Cullóid anfadhach ainigidhe scólta, –
Bunóc ceangailte is bean an tighe breóidhte,
Pusóid leagaithe ar smeachaidí teó aca,
Cuinneóg bhainne dhá greadadh le fórsa,
Is mullach ar lánmhias bánbhiadh is siúicre
Ag Muirinn Ní Cháimliaith báinliaigh an chrúca,
Bhí coiste cruinnighthe ag tuilleadh dem chomhursain
Chois na teine agus siosarnach dhamhsa.   540
Scaoilid cogar i bhfogus dom éisteacht: –
Míle moladh le Solus na Soillse!
Bíodh nach baileach a d'aibigh an chré seo
Do-chímse an t-athair 'n-a sheasamh 'n-a chéadfadh.
A bhfeiceann tu, a Shadhbh 'rú, luigheamh a ghéaga!
A dheilbh gan draghan a bhaill 's a mhéara!
Cumus na lámh ba dána dóirne!
Cuma na gcnámh is fás na feóla!

Do cheapadar cruinn gur shíolruigh an dúthchus
Maire mo ghnaoi agus íoghar mo ghnúise,   550
Feilleadh mo shrón' is glónradh m'éadain,
Deise mo chló mo shnódh agus m'fhéachain,
Leagadh mo shúl is go fiú mo gháire,
'S as-san do shiubhail ó chúl go sail é.
Amharc ná radharc ní bhfaghainn den chréice, –
Is baileach gan leigheas do mheillfeadh gaoth é! –
Ag cuideachta an teaghlaigh i bhfeidhil mo chaochta,
Siolladh dá laighead di leaghfaidhe an créatúir!
Do labhras garg 's do thagras Íosa,
Is stollta garbh do bhagras gríosach,   560
D'fhógras fearg le hainbhfios caínte,
'S is dóth gur chreathadar cailleacha an tighe romham.
De leisce an achrainn leagadar chugham é, –
Beir go haireach air, seachain ná brúigh é,
Is fuiris a suathadh, luaisc go réidh é,

My surprise event, without the blood from my heart in him –
A child of passion for me after the evening!
A tempestuous, peevish, fretful commotion, –
An infant swaddled and the woman of the house sick,
A medicinal draught laid on the warm live coals for them,
A churn of milk being whipped with force,
And a heap on a platter of beautiful food and sugar
For Muirinn Ní Cháimliath, lady physician of the hand,
A committee was gathered of more of my neighbours
Beside the fire and whispering about me.   540
They discharge a whisper close to my hearing: –
A thousand praises for the Light of Lights!
Although not quite has this clay fully matured
I see the father standing in him in his faculties.
Do you see, Saidhbh dear, the shape of his limbs!
His visage without moroseness, his limbs and his fingers!
The strength of the hands that would be bold fists!
The shape of the bones and the growth of the flesh!

They thought surely that the innate qualities sprang from
The comeliness of my appearance and the shape of my face,   550
The inclination of my nose and the cut of my forehead,
The niceness of my form, my complexion and my aspect,
The set of my eyes and even my laugh,
It is from me his movement from head to heel.
A sight or view I could not get of the whining child, –
It is entirely, without healing, that a draught would destroy him! –
From the company of the household with a view to my deception,
A puff such as that [and] the creature will be destroyed!
I spoke roughly and I entreated Jesus,
And fiercely and roughly I threatened to wreak havoc,   560
I proclaimed anger with reckless language,
And it seems that the hags of the house shook before me.
Loath to create a disturbance, they handed him to me, –
Carry him lightly, take care not to press him,
Easy is his upsetting, rock him smoothly,

Turraing do fuair sí ruaigh roimh ré é;
Seachain ná fáisc é, fág 'n-a luighe é,
Is gairid an bás do, is gearr do raghaidh sé;
Dá mairead go lá idir lámha 'n-a chló
'S an sagart ar fagh
áil níor bh'fhearr a bheith beó.   570

Do bhaineas an tsnaidhm dá choimhreach cumhdaigh
Is bhreathain me cruinn é sínte ar ghlúin liom,
A Muaireach d'airigh me tathacach tonnda é,
Fuair me feargach fearsadach lúitheach
Láidir leathan mo leanbh 'n-a ghuailnibh,
Sála daingeana is anchuid gruaige air!
Cluasa cruinnighthe is ingne fásta,
Chruadhdar a uilleanna a chroibh 's a chnámha,
D'aibigh a shúile is fiú a pholláirí,
'S d'airigh me a ghlúine lúthmhar láidir.   580
Coileán cumusach cuisleannach córach
Folláin fuinneamhach fulaingeach feólmhar.
Screadaim go hárd le gáir na tíre
Is leagaim dot láthair cás na ndaoine,
Breathain go caoin, is bí truaighmhéileach,
Beannaibh a gcinn is suim a gcéille;
Atharruigh an dlighe seo chuing na cléire
Is ainic an bhuidhean nár fríoth san ghéibheann.
Má laguigh an síolrach díonmhar daonna
I dtalamh dathaoibhinn fhíorghlais Éireann,   590
Is fuiris an tír d'aithlíonadh 'e laochaibh
D'uireasbha eangaighe gan bhrígh gan éifeacht, –
Cá bhfuil an gábha le gáir na bainse,
Cárta biotáille is págha lucht seinnte,
Sumaigh ar bórd go fóiseach taidhbhseach,
Glugar is gleó aca is ól dá shaighdadh,
Ó d'aibigh an t-adhbhar do bhronn Mac Dé
Gan sagart ar domhan dá dtabhairt dá chéile.
Is leathanmhar láidir lánmhar léadmhar
Fairsing le fagh
áil an t-álmhach saor so.   600

A fall that she got expelled him before time;
Take care, don't squeeze him, leave him lying,
Death is near him, shortly it will come;
If he will live until day in [someone's] hands in his condition
And the priest [then] available, it would not be better to be alive.   570

I took the knot from his protective binding
And I looked closely on him stretched on my knee,
By heaven, I found him substantial, blockish,
I found [him] manly, muscular, sinewy
Strong and broad, my child, in his shoulders,
Firm heels and a great deal of hair on him!
Formed ears and grown nails,
His elbows, his fists and his bones hardened,
His eyes and even his nostrils ripened,
And I noticed his knees muscular and strong.   580
A capable, strong-armed, well-proportioned pup
Healthy, spirited, hardy, fleshy.
I cry loudly the report of the country
And I lay in your presence the case of the people,
Look kindly and be compassionate,
[Regarding] the horns on their heads and the extent of their [good] sense;
Change this law, the clergy's yoke of oppression,
And protect the company that was not got within fetters.
If the well-protected human seed weakens
In the pleasant-hued, ever-green land of Ireland,   590
It's easy to refill the land with warriors
By doing without an obstacle that has no virtue or sense, –
Where is the need for the commotion of the wedding,
Quarts of spirits and the pay of musicians,
Plump youngsters at table, self-indulgent, vain,
Gurgling and noise from them and drink voraciously swallowed,
Since the embryo that the Son of God bestowed ripened
Without a priest in the world giving them [the parents] to each other.
Broad, strong, fully active, bold
Generous is this noble progeny to be found.   600

Is minic do-chímse bríoghmhar bórrtha
Cumusach líonta i gcroidhe 's i gcóir iad;
Créim ní fheicim ná daille ná caoiche
I léim ar leithre dar hoileadh ó mhnaoi ar bith;
Is mó 's is mire, 's is teinne 's is tréine
A gcló 's a gclisteacht ná dlisteanaigh éinne.

Is fuiris a luaidhimse d'fhuascailt suidhte
Is duine aca an uair seo ar fhuaid an tighe agam!
A bhfeiceann tu thall go ceannsa ciúin é!
Deisigh anall i dteannta an bhúird é.   610
Breathain go cruinn é, bíodh gurab óg é
Is dearbhtha suidhte an píosa feóla é,
Is preabaire i dtoirt i gcorp 's i gcnámh é,
Ca bhfuil a locht i gcois ná i láimh dhe?
Ní seirgtheach fann ná seandach feósach,
Leibide cam ná gandal geóiseach,
Meall gan chuma ná sumach gan síneadh é
Acht lannsa cumusach buinneamhach bríoghmhar.
Ní deacair a mheas nach spreas gan bhrígh
Bheadh ceangailte ar nasc ar teasc ag mnaoi,   620
Gan chnámh gan chumus gan chumadh gan chom,
Gan ghrádh gan chumann gan fuinneamh gan fonn,
Do scaipfeadh i mbroinn d'éanmhaighre mná
Le catachus draghain an groidhre breágh
Mar cuireann sé i bhfeidhm gan mhoill gan bhréig
Le cumus a bhaill 's le luigheamh a ghéag
Gur crobhaire é crothadh go cothrom gan cháime
Le fonn na fola is le fothram na sláinte.

Leis-sin ná hiarrse a riaghain réilteach
Meilleadh meiriad le riaghail gan éifeacht!   630
Scaoil 'o chodladh gan chochaill gan coimhreach
Síol an bhodaigh 's an mhogallfhuil mhaoidhteach,
Scaoil fá chéile de réir nádúra
An síolbhach séad 's an braon lábúrtha,

Often I see them vigorous and in bloom
Strong, satisfied in their hearts and in their power;
Blemish I do not see or dimness or blindness
In an illegitimate child given for rearing by any woman;
Bigger and livelier, and hardier and stronger
In form and in action than any legitimate person.

It's easy, I said, to prove for certain
And one of them at this time in my house!
Do you see him beyond, gentle and quiet!
Bring him here near the table.   610
Look at him attentively, although he is young
It's certainly certified that he is a piece of flesh,
He's a hearty person in size, in body and in bone,
Where is the flaw in foot or in hand of him?
[He] is not a weak, shrivelled person or a bearded antiquity,
A crooked, slovenly person or a paunchy gander,
A lump without shape or a plump person without length
But a capable, vigorous, substantial and lively youth.
It's not difficult to think that it's not a dry branch without force
Who would be tied on a chain for a task by a woman,   620
Without a bone, without ability, without a figure, without a waist,
Without love, without friendship, without vigour, without desire,
Who would beget in the womb of any healthy woman
With passionate concupiscence the fine, hearty fellow
As he demonstrates at once, without falsehood
With the power of his member and with the cut of his limbs
That he is a strong, able person created justly without fault
With desire of the blood and with the lustiness of health.

With that, do not ask, starry queen,
The destruction of a myriad by means of a rule without sense!   630
Make free to sleep without a cloak, without fetters
The seed of the churl and of the boastful noble blood,
Make free together according to nature
The seed of the precious ones and the base drop,

Fogair féilteach tré sna tíortha
D'óg is d'aosta saorthoil síolraidh.
Cuirfidh an dlighe seo gaois i nGaedhlaibh,
'S tiocfaidh an brígh mar bhí ina laochaibh,
Ceapfaidh sé com is drom is dóirne
Ag fearaibh an domhain mar Gholl mac Moirne,   640
Gealfaidh an spéir, beidh éisc i líonta,
Is talamh an tsléibhe go léir fé luíbhna,
Fir is mná go brách dá mhaoidhchain,
Ag seinnm do cháil le gárdus aoibhnis.'

Tar éis bheith tamall don ainnir ag éisteacht
Do léim'n-a seasamh go tapa gan foidhnne,
Do labhair sí leis agus loise'n-a súile
Is rabhartaí feirge feilice fútha: –
'Dar Coróin na Carraige mar'each le géilleadh
Dot chló dot aindeis's d'easnamh do chéille   650
Is d'am na hurraime'on chuideachta shéimh seo
An ceann lem ingin do sciobfainn det chaolscrog,
Do leagfainn anuas de thuairt fá'n mbórd thu
'S is fada le luadh gach cuairt dá ngeóbhainn ort
Go stróicfinn sreanga do bheathadh le fonn ceart,
'S go seólfainn t'anam go Acheron tonntach.
Ní fiú liom freagra freastail do thabhairt ort,
A shnamhaire fleascaigh nach aithis do labhartha!
Act'neósad feastain do mhaithibh na cúirte
An nós nur cailleadh an ainnir nár bh'fhiú thu: –   660
Bhí sí lag, gan bha gan phúntaibh,
Bhí sí abhfad gan teas gan clúdadh,
Cortha dhá saoghal, ar strae dhá seóladh
Ó phosta go pléar gan ghaol gan chomhghus,
Gan scíth gan spás de lá ná d'oidhche,
Ag stríocadh an aráin ó mhná nár chuibhe léi.
Do gheall an fear so dreas sócamhail di,
Do gheall an spreas di teas is clúdadh,
Cothrom glan is ba le crúdh dhi,

Declare regularly through the countries
For the young and for the mature freewill to propagate.
This law will put wisdom in the Gaels,
And the strength will come as it was in their warriors,
It will compose waist and back and fist
Into men of the world, like Goll mac Móirne,   640
The sky will brighten, fish will be in pools
And the ground of the mountain completely under herbs,
Men and women forever, on that account,
Singing your fame with the joy of pleasure.'

After listening a while the maiden
Leapt to her feet suddenly, without patience,
She spoke to him and anger in her eyes
And angry treacherous tides around her: –
'By the Crown of Carraig, were it not for yielding
To your character, your meanness, and your lack of sense   650
And out of due respect for this gracious assembly
With my nails I would snatch the head from your scrawny neck,
I would knock you down with a thud under the table
And long would be the speaking about every beating that I would put on you
I would tear the cords of your life with a right pleasure,
And I would send your soul to billowy Acheron.
It's not worth it to me to give an expected answer to you,
You creeper, you rascal, isn't your speech a disgrace!
But I will tell henceforth the nobles of the court
The way that the maiden you were not worthy of was ruined: –   660
She was poor, without cows, without pounds,
She was long without heat, without covering,
Wearied of her life, being blown astray,
From post to pillar, without kin, without relatives,
Without rest, without space, by day or night,
Cadging the bread from women who scorned her.
This man promised her a spell of comfort,
The dry twig promised her heat and covering,
Complete fair play to her and cows for milking,

Is codladh fada ar leabain chlúimh di,　　　　　　　　　670
Teallaighe teó agus móin a doíthin,
Fallaí fód gan leóithne gaoithe,
Fothain is díon ón sín 's ón spéir dhi,
Olann is líon le sníomh chum éadaigh.
Do b'fheasach don tsaoghal 's don phéist seo láithreach
Nach taitneamh ná téadhamh ná éanphuith grádha dho
Do cheangail an péarla maordha mná so
Acht easnamh go léir, – ba déirc léi an tsástacht!
Ba dúbhach an fuadar suairceas oidhche
Smúit is ualach duais is líonadh,　　　　　　　　　680
Lúithne luaidhe agus guailne caoila
'S glúine cruaidhe chomh fuar le hoidhre,
Cosa feóidhte dóighte ón ngríosaigh
'S colann bhreóidhte dhreóighte chríona.
A bhfuil stuaire beó ná feóidhfadh liath
Ag cuail dá short bheith pósta riamh?
Nár chuarduigh fós fá dhó le bliadhain
Cé buachaill óg í, feóil nó iasc?
'S an feóidhteach fuar so suas léi sínte
Dreóighte duairc gan buadh gan bíodhgadh.　　　　690
Óc! car mhuar di bualadh bríoghmhar
Ar nós ba dhual de uair san oidhche.
Ni dóth go dtuigthar gurab ise ba chiontach
Ná fós go gcliseadh ar luige 'n-a tonndacht
An maighre mascalach carthannach ciúintais –
Is deimhin go bhfeaca sí a mhalairt de mhúineadh.
Ní labharfadh focal dá mb'obair an oidhche
'S thabharfadh cothrom do stollaire bhríoghmhar.
Go brách ar siubhal níor dhiúltuigh riamh é,
Ar chnámh a cúil 's a súilibh iadhta.　　　　　　700
Ní thabharfadh preab le stailc mhíchuíbhsach,
Fogha mar chat ná straic ná scríob air,
Acht í go léir 'n-a slaod cóshínte,
Taobh ar thaobh 's a géag 'n-a thimcheall,
Ó scéal go scéal ag bréagadh smaointe,

Long sleeping on a bed of feathers for her,   670
Warm hearths and turf in plenty,
Walls of sod without a breath of wind,
Shelter and a roof from the weather and from the sky for her,
Wool and flax for spinning into clothes.
It was known to the world and to this pest present
That it was not pleasure nor warming nor any bit of love for him
That bound this stately pearl of a woman,
But a deficiency entirely, – alms were for her a sufficiency!
Gloomy was the activity of a night's jollity,
Gloom and a burden, sorrow and agitation,   680
Sinews of lead and narrow shoulders
And hard knees as cold as ice,
Feet withered, burnt from the embers
And a body ailing, decayed, old.
Is there a handsome girl alive who would not wither to grey
To be always married to a heap of bones of his sort?
Who moreover did not examine twice a year
Whether she was a young boy, meat or fish?
And this cold, withered old man stretched out by her,
Putrefied, surly, without virtue, without vigour.   690
O! how great for her a strong seizing
As would be natural once in the night.
It is not likely that it is understood that she was guilty
Or that she would yet fail in weakness, in inertness
The stately, friendly, calm lady –
It's certain that she tried an opposite instruction.
She would not speak a word if there were work of a night
And she would give on equal terms with a vigorous strong man.
Forever moving, she never refused him,
On her backbone and her eyes shut.   700
She wouldn't give a start with an immoderate sulk,
An attack like a cat or tear or scrape him,
But all of her luxuriantly stretched,
Side by side and her limbs around him,
Bit by bit coaxing his thoughts,

Béal ar bhéal 's ag méaracht síos air.
Is minic do chuir sí cos taobh 'nonn de,
Is chuimil a bruish ó chrios go glún de;
Do sciobadh an phluid 's an chuilt dá ghúnga
Ag spriongar 's ag sult le muirt gan súbhchus.   710
Níor chabhar dhi coigilt ná cuimilt ná fáscadh,
Fogha da hingin, dá huillinn, dá sála.
Is nár dham aithris mar chaitheadh sí an oidhche
Ag fáscadh an chnaiste, ag searradh 's ag síneadh,
Ag feacadh na ngéag 's an t-éadach fúithi,
A ballaibh go léir 's a déid ar lúithchrith,
Go loinnis an lae gan néall do dhúbhadh uirthi,
Ag imirt ó thaobh go taobh 's ag ionfairt.

Nach fuiris don lobhar so labhairt ar mhná
'S gan fuinneamh 'n-a chom ná cabhair 'n-a chnámha,   720
Má d'imthigh an mhodhmhail bhí trom 'n-a ghábha
'S gur deineadh an fhoghail seo gabhaimse a páirt.
A bhfuil sionnach ar sliabh ná iasc i dtráigh,
Ná fiolar le fiadhach ná fiadh le fán
Comh fada gan chiall le bliadhain ná lá
Do chaitheamh gan biadh 's a bhfiadhach le fagháil?
An aithnid díbh féin san tsaoghal so cá fhuil
An t-ainmhidhe claon ná an féithid fáin
Do phiocfadh an chré an fraoch nó an pháil
Is fiorthann 'n-a shlaoda 's féar le fagháil?   730
Aithris gan mhoill, a chladhaire cráidhte,
Freagair me, faghaimse feidhm it ráidhte: –
Ca bhfuil do dhíth ag suidhe chum béile?
Ar caitheadh le mí aici a dtigheas 'n-a féile!
An luigide an chúil nó an lughade an láithreach
Fiche milliún má shiubhail le ráithe ann?
Mairg it cheann a sheandaigh thonnda,
An eagal leat ganntan am do dhúla!
An dóth a ghliogaire buile gur bhaoghal duit
Ól na Sionainne tirim nó a taoscadh?   740

Mouth on mouth and fingering down him.
Often she put a leg beside and over him,
And rubbed her brush from thigh to knee of him;
She snatched the cover and the quilt from his loins
Toying and playing with the dead-weight without pleasure.   710
It was no help for her tickling or rubbing or squeezing,
An assault of her nails, of her elbows, of her heels.
It's a shame for me to tell how she spent the night
Squeezing, shaking and stretching the stout lump,
Twisting their limbs and the clothes under her,
All her limbs and her teeth quivering,
Until the lightening of the day without a wink of sleep on her,
Playing from side to side and tossing about.

It wouldn't be easy for this leper to speak about women
Who is without vigour in his body or support in his bones,   720
If the gentle lady who was seriously in need strayed
And this trespass was done, I take her part.
Is there a fox on a mountain or a fish in the sea,
Or an eagle on the hunt or a deer wandering
So long without sense for a year or a day
To go without food and their prey available?
Is it known to yourselves where in this world is
The perverse animal or creature astray
Who would choose the clay, the heather or the hedge
And wheatgrass in swathes and grass available?   730
Tell without delay, miserable rogue,
Answer me, I need your speech: –
Where is your loss sitting for a meal
If she spent a month in a house of plenty!
Is the corner smaller or is the place smaller
If twenty million walked for three months there?
Woe on your head, lethargic old man,
Do you fear scarcity at the time of your desire!
Does it seem likely, mad boaster, that there is a danger
[Of] drinking the Shannon dry or emptying it?   740

Trághadh na fairrge is tarraint an tsáile?
Is clár na mara do scaipeadh le scála?
Breathain in am ar leamhus do smaointe
Is ceangail do cheann le banda timcheall!
Seachain i dtráth, ná fág do chiall
Le heagla mná bheith fáilteach fial;
Dá gcaitheadh sí an lá le cách do riar
Bheadh tuilleadh's do sháith-se ar fagháil 'n-a ndiadh.

Mo chuma is mo chrádh badh bhreagh san éad
Ar lúbaire láidir lánmhear léadmhar   750
Shanntach sháithteach shásta sheasmhach
Ramsach ráflach rábach rabairneach,
Lascaire luaimneach, cuardóir coimseach,
Balcaire buan nó buailteóir bríoghmhar,
Act seanduine seanda crannda créimtheach,
Feamaire fann is feam gan féíle.
Is mithid dom chroidhe bheith líonta 'e léithe,
Is m'iongantus trí gach smaointe baotha
Cad do-bheir scaoilte ó choimhreach céile
In eagluis sinsir suim na cléire.   760
Mo chrádh gan leigheas, mo threighid dom fháscadh,
Is láidir m'fhoidhnne is laighead mo ráige,
Is méid a mbíom ar díth gan éinne,
Is méin ár gcroidhe fé shnaidhm na héide.
Nach bocht an radharc do mhaighdin ghábhmhair
Toirt is taidhbhse a mbaill 's a mbreaghtha,
Bloscadh a n-aghaidh agus soillse a ngáire,
Corp is coim is toill ar támhchrith,
Úireacht, áilneacht, bláth agus óige,
Ramhdus cnámh is meádhchan feóla,   770
Martus trom is drom gan suathadh,
Neart gan dobhta is fonn gan fuaradh.
Bíonn sealbh gach sógha aca ar bhórd na saoithe,
Earradh agus ór chum óil is aoibhnis,
Clúmh chum luighe aca is saill chum bídh aca,

Draining the sea and drawing up the brine?
And scattering the whole sea with a cup?
Notice in time the folly of your thinking
And tie a band around your head!
Beware in time, don't lose your reason
With fear of a woman being welcoming, generous;
If she spent the day with everyone in attendance
More and enough for you would be available after them.

My sorrow and my torment, jealousy would be fine there
In a strong, perfect, brave, agile man   750
Fierce, thrusting, pleasing, firm
Romping, given to raillery, vigorous, prodigal,
A nimble, rollicking person, a powerful visitor,
A long-lived, strong person or an effective thrasher,
But [not in] an aged, withered, decayed old person,
An infirm, weak-loined person and a stalk without pleasure.
It's time for my heart to be filled with greyness,
And my wonder through every vain thought
[Of] what is it that leaves free from the binding of a wife
In the ancestral church all of the clergy.   760
My torment without cure, my pang pressing me,
Strong is my patience and my anger a scarcity,
That there are so many who are in want, without anyone,
Longing is in our hearts because of the bond of the cloth.
Is it not a pitiful sight for a needy maiden
The mass and appearance of their limbs, and their beauty,
The radiance of their faces and the brightness of their laughter,
Body and waist and buttocks in a swooning trembling,
Freshness, beauty, flower and youth,
A stoutness of bone and a weight of flesh,   770
A heavy frame and a back without shaking,
Strength without doubt and desire without cooling.
They possess every luxury at the table of the eminent,
Goods and gold for drink and delight,
They have feathers for lying on and they have meat for food,

Plúr is milseacht meidhir is fíonta.
Is gnáthach cumusach iomadach óg iad
'S tá fhios againne gur fuil agus feóil iad.
Cumha ní ghlacfainn le cafairí coillte,
Snamhairí galair ná searraigh gan soillse,   780
Acht márlaidh bodacha, tollairí tréana,
I dtámhghail chodlata is obair gan déanamh!
Creidim gan bhréig gur mhéin le roinn díobh
Feilleadh le féile, daor ní bheinnse.
Cothrom, ní cóir an t-órd le chéile
Chrochadh le córda, ghóbhail ná dhaoradh,
Bás na droinge, is deimhin, ní ghrádhfinn,
Lán na luinge chum duine ní bháithfinn,
Cuid aca bíodh gur rícigh riamh
'S cuid eile bhíos gan ríomh gan riaghail,   790
Cinntigh chruadha gan truagh gan tréithe,
Fíochmar fuar is fuath do bhéithe.
Tuilleadh aca atá níos fearr 'ná a chéile,
Tuilte le grádh is le grása féile.
Is minic a buaidhtear buaibh is gréithe
Cuigeann is cruach de chuaird na cléire.
Is minic lem chuimhne maoidheadh a dtréithe
Is iomad dá ngníomhartha fírghlic féithe,
Is minic do chuala ar fhuaid na tíre
Siosarnach luaith dá luadh go líonmhar,   800
Is chonnairc me taidhbhseach roinn dá ramsa
Is uimhir dá gclainn ar shloinnte fallsa.
Baineann sé fáscadh as lár mo chléibh-se
A gcaithtar dá sláinte ar mhná treasaosta
Is turraing san tír chum díth na mbéithe,
Ar cuireadh gan bhrígh den tsíolrach naomhtha.
Is dealbh an diachair dianghuirt d'Éire
Ar chailleamair riamh le riaghail gan éifeacht!

Fágaim fút-sa a chnú na céille
Fáth na cúise is cumha na cléire.   810

Flour and dainties, mirth and wines.
Generally vigorous, proud, young they are
And we know they are blood and flesh.
I would not regret gelded praters,
Diseased cringers or young things without brightness,   780
But lusty youths, virile piercers,
In the lethargy of sleep and work not being done!
I believe sincerely that some of them desire
Turning to pleasure, [so] I would not be severe,
In fairness, it's not right the order altogether
To hang with a rope, to seize or to enslave,
The death of the group, it's certain, I would not love,
The full of a ship to a person I would not drown,
Some of them there are who were ever wastrels
And some of them not to be accounted for, without regulation,   790
Hard, mean persons without pity, without accomplishment,
Cruel, cold, and with hatred of women.
There are many of them that are better than these,
Flooded with love and with grace, generosity.
Often have cattle and gifts been gained
The contents of a churn and a rick from a visit of the clergy.
Often in my memory their qualities were praised
And a great number of their always-clever deeds of lust,
Often I heard throughout the land
A frenzied whispering being stirred up abundantly,   800
And I saw plainly some of their romping
And a number of their children with false surnames.
It wrings the centre of my bosom
That their health is spent on women fairly advanced in age
It's a misfortune in the country to the detriment of the women,
The sowing without efficacy of the saintly seed.
Miserable the bitter sorrow for Ireland
That we have always lost from a pointless rule!

I leave [it] with you, nut of wisdom,
The reason for the circumstance and predicament of the clergy.   810

Is meallta meillte luighid dom dhóith-se.
Is dall gan radharc me, soillsigh m'eólus,
Aithris, ó's cuimhin leat, caínt na bhfáidhe
Is apstol an Ríogh ba bhíodhgach ráidhte.
Ca bhfuil na comhachta d'órduigh an Dúileamh, –
Is calcadh na feóla i gcoróin na cumha so;
Pól dar liúm ní dubhairt le héinne
An pósadh dhiúltadh acht drúis do shéanadh,
Scaradh let ghaol dá mhéid do ghnaoi
Is ceangal let shaoghal is claedh let mhnaoi.   820
Is obair gan bhrígh do mhnaoi mar táimse
Focal den dlighe seo shuidheamh 'ot láthair,
Is cuimhin leat féín a phéarla an taidhbhse
Suidheamh gach scéil is léir dhuit soillseach
Binnghuth buan is buadh na mbréithre
Is caínt an Uain ná luadhfar bréagach,
Dia nár bh'áil leis máthair aonta,
Is riaghail gach fáidh i bhfábhar béithe.

Guidhm go hard tu, a fháidhbhean tsídhthe,
A shíolrach neámhdha a bharr na ríghthe,   830
A shoillse glóire a choróin na sluaighte,
Éist lem ghlór-sa, fóir is fuar dhúinn;
Meáidh it intinn díth na mbéithe
Is práinn na mílte brídeach aonta,
Is toicibh mar táid ar bhrághaid a chéile
Ag borradh is ag fás mar ál na ngéanna;
An tál is lugha tá ag siubhal na sráide,
Garlaigh dhubha is giúnach gránna,
An aga dá laighead má gheibhid a ndóithin
Glasradh, meidhg, is bleaghdair bórrfaid;   840
D'urchar nimhe le haois gan éifeacht
Tiocfa na cíocha, sceinnfid, scéidhfid.

Scalladh mo chléibh! is baoth mo smaointe!
Ag tagairt ar chéile i gcaorthaibh teinte!

Defrauded and destroyed, they swear [their vows], it seems to me,.
I am blind without a view, enlighten my understanding;
Recite, since you remember, the speech of the prophets
And of the apostle of the King whose words were vigorous.
Where are the authorities [saying] that the Creator ordered, –
That the flesh stagnate in this throne of loneliness;
Paul, it seems to me, did not tell anyone
To forsake marriage but to abstain from adultery,
To separate from your kindred, if it's much to your liking
And [be] bound for your life and cleave to your woman.   820
It's work without meaning for a woman as I am
To set the words of this law before your presence,
You yourself know, pearl of magnificence,
The proving of every matter, it's plain to you clearly
[With] an ever-sweet voice and a gift of the words
And the speech of the Lamb that one will not mention falsely,
[That] God did not want a single mother,
The rule of every prophet is in favour of women.

I beseech you loudly, prophetess of the fairies,
Heavenly seed from the branch of the kings,   830
Light of glory, crown of the crowds,
Listen to my voice, help and relieve us;
Weigh in your mind the deprivation of women
And the need of the thousands of single maidens,
Who are falling as they are on the necks of each other
Increasing and growing like a brood of geese;
The smallest progeny who are walking the street,
Dark urchins who are close-cropped, ugly,
In a small period of time, if they get their sufficiency
Of green stuff, whey and curdled milk, they will grow;   840
Like a bolt from the blue in an inconsiderable space of time
The breasts will come, will start, will erupt.

Scalding of my bosom! foolish are my thoughts!
Mentioning a spouse [while] among masses of sparks!

[159]

Is deacair dam súil le súbhchus d'fhagháil
'S gan fear in aghaidh triúir san Mhumhain dá mná.
Ó tharla an ceanntar gann so gábhmhar,
Fánlag fann,'s an t-am so práinneach,
Fódla follamh is fothram ag fiadhaile,
Is óige an phobail ag cromadh is ag liathadh,   850
Aonta fada go dealbh gan foidhnne
D'éinne ar talamh is fear éigin faghaimse.
Ceangail i dtráth go tláith fén úghaim iad,
'S as san go bráthach fágtar fúinne iad.'

D'éirigh an mhánla ar bharr a bínse,
'S do shoillsi' an lá san áit 'n-a timcheall,
B'áluinn óg a cló 's a caoindreach,
B'árd a glór ba bheó is ba bhíodhgach.
D'fháirc a dóirne is d'órduigh deimhneach
Báille ar bórd ag fógairt *Silence*.   860
Adubhairt a béal bhí ag séideadh soillse, –
An chúirt go léir go faon ag éisteacht: –
'Do-gheibhimse díreach brígh chum buaidhte
Is feidhm it chaínt-se a bhrídeach bhuartha.
Chím, 's is dóth gur dóighte an radharc liom,
Síolrach Órfhlaith Mhóire is Mheidhbhe,
An seifteóir caol 's an créatúir cladhartha,
An ceisteóir claon 's an déirceóir doigheartha,
Súgh na táire is tál na coimse
Ag súil le sárfhuil sámh na saoithe.   870

Achtaimíd mar dhlighe do bhéithe
An seacht fó thrí gan coimhreach céile
Do tharraing ar cheann go teann gan truaighe
'S a cheangal don chrann so i dteannta an tuama.
Bainigidhe lom de a chobhail 's a chóta,
'S feannaigidhe a dhrom 's a chom le córda.
An chuid aca thárla báithte i mbliadhnta
Is cheileas go táir an táirnge tiarpa,

It's difficult for me to hope to find joy
And not a man for three women in Munster.
Since it happens that this meagre district is needy,
Men enfeebled, and the time urgent,
Ireland empty and a commotion from upstarts,
And the youth of the people stooping and turning grey,   850
Long single, destitute, without patience
For anyone on earth until I get some man.
Bind them in time tenderly in harness,
And from then until forever leave them to us.'

The stately maid at the head of the bench rose,
And the day in the place shone around her,
Lovely, young were her shape and her fair countenance,
Noble was her voice, it was lively and it was vigorous.
She clenched her fists and ordered decisively
The bailiff at the table to announce *Silence*.   860
Her voice, which was sounding clearly, said, –
The entire court quietly listening: –
'I find truly the essence of victory
And power in your speech, perturbed maiden.
I see, and bitter seems the sight for me,
The progeny of Órla, Mór and Medhbh,
The sharp contriver and the cowardly creature,
The biased examiner and the annoying beggar,
The product of baseness and the offspring of mediocrity
Aspiring to the tranquil, superior blood of eminent people.   870

We decree as a law for women
[That] the twenty-one-year-old without the bond of a spouse
Be dragged by the head fiercely without pity
And be tied to this tree beside the tomb.
Strip him bare of his shirt and his coat,
And flay his back and his waist with a cord.
[For] those of them drowned in years
And who hide basely the posterior's nail,

Chuireas amugha gan subhchus d'éinne
Buile na hútha is lúth a ngéaga,   880
Do mheilleas a gcáil is fagháíl ar mhnaoi aca
Ag feitheamh gan fáth ar bharr na craoibhe,
Fágaim fúibh-se tionnscal páise
A mhná na dúla dúbhadh le dálgus;
Ceapaigidhe fírnimh teinte is táirngibh,
Caithigidhe smaointe is inntleacht mhná leis,
Cuiridh bhur gcomhairle i gcomhar le chéile,
'S tugaimse comhachta an fórsa dhéanamh.
Do-bheirim gan spás díbh páis na gciantach, –
Is beag liom bás gan barrghoin pian dóibh.   890
Ní chuirimse i bhfáth de bharr mo chaínte
An foirbhtheach fálta cáslag claoidhte,
An gabhal gan gotha ná an gola gan geall shuilt,
An toll gan toradh ná an tormach fallsa,
Acht léigthar an óige i gcóir chum síolraidh
'S déanfa an sórt so clóca is díon dóibh.
Is minic do-chímse rinnsigh bhaotha
Ag tuitim le tigheas, is bímse buidheach díobh,
Gabhtha le mná de lá agus d'oidhche
Ag cosnamh a gcáíl's an scáith a ngníomhartha;   900
Ag seasamh 'n-a bhfeidhil's a bhfeidhm go fálta,
A n-ainm ar chloinn is bheinnse sásta.
Do chuala siolla is do cuireadh i bhásta é –
Is fuath liom boineannach iomadach ráidhteach –
Labhair go réidh is glaeidh go híseal,
Bas ar do bhéal, is baoghal bheith caínteach!
Seachain go fóill na comhachtaigh íogmhar
Is caithfe siad pósadh fós pé chífeas.
Tiocfaidh an lá le lánchead comhairle
'S cuirfidh an Pápa lámh na gcomhacht air,   910
Suidhfe an chuideachta ar thiubaist na tíre,
Is scaoilfar chugaibh fé urchall coimhrigh
Fiadhntus fola agus fothram na feóla
Is mian bhur dtoile na tollairí teó so.

And render ineffective without pleasure to anyone
The craze of the scrotum and vigour of their members,   880
Who destroy their means and leave women
Waiting without reason at the top of the branch,
I leave to you a plan of affliction
O women of the desire blighted with longing;
Seize the true venom of fire and nails,
Use the thoughts and intellect of women for this,
Putting your counsels in cooperation together,
And I grant power to do the violence.
I grant you instantly the affliction of the old men, –
Little to me is death without the height of wounding and pain for them.   890
I consider of no importance as a point of my talk
The feeble, spent, exhausted old men,
The groin without a spear or the penal orifice without promise of pleasure,
The hole without issue or the false swelling,
But let the youth be ready for propagating
And make this sort [old men] a cloak and shelter for them.
Often I see foolish dawdlers
Setting up a household, and I am grateful to them,
Yoked to women by day and by night
Protecting their reputations and the shelter for their deeds;   900
Attending to their vigilance and their duty feebly,
Their names on offspring, and I would be satisfied.
I heard a syllable and it was put to waste –
I hate a female of too much talking –
Speak evenly and call humbly,
A hand on your mouth, it's a danger to be talkative!
Shun awhile the cruel, powerful persons
And they will have to marry still, whatever will happen.
The day will come with full permission of a council
And the Pope will put the hand of authority on it,   910
The assembly will meet on the misfortunes of the country,
And released to you under shackles will be
Wildness of blood and lustiness of the flesh
And desire of your will, these warm piercers.

Éanduine eile dar hoileadh ó mhnaoi ar bith –
Léighidh a ndeirim is feicim do bhíodhga;
Ar shlighe mo chumuis ná fulaing i gcaoi ar bith
Sraoill gan urraim ná Muirinn i mbríste,
Acht leanaidh san tóir na feoidhtigh liatha
Is glanaigidhe Fódla ón sórt so fiadhaile!   920

Caithfe me gluaiseacht uaibh chum siubhail,
Is fada mo chuairt-se ar fhuaid na Mumhan;
An turus tá romham ní fhoghnann moill do,
Is iomad den gnó annso fós gan éisteacht.
Casfa me arís 's is fíor nách fáilteach
D'fhearaibh nach díon me thigheacht don áit seo;
An chuid aca atá go táir n-a smaointe,
Fuireann nach fuláis leó a gcáil bheith sínte,
Mhaoidheas le fothram a gcothrom ar bhéithe,
Chífe an pobul a gcogair 's a sméide.   930
Is taitneamhach leó 's is dóth gur laochus
Scannal na hóige pósta is aonta,
Mian a dtoile ní sporann a gcionta,
Bréantus fola ná borradh na drúise,
Taitneamh don ghníomh ná fíoch na féithe
Acht magadh na mílte, maoidheamh a n-éachta.
Ní saínnt dá sógh bheir beó na céadta
Acht caínt is gleó agus mórtus laochuis,
Mustar is ábhacht is ráíg gan riaghail,
'S a gcumus go tláth gan tál gan triall,   940
Go tuisealach tárrlag támh 'n-a n-iall,
'S cuthach le gábha ar a mná 'n a ndiaidh.
Glacfadh go réidh an méid seo láithreach,
Caithfe me géilleadh 'o mhéid mo phráinneach,
Cuirfe me an bhuidhean so i gcuing 's in ughaim
Nuair thiocfa me arís san mí seo chughainn.'

Do breathain me cruinn an ríghbhean réilteach,
'S do laguigh mo chroidhe le linn bheith réidh dhi,

Any other person who was reared by any woman –
Consider what I say and let me see your vigour;
By way of my power, don't put up with in any way
An untidy person without honour or a Muirinn in trousers,
But follow the trail of the grey, withered old men
And cleanse Ireland of this sort of weeds!   920

I have to set out travelling from you,
Long is my visit throughout Munster,
The journey that is before me delay does not serve,
And much of the business here still without a hearing.
I will return again and, it's true, not agreeably
For men [for whom] I am not a protector coming to this place;
Some of them who are vile in their thoughts,
A group for whom it's necessary that their renown be extended,
Who boast with lustiness of their treatment of women,
The public will see through their whispers and their winking.   930
It pleases them and it seems that it's heroism
The disgrace of the young, married and single,
The desire of their will does not spur their passions,
Sensuality or the swelling of lust,
Pleasure in the act or fury of the vein
But mockery of the thousands, boasting of their deeds.
Fierce desire for their pleasure does not at all grip hundreds
But talk and clamour and boasting of heroism,
Arrogance and mirth and frivolity without restraint,
And their ability weak, without flowing, without attempting,   940
Tottering, weak-bellied, numb in their thong,
And rage with distress for their women accordingly.
I will readily take up this matter presently,
I must yield this much to my urgency,
I will put this gang in yoke and in cellar
When I will come back again next month.'

I looked closely at the starry queen,
And my heart weakened while she was finishing,

D'airigh me dásacht ghránmhar éigin
Is pairithis bháís im chnámha's im chéadfadh; 950
Chonnairc me an tír's an tigheas ar luascadh,
Is fuinneamh a caínte ag rinnce im chluasa.
Tagann an bíoma bíodhgach báille,
Is leathain mo líthe ar shíneadh a láimhe;
Tharraing ar chluais go stuacadh stórtha
Stracaithe suas léi ar uachtar bóird me.
Preabann an bháb so chráidh an t-aonta,
Greadann a lámha's is árd do léim sí.
Is aibidh adubhairt – 'A chrústa críona
Is fada me ag súil let chúl-sa chíoradh, 960
Is minic do sluigheamh thu, a chroidhe gan daonnacht,
Is mithid duit stríocadh 'o dhlighe na mbéithe.
Cosaint cá bhfaghaidh tu in agaidh na cúise?
Focal níor thuill tu a leadhb gan lúithchlis.
Ca bhfuil do shaothar saor le suidhmhchan?
Ca bhfuil na béithe buidheach det gníomhartha?
Breathainse a bhaill seo a mhaighdean mhaordha, –
Ainimh ní bhfaghaimse mheill ar bhéihe é;
Breathain go cruinn a ghnaoi's a ghéaga
Ó bhaitheas a chinn go boinn a chaolchos. 970
Bíodh gurab ainimheach anmhíchúmtha é
Chímse ceangailte a bharra gan diúltadh.
A ghile ní ghrádhfinn, b'fhearr liom buidhe é,
Is cuma na gcnámh – ní cháinfinn choidhche
Duine mbeadh dronn 'n-a dhrom is fánadh –
Is minic sin togha fir cromshlinneánach;
Ba mhinic sin gambach lannsa gníomhach
Is ioscada cam ag strampa bríoghmhar.
Is fáithibh foilightheach uireasbhach éigin
D'fhág an doirbhtheach foirbhthe in aonta, 980
Is méid a cheana idir mhaithibh na tíre, –
A réim le sealad i gcaradus daoine,
Seinnm ar cheólta spórt is aoibhneas
Imirt's ól ar bhórd na saoithe,

I felt some horrid violence
And the paralysis of death in my bones and in my senses;   950
I saw the country and the household shaking,
And the force of her speech dancing in my ears.
The powerful tall person of the bailiff comes,
And my colouring spreads upon the stretching forth of her hand;
She pulled [me] by the ear roughly, stubbornly
Dragging me up with her to the head of the table.
This maiden who tormented the unmarried jumps up,
Strikes her hands and it's high she leapt.
And quick-wittedly she said – 'old clod,
It's long I'm hoping to rake your back,   960
It's often that you were exhorted, heart without humanity,
It's time for you to submit to the law of women.
Where will you get a defence against the case?
You did not deserve a word, useless person without dexterity.
Where is your noble work established?
Where are the women gratified by your actions?
Look at his limbs, stately maidens, –
A defect I don't see spoiling him for women;
Examine carefully his countenance and his limbs
From the crown of his head to the soles of his thin feet.   970
Although he is blemished, very badly formed
I see those that he is superior to married without question.
His whiteness I would not love, I would prefer him sunburnt,
And the shape of his bones – I would never revile
A person who would have a hump on his back and a droop –
Often a choice man is stoop-shouldered;
Often a long-legged man would be a vigorous blade
And a crooked, weak-kneed person would have a lively stump.
There are some hidden, deficient reasons
[That] left the discontented person an unmarried old man,   980
Much is his regard among the nobles of the country, –
His position for a while in the affection of the people,
Making music, sport, and pleasure
Playing and drinking at the table of the nobles,

I gcomhar na fuirinne fuineadh as féile,
An snamhaire ar b'fhuiris dom urraim-se géilleadh.
Is taidhbhseach taitneamhach tairbheach tréitheach
Meidhrach meanmnach a ainm's is aerach.
Ainmhidhe 'et shórt níor órduigh an Tiarna, –
Geanmnaidhe fós i gcomhgar liathe!   990
Creathaim go bonn le fonn do dhaortha,
Is gairid an chabhair do labhartha baotha,
Is coir módh is díreach suidhte it éadan –
Deich fó thrí gan coimhreach céile.
Éistigh lium-sa a chlú na bhfoidhnneach,
Faghaimse congnadh i gcúis na maighdne;
An crádh's an dúladh mhúch gan bhrígh me,
A mhná na múirne, is rún liom íoc air.
Congnaidh deirim libh, beiridh air, tóg é,
A Úna goirim thu's fagh dham córda;   1000
Ca bhfuil tu a Áine, ná bí ar iarraidh!
Ceangailse, a Mháire, a lámha ar dtaobh thiar de!
A Mhuirinn, a Mheadhbh, a Shaodhbh's a Shíle,
Cuiridh i bhfeidhm le doighearthaibh díograis
Barr gach scóla d'órduigh an tsídhbhean,
Báithidh sa bhfeóil gach córda snaidhmeach,
Tómhais go fial na pianta is cruaidhe
Le tóin's le tiarpa Bhriain, gan truagh ar bith;
Tóg na lámha is árduigh an sciúirse,
Is sómpla sámh é a mhná na múirne!   1010
Gearraigidhe doimhin, níor thuill sé fábhar!
Bainidh an leadhb ó rinn go sáil de!
Cloistear a chling i gcríochaibh Éibhir
'S critheadh a gcroidhe 'sna críontaigh aonta.
Is ciallmhar ceart an t-acht é, saoilim,
Bliadhain an aicht seo is ceart a scríobhadh dhúinn: –
Réidhtigh, ceil, nó goid de sceimhle
Céad is deich fé leith as mile,
Dúbail ceart an freastal fuidhlaigh,
Is thúirling Mac an tseachtmhain roimhe-sin.   1020

Before the company at feast-day,
It would be easy for me to yield respect to the crawler.
[He] is attractive, pleasing, useful, clever
Merry, spirited his name and he is lively.
A brute of your sort the Lord did not order, –
Chaste still near to grey!   990
I tremble to the sole with desire for your being condemned,
Little is the help from your foolish talk,
The situation is a crime, and truly evident in your face –
Thirty without the yoke of a spouse.
Listen to me, glory of the patient,
Let me have help in the matter of the virgin;
The torment and the unsatisfied desire [that] left me without force,
 O women of spirit, it is my intention to avenge him for.
Help, I say to you, seize him, take him,
Úna, I call on you, and get a cord for me;   1000
Where are you, Áine, don't be missing!
Máire, tie his hands behind him!
Muirinn, Meadhbh, Sadhbh and Síle,
Put into action with flames of eagerness
The height of every torment that the sky-woman ordered,
Drown in the flesh every knotted cord,
Measure out generously the pains and hardship
On Brian's bottom and backside, without any pity;
Lift the hands and raise the scourge,
He is a splendid example, women of spirit!   1010
Cut deeply, he did not earn a favour!
Take the hide from him from top to heel!
May his knell be heard to the ends of Éibhear
And shake their hearts in the single old people.
Sensible and right is the act, I think,
The year of this act it is right to record for us: –
Regulate, conceal, or remove your dread
A hundred and ten from a thousand,
Double rightly the remainder,
And the Son descended the week before that.   1020

[169]

Glacann sí a peann's mo cheann-sa suaidhte
Ar eagla m'fheannta is scannradh an bhuailte;
An feadh do bhí sí ag scríobhadh an dáta
Is maithibh an tighe aici suidhte ar gárdain,
Do scaras lem néill, do réidheas mo shúile,
'S do phreabas de léim ón bpéin'om dhúiseacht!

She takes her pen and my head is weak
For fear of my flaying and terror of the beating;
While she was writing the date
And the nobles of the house seated by her on guard,
I started from my sleep, I cleared my eyes,
And I jumped with a bound from the pain upon my awaking!

Bibliography

PUBLISHED TRANSLATIONS OF CÚIRT AN MHEÁN OÍCHE
(alphabetical by translator; complete translations unless otherwise noted)

The Midnight Court: A New Translation of 'Cúirt an Mheán Oíche'. Trans. Ciaran Carson. Oldcastle, Co. Meath: Gallery Press, 2005.

Cúirt an mheodhon oidhche: The Midnight Court: Done into Dublin English. Trans. Yam Cashen. Dublin: Ashfield, 2005.

On Trial at Midnight: Cúirt an Mheán Oíche / The Midnight Court. Trans. Bowes Egan. Dublin: Brehon Press, 1985.

The Midnight Verdict. Trans. Seamus Heaney. Oldcastle, Co. Meath: Gallery Press, 1993. [Partial]

'The Midnight Court.' In *An Duanaire: 1600–1900: Poems of the Dispossessed*. Ed. Seán Ó Tuama. Trans. Thomas Kinsella. Mountrath, Portlaoise: Dolmen Press, 1981. [Partial]

'The Midnight Court.' In *The New Oxford Book of Irish Verse*. Ed. and trans. Thomas Kinsella. Oxford and New York: Oxford Univ. Press, 1986.

'The Midnight Court.' Trans. Lord Longford. *Poetry Ireland*. No. 6. July, 1949. Pp. 6–28.

Cúirt an Mheadhon Oídhche: The Midnight Court. Trans. David Marcus. Dublin: Dolmen Press, 1953. Rpt. in *The Midnight Court / Cúirt an Mheán Oíche: A Critical Edition*. Ed. Brian Ó Conchubhair. Syracuse, N.Y.: Syracuse Univ. Press, 2011.

The Midnight Court: A Rhythmical Bacchanalia from the Irish of Bryan Merryman. Trans. Frank O'Connor. London, Dublin: Maurice Fridberg, 1945. Rpt. with revisions as 'The Midnight Court' in *Kings, Lords, and Commons: Irish Poems from the Seventh Century to the Nineteenth Century*. Dublin: Gill and Macmillan, 1959. Also rpt. in *The Midnight Court and Other Poems Translated from the Irish*. New York: Open Road Integrated Media, 2014. [Digital book]

The Midnight Court. Trans. Cosslett Ó Cuinn. Dublin and Cork: Mercier Press, 1982.

The Midnight Court: Literally Translated from the Original Gaelic. Trans. Michael C. O'Shea. Boston: 1897.

Cúirt an Mheán Oíche: The Midnight Court. Trans. Patrick C. Power. Cork: Mercier Press, 1971.

Cúirt An Mheán-Oíche: The Midnight Court and The Adventures of a Luckless Fellow. Trans. Percy Arland Ussher. London: Jonathan Cape; New York: Boni and Liveright, 1926.

Cúirt an Mheádhoin-Oidhche. Trans. Denis Woulfe. *The Irishman* (Dublin). Vol. XXII. Nos. 34–49. 21 February–5 June, 1880. Rpt. with revisions in *Cúirt an Mheon-Oíche*. Ed. Liam P. Ó Murchú. Baile Átha Cliath: Clóchomhar, 1982; and as *The Midnight Court: Traditional Gaelic Burlesque Poem, translated into English by Dennis* [sic] *Woulfe*. Ed. Donal Ó Siodhacháin. Cork: Irish and Celtic Publications, 1990.

EDITIONS OF CÚIRT AN MHEÁN OÍCHE
(in order of publication)

Mediae Noctis Consilium: Poema Heroico-Comicum. Dublin: John O'Daly, 1850.

Mediae noctis consilium: a heroic comic poem in Irish-Gaelic by Bryan Macgilla Meidhre. Dublin: M.H. Gill and Son, 1879. [Reprint of 1850 edition]

Mediae Noctis Consilium: Cúirt an Meadhoin Oidhche. Dublin: Pádraig Ó Briain, 1893. [Reprint of 1850 edition]

'Brian Merriman's *Cúirt An Mheadhóin Oidhche*.' Ed. L.C. Stern. *Zeitschrift für Celtische Philologie*. Vol.V. 1905. Pp. 193–415. [Includes a translation into German]

The Midnight Court: Cúirt an mheandoin oidhche. Dublin: Celtic Press, 1909. [Partial]

Cúirt an Mheadhon Oidhche. Ed. Risteárd Ó Foghludha. Intro. Piaras Béaslaí. Dublin: Hodges, Figgis, 1912.

Giotaí as Cúirt an Mheodhn-Oidhche. Ed. Conall Cearnach (Feardorcha Ó Conaill). Baile Átha Cliath, Corcaigh: Comhlacht Oideachais na hÉireann, nd (1927). [Partial]

Cúirt an Mheadhón Oidhche. Ed. Risteárd Ó Foghludha. Dublin: Hodges, Figgis, 1949.

Cúirt An Mheán Oíche. Ed. Dáithí Ó hUaithne. Baile Átha Cliath: Dolmen Press / Cumann Merriman, 1968.

The Midnight Court: Cúirt an Mheán-Oíche. Ed. Patrick C. Power. Cork: Mercier Press, 1971.

Cúirt an Mheon-Oíche. Ed. Liam P. Ó Murchú. Baile Átha Cliath: Clóchomhar, 1982.

SECONDARY WORKS, GENERAL

Béaslaí, Piaras. 'Merriman's Secret: An Interpretation.' Preface to *Cuirt an Mheadhon Oidhche*. Ed. Risteárd O Foghludha. Dublin: Hodges Figgis, 1912. Pp. 1–19.

Benjamin, Walter. 'The Task of the Translator.' In *Translation Studies Reader*. Ed. Lawrence Venuti. London and New York: Routledge, 2000. Pp. 15–23.

Breatnach, R.A. '"The End of a Tradition": A Survey of Eighteenth-Century Gaelic Literature.' *Studia Hibernica*. Vol. I. 1961. Pp. 128–50.

Buttimer, Neil. 'Literature in Irish, 1690–1800.' In *The Cambridge History of Irish Literature*. Eds. Margaret Kelleher and Philip O'Leary. Vol. I. Cambridge: Cambridge Univ. Press, 2006. Pp. 320–71.

Chayfitz, Eric. *The Poetics of Imperialism: Translation and Colonization from The Tempest to Tarzan*. New York: Oxford Univ. Press, 1991.

Colum, Padraic. 'Introduction.' 'The Midnight Court.' Trans. Lord Longford. *Poetry Ireland*. No. 6. July, 1949. Pp. 3–4.

Corkery, Daniel. 'Brian Merriman.' In *The Hidden Ireland: A Study of Gaelic Munster in the Eighteenth Century*. Dublin: Gill & Son, 1924. Pp. 222–39.

Corkery, Daniel. *The Fortunes of the Irish Language.* Cork: Mercier Press, 1954.

Croghan, Martin J. 'Sexuality in *The Midnight Court* and *Ulysses.*' In *Troubled Histories, Troubled Fictions: Twentieth-Century Anglo-Irish Prose.* Eds. Theo D'haen and José Lanters. Amsterdam, Atlanta, Ga.: Rodopi, 1995. Pp. 19–30.

Cronin, Michael. *Translating Ireland: Translation, Languages, Cultures.* Cork: Cork Univ. Press, 1996.

Crowley, Tony. *The Politics of Language in Ireland 1366–1922: A Source Book.* London: Routledge, 2000.

de Blacam, Aodh. *Gaelic Literature Surveyed.* 2nd ed. Dublin, Belfast: Phoenix, nd [1927].

Dillon, Charlie, and Ríona Ní Fhrighil, eds. *Aistriú Éireann.* Belfast: Queens Univ. Press, 2008.

Eco, Umberto. *Mouse or Rat? Translation as Negotiation.* London: Weidenfeld and Nicolson, 2003.

Eglinton, John. *Bards and Saints.* Dublin: Maunsel, 1906.

Greene, David. *The Irish Language: An Ghaeilge.* Dublin: Three Candles, 1966.

Griffin, Michael. 'The Two Enlightenments of Brian Merriman's County Clare.' In *The Midnight Court / Cúirt an Mheán Oíche.* Ed. Brian Ó Conchubhair. Syracuse, N.Y.: Syracuse Univ. Press, 2011. Pp. 59–69.

Holmes, James S., et. al., eds. *Literature and Translation: New Perspectives in Literary Studies.* Leuven: Acco, 1978.

Holmes, James S., et. al., eds. *The Nature of Translation: Essays on the Theory and Practice of Literary Translation.* The Hague: Moulton, 1970.

Kiberd, Declan. 'Brian Merriman's Midnight Court.' In *Irish Classics.* Cambridge, Mass.: Harvard Univ. Press, 2001. Pp. 184–201.

Kiberd, Declan. *Idir Dhá Chultúr.* Dublin: Coiscéim, 1993.

Lefevere, André. 'Literary Theory and Translated Literature.' *Dispositio.* Vol. VII. 1982. Pp. 3–22.

Lefevere, André. *Translating Poetry: Seven Strategies and a Blueprint.* Assen: Van Gorcum, 1975.

Mathews, Jackson. 'Third Thoughts on Translating Poetry.' In *On Translation.* Ed. Reuben A. Brower. New York: Oxford Univ. Press, 1966. Pp. 67–77.

McKibben, Sarah E. 'Courting an Elusive Masterwork: Reading Gender and Genre in *Cúirt an Mheán Oíche.*' In *The Midnight Court / Cúirt an Mheán Oíche.* Ed. Brian Ó Conchubhair. Syracuse, N.Y.: Syracuse Univ. Press, 2011. Pp. 70–7.

McKibben, Sarah E. *Endangered Masculinities in Irish Poetry 1540–1780.* Dublin: Univ. College Dublin Press, 2010.

Mercier, Vivian. *The Irish Comic Tradition.* Oxford: Clarendon Press, 1962.

Nic Dhiarmada, Bríona. 'Approaching *Cúirt an Mheán Oíche / The Midnight Court.*' In *The Midnight Court / Cúirt an Mheán Oíche.* Ed. Brian Ó Conchubhair. Syracuse, N.Y.: Syracuse Univ. Press, 2011. Pp. 78–89.

Ó Conchubhair, Brian. 'Introduction: Brian Merriman's Daytime Milieu.' In *The Midnight Court / Cúirt an Mheán Oíche.* Ed. Brian Ó Conchubhair. Syracuse, N.Y.: Syracuse Univ. Press, 2011. Pp. xiii-xxvi.

Ó Crualaoich, Gearóid. 'The Vision of Liberation in *Cúirt an Mheán-Oíche.*' In *Folia Gadelica, aistí ó iardhaltaí leis a bronnadh ar R.A. Breatnach.* Eds. Pádraig de Brún, et al. Cork: Cork Univ. Press, 1983. Pp. 95–104.

Ó Cuív, Brian. 'Irish Language and Literature 1691–1845.' In *A New History of Ireland: IV: Eighteenth-Century Ireland: 1691–1800.* Eds. T. W. Moody and W. E. Vaughan. Oxford: Clarendon Press, 1986. Pp. 374–423.

Ó Foghludha, Risteárd. 'Brian Merriman.' Preface to *Cúirt an Mheadhón Oidhche*. Ed.
    Risteárd Ó Foghludha. Dublin: Hodges, Figgis, 1949. Pp. 6–12.

Ó Murchú, Liam P. 'Merriman's *Cúirt an Mheoníche* and Eighteenth-Century Irish Verse.' In
    A Companion to Irish Literature, Vol. I. Ed. Julia M. Wright. Chicester, West Sussex:
    Wiley-Blackwell, 2010. Pp. 178–92.

Ó Murchú, Liam P. *Merriman: I bhFábhar Béithe*. Baile Átha Cliath: Clóchomhar, 2005.

O'Rahilly, Thomas F. Rev. of *Cúirt an Mheadhon Oidhche*, ed. Risteárd Ó Foghludha.
    Gadelica. Vol. I. 1912. Pp. 190–204.

Ó Tuama, Seán. 'Brian Merriman and his *Court*.' *Irish University Review*. Vol. II. 1981. Pp.
    149–164. Rpt. in *Repossessions: Selected Essays on the Irish Literary Heritage*. Cork:
    Cork Univ. Press, 1995. Pp. 63–77.

Ó Tuama, Seán. 'Réamhrá.' *Cúirt an Mheán Oíche*. Ed. Dáithí Ó hUaithne. Baile Átha Cliath:
    Dolmen Press / Cumann Merriman, 1968. Pp. 7–16.

Partridge, A.C. *Language and Society in Anglo-Irish Literature*. Dublin: Gill and
    Macmillan, 1984.

Schirmer, Gregory A. *After the Irish: An Anthology of Poetic Translation*. Cork: Cork Univ.
    Press, 2009.

Sewell, Frank. 'Between two languages: poetry in Irish, English and Irish English.' In
    Cambridge Companion to Contemporary Irish Poetry. Ed. Matthew Campbell.
    Cambridge: Cambridge Univ. Press, 2003. Pp. 149–68.

Shields, Kathleen. *Gained in Translation: Language, Poetry and Identity in Twentieth-Century
    Ireland*. Bern: Peter Lang, 2000.

Smith, Stan. *Irish Poetry and the Construction of Modern Identity*. Dublin: Irish Academic
    Press, 2005.

Steiner, George. *After Babel: Aspects of Language and Translation*. Oxford and New York:
    Oxford Univ. Press, 1975, 1992, 1998.

Titley, Alan. '*Cúirt an Mheán Oíche*: A Wonder of Ireland.' In *The Midnight Court / Cúirt an
    Mheán Oíche*. Ed. Brian Ó Conchubhair. Syracuse, N.Y.: Syracuse Univ. Press, 2011.
    Pp. 47–58.

Tymoczko, Maria. *Translation in a Postcolonial Context*. Manchester: St Jerome, 1999.

Venuti, Lawrence, ed. *The Translation Studies Reader*. London and New York: Routledge, 2000.

Welch, Robert. 'Poetry, Fear, and Translation: Versions of Merriman.' In *Brian Merriman
    and His World: Merriman ar an mbinse*. Eds. Máirín Ní Dhonnchadha, Gearóid
    Ó Tuathaigh, and Patrick Crotty. Dublin: Four Courts Press (forthcoming).

Williams, J. E. Caerwyn, and Máirín Ní Mhuiríosa. *Traidisiún Liteartha na nGael*. Baile Átha
    Cliath: Clóchomhar, 1979.

Yeats, W.B. 'Preface.' *The Midnight Court and The Adventures of a Luckless Fellow*. Trans.
    Percy Arland Ussher. London: Jonathan Cape, 1926. Pp. 5–12.

WORKS BY AND ABOUT INDIVIDUAL TRANSLATORS

Alexander, Neal. *Ciaran Carson: Space, Place, Writing*. Liverpool: Liverpool Univ. Press, 2010.

Badin, Donatella Abbate. *Thomas Kinsella*. New York: Twayne, 1996.

Binchy, D. A. 'The Scholar-Gipsy.' In *Michael / Frank: Studies on Frank O'Connor*.
    Ed. Maurice Sheehy. New York: Alfred Knopf, 1969. Pp. 16–22.

Brown, John. *In the Chair: Interviews with Poets from the North of Ireland*. Cliffs of Moher: Salmon, 2002. Pp. 141–52. [Ciaran Carson]

Carson, Ciaran. *Fishing for Amber: A Long Story*. London: Granta, 1999.

Carson, Ciaran. *The Star Factory*. New York: Arcade Publishing, 1997.

Carson, Ciaran. '*Sweeney Astray*: Escaping from Limbo.' In *The Art of Seamus Heaney*. Ed. Tony Curtis. Chester Springs, Pa: Dufour, 1985. Pp. 141–8.

Carson, Ciaran. '"Whose Woods These Are …": Some Aspects of Poetry and Translation.' *The Yellow Nib*. No. 2. 2006. Pp. 112–27.

Cowell, John. *No Profit but the Name: The Longfords and the Gate Theatre*. Dublin: O'Brien Press, 1988.

Curtis, Tony, ed. *The Art of Seamus Heaney*. Chester Springs, Pa: Dufour, 1985.

Finlay, Alison. 'Putting a Bawn into *Beowulf*.' In *Seamus Heaney: Poet, Critic, Translator*. Eds. Ashby Bland Crowser and Jason David Hall. Basingstroke and New York: Palgrave Macmillan, 2007. Pp. 136–54.

Greene, David. 'Poet of the People.' In *Michael / Frank: Studies on Frank O'Connor*. Ed. Maurice Sheehy. New York: Alfred Knopf, 1969. Pp. 137–9.

Harmon, Maurice. *Thomas Kinsella: Designing for the Exact Needs*. Dublin: Irish Academic Press, 2008.

Heaney, Seamus. 'The God in the Tree.' In *The Pleasures of Gaelic Poetry*. Ed. Seán Mac Réamoinn. London: Allen Lane, 1982. Pp. 25–34.

Heaney, Seamus. 'Orpheus in Ireland: On Brian Merriman's *The Midnight Court*.' In *The Redress of Poetry*. New York: Farrar, Straus and Giroux, 1995, Pp. 38–62.

Heaney, Seamus, and Robert Haas. *Sounding Lines: The Art of Translating Poetry*. Berkeley, Calif.: Doreen B. Townsend Center for the Humanities, 2000.

Jackson, Thomas H. *The Whole Matter: The Poetic Evolution of Thomas Kinsella*. Syracuse, N.Y.: Syracuse Univ. Press; Dublin: Lilliput Press, 1995.

John, Brian. *Reading the Ground: The Poetry of Thomas Kinsella*. Washington, D.C.: Catholic Univ. Press, 1996.

Kennedy-Andrews, Elmer, ed. *Ciarán Carson: Critical Essays*. Dublin: Four Courts Press, 2009.

Kennelly, Brendan. 'Little Monastaries.' In *Michael / Frank: Studies on Frank O'Connor*. Ed. Maurice Sheehy. New York: Alfred Knopf, 1969. Pp. 103–13.

Kiberd, Declan. 'Merry Men: the Afterlife of the Poem.' In *Frank O'Connor: Critical Essays*. Ed. Hilary Lennon. Dublin: Four Courts Press, 2007. Pp. 114–28.

Kinsella, Thomas. 'Another Country.' In *The Pleasures of Gaelic Poetry*. Ed. Seán Mac Réamoinn. London: Allen Lane, 1982. Pp. 175–82.

Kinsella, Thomas. 'The Divided Mind.' In *Irish Poets in English: The Thomas Davis Lectures on Anglo-Irish Poetry*. Ed. Sean Lucy. Dublin and Cork: Mercier Press, 1972. Pp. 208–218.

Kinsella, Thomas. *The Dual Tradition: An Essay on Poetry and Politics in Ireland*. Manchester: Carcanet, 1995.

Kinsella, Thomas. 'The Irish Writer.' In *Davis, Mangan, Ferguson? Tradition and the Irish Writer*. Dublin: Dolmen Press, 1970. Pp. 57–70.

Luke, Peter, ed. *Enter Certain Players: Edwards-MacLiammóir and the Gate 1928–1978*. Dublin: Dolmen Press, 1978.

Matthews, James. *Voices: A Life of Frank O'Connor*. New York: Atheneum, 1983.

Marcus, David. *Oughtobiography: Leaves from the Diary of a Hyphenated Jew*. Dublin: Gill and Macmillan, 2001.

McKeon, Jim. *Frank O'Connor: A Life*. Edinburgh: Mainstream, 1998.

Murphy, Andrew. 'Heaney and the Irish Poetic Tradition.' In *The Cambridge Companion to Seamus Heaney*. Ed. Bernard O'Donoghue. Cambridge: Cambridge Univ. Press, 2009. Pp. 136–49.

Ní Dhomhnaill, Nuala. 'The English for Irish.' *The Irish Review*. No. 4. 1988. Pp. 116–18. [Ciaran Carson]

O'Brien, Eugene. *Seamus Heaney: Creating Irelands of the Mind*. Dublin: Liffey Press, 2002.

O'Brien, Eugene. *Seamus Heaney and the Place of Writing*. Gainseville, Fla.: Univ. of Florida Press, 2002.

O'Brien, Eugene. *Seamus Heaney: Searches for Answers*. London and Dublin: Pluto Press, 2003.

O'Driscoll, Denis. *Stepping Stones: Interviews with Seamus Heaney*. New York: Farrar, Straus and Giroux, 2008.

Ó Cuinn, Cosslett. 'Merriman's Court.' In *The Pleasures of Gaelic Poetry*. Ed. Seán Mac Réamoinn. London: Allen Lane,1982. Pp. 113–26.

Ó Murchú, Liam P. 'Aistriúchán / áin Frank Ó Connor de *Chúirt an Mheán Oíche* le Brian Merriman.' In *Aistriú Éireann*. Eds. Charlie Dillon and Ríóna Ní Fhrighil. Béal Feirste: Cló Ollscoil na Banríona, 2008. Pp. 131–45.

Ormsby, Frank. 'Ciaran Carson interviewed by Frank Ormsby.' *Linen Hall Review*. Vol. VIII. No. I. 1991. Pp. 5–8.

Risteárd Ó Glaisne. *Cosslett Ó Cuinn*. Baile Átha Cliath: Coiscéim, 1996.

Pakenham, Lord. *Avowed Intent: An Autobiography of Lord Longford*. London: Little, Brown, 1994.

Pakenham, Lord. *Born to Believe: An Autobiography*. London: Jonathan Cape, 1953.

Power, Patrick C. *A Literary History of Ireland*. Cork: Mercier Press, 1969.

Power, Patrick C. *The Story of Anglo-Irish Poetry (1800–1922)*. Cork: Mercier Press, 1967.

Stanford, Peter. *Lord Longford: A Life*. London: William Heinemann, 1994.

Titley, Alan. 'The Interpretation of Tradition.' In *Frank O'Connor: New Perspectives*. Eds. Robert C. Evans and Richard Harp. West Cornwall, Connecticut: Locust Hill Press, 1998. Rpt. in *Frank O'Connor: Critical Essays*. Ed. Hilary Lennon. Dublin: Four Courts Press, 2007. Pp. 218–32.

Turner, Paul. 'The Cure at Troy: Sophocles or Heaney?' In *Seamus Heaney: Poet, Critic, Translator*. Eds. Ashby Bland Crowser and Jason David Hall. Basingstroke and New York: Palgrave Macmillan, 2007. Pp. 121–35.

Ussher Arland. *The Face and Mind of Ireland*. 1949; New York: Devin-Adair, 1950.

Ussher, Arland. *The Journal of Arland Ussher*. Ed. Adrian Kenny. Dublin: Raven Arts, 1980.

Ussher, Arland. *Three Great Irishmen: Shaw, Yeats, Joyce*. New York: Devin-Adair, 1953.

Notes

INTRODUCTION

1. Alan Titley, 'Cúirt an Mheán Oíche: A Wonder of Ireland,' in *The Midnight Court / Cúirt an Mheán Oíche*, ed. Brian Ó Conchubhair (Syracuse, N.Y.: Syracuse Univ. Press, 2011), describes Merriman's poem as 'the most famous Irish poem of all' (p. 47). Aodh de Blacam, *Gaelic Literature Surveyed*, 2nd ed. (Dublin, Belfast: Phoenix, n.d. [1927]), says that *Cúirt an Mheán Oíche* is esteemed by many critics as the most original and artistic piece of work in late Modern Irish' (p. 334). And Sean Ó Tuama, 'Brian Merriman and his *Court*,' *Irish University Review*, Vol. II (1981); rpt. in *Repossessions: Selected Essays on the Irish Literary Heritage* (Cork: Cork Univ. Press, 1995), describes *Cúirt an Mheán Oíche* as 'undoubtedly one of the greatest comic works of literature, and certainly the greatest comic poem ever written in Ireland' (p. 64).

2. Because the year 1780 is given at the end of *Cúirt an Mheán Oíche* as the time of the sitting of Aoibheall's court, most critics have taken it to be the date of the poem's composition. But Breandán Ó Buachalla has argued that there's no reason to assume that the poem was completed in 1780: 'It could be twenty years earlier, it could be twenty years later – my sense is that it's earlier' (unpublished lecture given in 2005, cited in Brian Ó Conchubhair, 'Introduction: Brian Merriman's Daytime Mileu,' *The Midnight Court / Cúirt an Mheán Oíche*, ed. Ó Conchubhair, p. xvi).

3. There are two essays considering Frank O'Connor's translation: 'Merry Men: the Afterlife of the Poem,' by Declan Kiberd, in *Frank O'Connor: Critical Essays*, ed. Hilary Lennon (Dublin: Four Courts Press, 2007), pp. 114–28, and 'Aistriúchán / áin Frank O' Connor de *Chúirt an Mheonoíche* le Brian Merriman,' by Liam P. Ó Murchú, in *Aistriú Éireann*, eds. Charlie Dillon and Ríóna Ní Fhrighil (Belfast: Queens Univ. Press, 2008), pp. 131–45. Kiberd's essay considers O'Connor's translation, in part, as 'an occluded autobiographical work' (p. 121), while also paying some attention to the translations of Arland Ussher, Cosslett Ó Cuinn, Seamus Heaney, and Ciaran Carson. Ó Murchú's essay is largely an examination of differences between the 1945 edition of O'Connor's translation and the version published in *Kings, Lords and Commons* in 1959. An essay on Merriman's translators in general, 'Poetry, Fear, and Translation: Versions of Merriman,' by Robert Welch, is forthcoming in *Brian Merriman and His World: Merriman ar an mbinse*, eds. Máirín

Ní Dhonnchadha, Gearóid Ó Tuathaigh, and Patrick Crotty (Dublin: Four Courts Press). I am grateful to Professor Welch for the letting me read this essay in typescript.

4. With the exception of Seamus Heaney's partial version, the translations considered in this study are complete translations of Merriman's poem. There are two complete published translations not examined here, on the ground they are of little poetic interest: *On Trial at Midnight*, by Bowes Egan (Killybegs: Brehon Press, 1985), and *Cúirt an mheodhon oidhche: The Midnight Court: Done into Dublin English*, by Yam Cashen (Dublin: Ashfield, 2005). Also, according to Brendan Behan's biographer, Behan turned up one night in 1952 at McDaid's in Harry Street, and recited, in its entirety, his complete translation of Merriman's poem. Three days later, Behan was reportedly in a fight in the Conservative Club in York Street, and the manuscript of his translation was lost, although the opening twenty-two lines of it appeared six years later in his autobiographical work *Borstal Boy* (Ulick O'Connor, *Brendan Behan* [London: Hamish Hamilton, 1970], p. 122).

5. Yeats's comments on the connection between Swift and Merriman are to be found in his preface to Arland Ussher's translation of *Cúirt an Mheán Oíche* (*The Midnight Court and The Adventures of a Luckless Fellow* [London: Jonathan Cape, 1926], pp. 5–7). A.C. Partridge says that Merriman's couplets are 'reminiscent of the writing of Swift and Goldsmith' (*Language and Society in Anglo-Irish Literature* [Dublin: Gill and Macmillan, 1984], p. 143). And Vivien Mercier, referring to Yeats' comments, says, 'it is hard to see where else Merriman could have encountered a court in which each sex blames the other for the decay of love', and adds that Merriman's line could easily be considered an imitation of Swift's octosyllabic line (*The Irish Comic Tradition* [Oxford: Clarendon Press, 1962], pp. 193–4).

6. *After Babel: Aspects of Language and Translation* (Oxford and New York: Oxford Univ. Press, 1975, 1992, 1998), p. 317.

7. Ó Tuama, 'Brian Merriman and his *Court*,' says of Merriman's poem that 'scores of copies were transcribed and reproduced in the immediate years after its composition: it was read with avidity, discussed, and frequently added to' (p. 64). Bríona Nic Dhiarmada, 'Approaching *Cúirt an Mheán Oíche* / *The Midnight Court*,' in *The Midnight Court* / *Cúirt an Mheán Oíche*, ed. Ó Conchubhair, says that numerous manuscript copies were circulating not just in Merriman's lifetime, but far into the nineteenth century as well (p. 79). Indeed, Liam P. Ó Murchú has argued that the poem 'reached the zenith of its popularity in the first half of the nineteenth century' ('Merriman's *Cúirt an Mheoníche* and Eighteenth-Century Irish Verse', in *A Companion to Irish Literature*, Vol. 1, ed. Julia M. Wright [Chicester, West Sussex: Wiley-Blackwell, 2010], p. 179). From the middle of the nineteenth century on, the poem has been published in printed editions no fewer twelve times – in 1850, 1879, 1893, 1905 (with a German translation), 1900 (a bowdlerized edition for use in the schools), 1909, 1912, 1927 (another bowdlerized edition), 1949, 1968, 1971 and 1982. See the Bibliography for a detailed list of these editions.

Given the considerable reputation of *Cúirt an Mheán Oíche*, it's surprising how much obscurity still surrounds its author. The year of Merriman's birth has been given variously as 1747, 1749 and 1750. According to one scholar, he was born into a Protestant family (Partridge, *Language and Society in Anglo-Irish Literature*, p. 143), and according to others, he was illegitimate (Ó Tuama, 'Merriman and His Court', p. 75). Even his name is not certain; the Irish version has been variously given as Mac Gillameidre, Mac Giolla Meidhre and Mac Manaman, and anglicized versions include Bryan Merryman, Bryan Merriman, and Brian Merriman. His birthplace is said by some to be Ennistymon,

Co. Clare, but by others to be the parish of Clondagad, some fifteen kilometres southwest of Ennis. His family is said to have moved to Feakle, near Lough Graney in east Clare, when Merriman was quite young, although one nineteenth-century scholar has said that Merriman, a 'wild youth and fond of amusement', left his father's house when he was a young man and settled by himself near Feakle (Seán Ó Dálaigh, in *Poets and Poetry of Munster* [2nd series], 1860; quoted in Liam P. Ó Murchú, 'An Réamhra' ('Introduction'), *Cúirt an Mheon-Oíche*, ed. Ó Murchú (Baile Átha Cliath: Clóchomhar, 1982, p. 13). Most accounts say Merriman taught school near Feakle, in a hedge school possibly, and may have tutored some of the local gentry, while also doing a little farming. He presumably wrote *Cúirt an Mheán Oíche* while living in Clare, and then, sometime later, moved to Limerick, where he taught mathematics, and where he died, according to three local newspapers, on the 29th of July, 1805 (Ó Murchú, *Cúirt*, p. 13). Only two other poetic works, both minor, have been attributed to him. For a summary of the various accounts of Merriman's life, see Ó Murchú, *Cúirt*, pp. 11–14.

8. 'Orpheus in Ireland: On Brian Merriman's *The Midnight Court*,' *The Redress of Poetry* (Farrar, Straus and Giroux, New York, 1995), p. 53.

9. Gearóid Ó Crualaoich has described the theme of Merriman's poem as 'a civil and psychological liberation of the individual' ('The Vision of Liberation in *Cúirt an Mheán-Oíche*,' *Folia Gadelica, aistí ó iardhaltaí leis a bronnadh ar R.A. Breatnach* [Cork Univ. Press, 1983], p. 99). John Eglinton, writing in 1906, described Merriman as 'this Irish free-thinker of the eighteenth century' (*Bards and Saints*, [Dublin: Maunsel, 1906], p. 54). And Alan Titley, 'The Interpretation of Tradition,' *Frank O'Connor: Critical Essays*, says of Merriman's poem: 'It is funny, bawdy, explicit, dramatic and intelligent and in one declamation seems to destroy the stereotype of the repressed and puritanical peasant. That is to say, it is a poem which represents the direct opposite of the regnant assumptions of those ignorant of Irish culture' (p. 227). On the other hand, Liam P. Ó Murchú argues that Aoibheall is speaking for Merriman when she attributes the decline of the Gaelic aristocracy to mixed marriages between the nobility and the lower classes (*Merriman: I bhFábhar Béithe* [Baile Átha Cliath: Clochomhar, 2005], p. 106).

10. Ó Murchú says that Merriman 'developed and harnessed in an unprecedented manner the well-established *caoineadh* measure, giving to the end product a rushing fluency' ('Merriman's *Cúirt an Mheonoíche* and Eighteenth-Century Irish Verse,' p. 190). The standard *caoineadh* measure consists of four-line stanzas, with each line carrying four stresses. The four lines are connected through terminal assonance falling on the last accented vowel of each line, and internal assonance occurs between the second and third accented vowels in each line.

11. *Cúirt an Mheon-Oíche*, pp. 79–81.

12. 'Introduction,' *An Duanaire: 1600–1900: Poems of the Dispossessed*, ed. Seán Ó Tuama, trans. Thomas Kinsella (Mountrath: Portlaoise: Dolmen, 1981), p.xxxv.

13. 'Foreword,' *The Midnight Court: A New Translation of 'Cúirt an Mheán Oíche'* (Oldcastle, Co. Meath: Gallery Press, 2005), p. 11.

14. 'Orpheus in Ireland,' p. 48.

15. Merriman's diction manages to occupy, as Declan Kiberd has put it, 'an teorainn dhoiléir sin idir an litríocht "liteartha" agus an litríocht bhéil' ('that indistinct border between "literary" literature and the literature of speech') (*Idir Dha Chultúr* [Dublin: Coiscéim, 1993], p. 34).

16. Ó Murchú says that this practice is 'frémhaithe i nós na gnáthchainte agus cuireann sé go mór fuinneamh na véarsaíochta' ('rooted in the custom of ordinary speech and it contributes much to the vigour of the verse' (*Cúirt an Mheon-Oíche*, p. 77). Ó Murchú sees Merriman's use of these lists as part of an effort to represent the life of the people in east Clare with realistic accuracy (*I bhFábhar Béithe*, pp. 93–4).

17. 'Introduction,' *An Duanaire*, p. xxxv.

18. 'Sweeney Astray: Escaping from Limbo,' in *The Art of Seamus Heaney*, ed. Tony Curtis (Chester Springs, Pa.: Dufour, 1985), p. 143.

19. The artist Pauline Bewick produced in 2007 a set of eleven large-scale paintings entitled 'The Visual Translation of"The Midnight Court"'.

20. 'Third Thoughts on Translating Poetry,' in *On Translation*, ed. Reuben A. Brower (New York: Oxford Univ. Press, 1966), p. 68.

21. *After Babel*, p. xvi.

22. Eco, *Mouse or Rat? Translation as Negotiation* (Weidenfeld and Nicolson, 2003), p. 192.

DENIS WOULFE: CULTURAL LOSS AND METRICAL FINESSE

1. *Cúirt an Mheon-Oiche*, ed. Liam P. Ó Murchú (Baile Átha Cliath: An Clóchmhar, 1982), p. 84. Ó Murchú says that what biographical information we have about Woulfe is based on notes written by a scribe from Co. Clare on a manuscript of seven of Woulfe's poems (LS 63, Leabharlann Choláiste na hOllscoile, Corcaigh).

2. On one of the manuscript copies of Woulfe's translation, held by the library at University College Dublin, the date 1789 is written into the margins, and Andrew Carpenter has argued on this basis that the translation was probably made that year, nine years after the original was written. (*Verse in English from Eighteenth-Century Ireland*, ed. Andrew Carpenter [Cork: Cork Univ. Press, 1998], p. 446.)

3. Tomás Ó Rathaille, review of Risteárd Ó Foghluda, ed., *Cúirt an Mheadhon Oidhche* (Dublin: Hodges, Figgis 1912), in *Gadelica*, Vol. I (1912), says the printed text of Woulfe's translation from an unidentified and undated Clare newspaper, along with the text of the translation printed in *The Irishman* in 1880, are pasted into one of the manuscripts of Woulfe's translation held by the National Library in Dublin (p. 202). Woulfe's translation appeared in serial form in the following editions of *The Irishman*, Vol. XXII, 1880, published in Dublin: No. 34 (21 February), p. 138 (the editor's introduction to the poem); No. 35 (28 February), p. 554; No. 36 (6 March), p. 570; No. 37 (13 March), p. 586; No. 38 (20 March), p. 602; No. 41 (10 April), pp. 650–1; No. 43 (24 April), p. 667; No. 44 (1 May), pp. 698–9; No. 45 (8 May), pp. 714–15; No. 46 (15 May), pp. 730–1; No. 47 (22 May), p. 747; No. 48 (29 May), p. 762; and No. 49 (5 June), p. 779. There are numerous differences of grammar and spelling between this version and the one that appears in Ó Murchú's modern edition, and a number of more substantial differences in wording. In any case, the editor of *The Irishman* was not, it seems, very appreciative of Woulfe's translation, or of Merriman's poem. 'The original has often been instanced as an example of rhythmical jingle, and alliteration allowed to run riot,' he says in introducing Woulfe's translation. 'This characteristic feature Woulfe has, in many instances, successfully endeavoured to imitate in his translation' (*The Irishman*, No. 34 [21 February 1880], p. 138).

4. Seán Ó Tuama, 'Brian Merriman and His *Court*,' *Irish University Review*, Vol. II (1981);

rpt. *Repossessions: Selected Essays on the Irish Literary Heritage* (Cork: Cork Univ. Press, 1995), has argued, for example, that the social and political problem of declining population was less a reason for writing the poem than Merriman's own personal problems, emanating from the questionable circumstances of his birth (p. 75).

5. *Cúirt an Mheon-Oíche*, ed. Ó Murchú, ll. 77–92. It's not possible to determine which version of the original Woulfe was working from, although it must have been a manuscript copy, as the poem was not published until 1850. All citations from the original are from Ó Murchú's edition, the most reliable modern edition of the poem.

6. All literal translations from Merriman's Irish in this book are the author's. See the Appendix for a literal translation of the entire poem.

7. Ó Murchú, ll. 77–92. All further references to Woulfe's translation are to the version included in Ó Murchú's edition. The text of Woulfe's translation as it appears in Ó Murchú was reprinted in *The Midnight Court: traditional Gaelic burlesque poem, translated into English by Dennis* [sic] *Wolfe*, ed. Donal Ó Siodhacháin (Cork: Irish and Celtic Publications, 1990).

8. *The Hidden Ireland: A Study of Gaelic Munster in the Eighteenth Century* (Dublin: Gill, 1924), p. 229. Seán Ó Tuama has said that the diction of *Cúirt an Mheán Oíche* indulges in a 'bombastic vituperative vein' often found in the Irish-language tradition ('Brian Merriman and his *Court*,' p. 73).

9. Corkery says that the opening of Merriman's poem is itself not original or striking: 'his opening lines, the description of a fine morning by the shores of Loch Gréine, are not, one thinks, really poetic: they are the commonplace – nature apprehended by a spirit only slightly raised' (*Hidden Ireland*, p. 238).

10. Ó Murchú says Woulfe's phrase is probably the best guess that can be made for *cuile na móna* (p. 54).

MICHAEL C. O'SHEA: NATIONALISM UNLEASHED

1. *The Midnight Court, Literally Translated from the Original Gaelic* (Boston: 1897), p. vi.

2. In the introduction to his translation, O'Shea says he undertook his translation after being presented with 'a fine copy of the first edition, printed in Irish-Gaelic A.D. 1800' (p. v). In fact, the first edition of the poem was published by John O'Daly in 1850 under the title *Mediae Noctis Consilium: Poema Heroico-Comicum*.

3. According to an anonymous article, 'Notes from Ireland,' in *The Gael (An Gaodhal)*, published in New York in 1903, O'Shea and P. J. Daly, one of the other editors of the Boston periodical the *Irish Echo*, were from Co. Kerry, and worked for the Gaelic League (Vol. XXII, January, 1903, p. 29).

4. O'Shea says in the introduction to his translation that it was done while he was living in Beverly, Massachusetts (*Midnight Court*, p. v).

5. *The Irish Echo*, Vol. I, No. 1 (January 1886), p. 1.

6. *Irish Echo*, Vol. II, No. 17 (June 1889), p. 4. O'Shea's name disappeared without comment from the masthead in the issue of July, 1890. The magazine lasted until April, 1894, when it was replaced by a periodical entitled *An Mac-Alla Éireannach (The Irish Echo)*.

7. All too characteristic are these lines, from a poem entitled 'Cheering Address to the Reviving Gaelic Language':

Lov'd Gaelic O! my mother tongue,
Lift high thy strain once more,
And cease to wail o'er woes and wrong,
O'er tales of grief and gore;
The chain of silence hard and chill
'Neath which thou long hast lain,
No more thy free shout on the hill
Shall rigidly restrain. (*Irish Echo*, Vol. II, No. 10 [October 1888], p. 4).

8. *Midnight Court*, p. vi.
9. *Midnight Court*. All further references to O'Shea's translation are to this edition.
10. *Mediae Noctis Consilium: Poema Heroico-Comicum* (Dublin: John O'Daly, 1850), p. 7. All further references to *Cúirt an Mheán Oíche* are to this edition.
11. In *Cúirt an Mheon-Oíche*, ed. Liam P. Ó Murchú (Baile Átha Cliath: Clóchomhar, 1982), ll. 603–614. Further references to Woulfe's translation are to this edition.
12. The address was given to mark the re-opening of a school for teaching Irish in Boston, and was reprinted in *The Irish Echo*, No. 22 (October 1887), p. 7.

ARLAND USSHER: ON BEHALF OF THE ASCENDANCY AND LIBERAL HUMANISM

1. *The Twilight of Ideas and Other Essays* (Dublin: Sandymount Press, 1948).
2. *The Journal of Arland Ussher*, ed. Adrian Kenny (Dublin: Raven Arts, 1980), p. 5.
3. *Journal*, p. 5.
4. *The Face and Mind of Ireland* (1949; New York: Devin-Adair, 1950), p. 145.
5. *Face and Mind*, p. 146. The two collections are *Caint an tSean-Shaoghail* (1942) and *Cúrsaí an tSean-Shaoghail* (1948).
6. *Face and Mind*, p. 145.
7. *Face and Mind*, p. 176.
8. Declan Kiberd has argued that in translating *Cúirt an Mheán Oíche*, Ussher was insisting that he 'had as valid a claim on Gaelic tradition as any other social group on the island' ('Merry Men: the Afterlife of the Poem,' in *Frank O'Connor: Critical Essays*, ed. Hilary Lennon [Dublin: Four Courts Press, 2007], p. 125).
9. This argument has been made by Gerry Smyth, in *Decolonisation and Criticism: The Construction of Irish Literature* (London: Pluto Press, 1998). Smyth says that Ussher's work threatened to 'fracture the discursive boundaries between Irish and non-Irish experience (p. 204).
10. *Face and Mind*, p. 10.
11. Introduction, *The Midnight Court and The Adventures of a Luckless Fellow*, trans. Percy Arland Ussher (London: Jonathan Cape, 1926), p. 5. This volume includes Ussher's translation of *Cúirt an Mheán Oíche* and of 'Eachtra Ghiolla an Amaráin', by Donnchadh Ruadh Mac Conmara (1715–1810). Ussher dropped the 'Percy' in later writings. Yeats is not the only reader of Merriman's poem to see 'Cadenus and Vanessa' behind it. Seán Ó Tuama, 'Brian Merriman and his Court,' *Irish University Review*, Vol. II, 1981; rpt. in *Repossessions Selected Essays on the Irish Literary Heritage* (Cork: Cork Univ. Press, 1995), says that 'Cadenus and Vanessa' is one of the last expressions in English literature of the

medieval court-of-love tradition, and that *Cúirt an Mheán Oíche* very much belongs to that tradition (p. 64). Vivian Mercier, in *The Irish Comic Tradition* (London: Oxford Univ. Press, 1962), says of 'Cadenus and Vanessa': 'it is hard to see where else Merriman could have encountered the idea of a court in which each sex blames the other for the decay of love' (p. 193).

12. *Journal*, p. 5.

13. *Journal*, p. 28.

14. This point has been suggested by Declan Kiberd, who has argued that Ussher's translation of *Cúirt an Mheán Oíche* 'managed to lodge the claims for a more humanist attitude within the context of well-mannered metrification' ('Merry Men,' p. 125).

15. *Cúirt an Mheadhon Oichde*, ed. Risteárd Ó Foghludha (Dublin: Hodges, Figgis, 1912), ll. 65–68. It's likely that this is the version that Ussher used for his translation as the edition was published about a decade before Ussher would have been working on it. All further references to Merriman's text in this chapter are taken from this edition.

16. *Midnight Court and Adventures*, p. 18. All citations of Ussher's translation are from this edition.

17. *Cúirt an Mheon-Oíche*, ed. Liam P. Ó Murchú (Baile Átha Cliath: An Clóchomhar, 1982), ll. 311–16. Further references to Woulfe's translation are from this edition.

18. *Face and Mind*, p. 172.

19. Robert Welch, 'Poetry, Fear, and Translation: Versions of Merriman,' in *Brian Merriman and His World: Merriman ar an mbinse*, eds. Máirín Ní Dhonnchadha, Gearóid Ó Tuathaigh, and Patrick Crotty (Dublin: Four Courts Press, forthcoming), says of Ussher's translation of this passage: 'Ussher suppresses all the disgrace, the violent sex, the abandonment.' I am grateful to Professor Welch for letting me see a typescript of this essay.

FRANK O'CONNOR: RESTORING THE NATION

1. Alan Titley, 'The Interpretation of Tradition,' in *Frank O'Connor: Critical Essays*, ed. Hilary Lennon (Dublin: Four Courts Press, 2007), says that O'Connor's translations are 'among the best translations of Irish poetry that we have' (p. 219).

2. Ussher once complained facetiously, in a letter to the *Irish Times* that was part of a lengthy correspondence that followed the decision of the Appeal Board, in 1946, not to overturn the original ban on O'Connor's translation of Merriman, that he was 'a trifle aggrieved that the Board did not give me the same public advertisement as it has given to my friend Frank O'Connor' (12 September 1946, p. 7). The correspondence, consisting of forty-four letters and one leader, was often vitriolic, and ran in the *Times* for nearly three months. Although many of the letter-writers were defending O'Connor, the other side was well represented. One member of the Appeal Board, James Hogan, wrote that O'Connor's translation went beyond the immorality of the original to 'sound a note of blasphemy' (*Irish Times*, 27 July 1946, p. 8), and Risteárd Ó Foghludha, who had published an edition of the original in 1912 – probably the edition that O'Connor based his translation on – declared that O'Connor's translation was 'a misrepresentation, distortion of the sense, a false picture, and, in one line in particular, theologically offensive' (*Irish Times*, 12 August 1946, p. 5).

3. *An Only Child* (1961; London: Pan Books, 1970), p. 123.

4. *An Only Child*, p. 135.

5. The translation was of 'Heureux Qui Comme Ulysse' by the sixteenth-century French poet Joachim Du Bellay. O'Connor himself was quite sceptical about what he had done, calling his work 'a translation from one language the author didn't know into another he didn't know – or at best, knew most imperfectly' (*An Only Child*, pp. 150–1).

6. *My Father's Son* (1968; London: Pan Books, 1971), p. 21.

7. In the extended correspondence generated in 1946 over the decision of the Appeal Board not to overturn the Censorship Board's ban on his translation of *Cúirt an Mheán Oíche*, O'Connor said, 'I do not *pose* as a Celtic scholar' (Letter to *Irish Times*, 29 July 1946, p. 5).

8. 'The Scholar-Gipsy,' in *Michael / Frank: Studies on Frank O'Connor*, ed. Maurice Sheehy (New York: Alfred Knopf, 1969), p. 18.

9. 'Interpretation of Tradition,' p. 232.

10. James Matthews, in *Voices: A Life of Frank O'Connor* (New York: Atheneum, 1983), has made this argument (p. 223).

11. *Leinster, Munster and Connaught* (London: Robert Hale, nd), pp. 230–232. Alan Titley, 'Interpretation of Tradition,' says that Merriman's poem 'in one declamation seems to have destroyed the stereotype of the repressed and puritanical peasant' (p. 227). And Declan Kiberd has argued that O'Connor saw Merriman's poem 'as one way of proving to puritanical nationalists that they had no real interest in a revival of authentic Gaelic tradition' ('Merry Men: the Afterlife of the Poem,' in *Frank O'Connor: Critical Essays*, p. 124).

12. An edition published in 1909 and entitled *The Midnight Court: Cúirt an Mheadhoin Oidhche*, contained only 606 lines of the 1026-line original, and described itself as 'specifically prepared for the use of the schools'. In 1927, *Giotaí as Cúirt an Mheodhn-Oidhche*, edited by Conall Cearnach (Feardorcha Ó Conaill), offered the reader just 615 lines of Merriman's poem.

13. Liam P. Ó Murchú, 'Aistriúchán / -áin Frank O'Connor de *Chúirt an Mheonoíche* le Brian Merriman,' in *Aistriú Éireann*, eds. Charlie Dillon and Ríóna Ní Fhrighil (Belfast: Queens Univ. Press, 2008), argues that O'Connor allowed his dissatisfaction with the clergy and the state to interfere with his translation, and that, in particular, he invested his translation with an anti-clericalism not present in Merriman's poem (p. 138).

14. *Cúirt an Mheadhon Oidhche*, ed. Risteárd Ó Foghludha (Dublin: Hodges, Figgis, 1912), ll. 789–792. It's likely that this is the edition that O'Connor was working from, as Ó Murchú argues in 'Aistriúchán / -áin Frank O'Connor' (p. 140). It's also possible, Ó Murchú says, that O'Connor had access to a version of Merriman's poem edited by L. Christian Stern, and published in 1905 in *Zeitschrift für Celtische Philologie*, Vol. V, pp. 193–415. Further references to Merriman's poem in this chapter are to Ó Foghludha's edition.

15. *The Midnight Court: A Rhythmical Bacchanalia from the Irish of Bryan Merriman*, trans. Frank O'Connor (London, Dublin: Maurice Fridberg, 1945), p. 41. Further references to O'Connor's translation are to this edition. For a comparison between this text and the revised text of the translation that appeared in O'Connor's collection of translations entitled *Kings, Lords and Commons* (1959), see Ó Murchú, 'Aistriúchán / -áin Frank O'Connor,' especially pp. 131–6.

16. In *An Only Child*, O'Connor recalls that during his first night in Gormanstown Internment Camp, his encounter with an anti-Treaty soldier who had been severely beaten by a member of the Free-State forces made him lament that 'this was all our romanticism came to' (p. 192).

17. Kiberd, 'Merry Men', says that O'Connor turned to translation from the Irish in part out

of the hope that 'in connecting people with their buried past, texts of the Irish language could help to create a more liberal and tolerant society' (p. 115).

18. O'Connor once said that Merriman very likely belonged to United Ireland, and that his apparent failure to write anything after *Cúirt an Mheán Oíche* may have had something to do with the failure of the United Ireland rebellion at the end of the eighteenth century (*Leinster, Munster and Connaught*, pp. 226, 232).

19. Declan Kiberd has argued that Merriman's treatment of 'lost manhood, lost procreativity, lost self-belief' was 'all too real for Frank O'Connor and his generation of veterans of the War of Independence' ('Merry Men,' p. 115).

20. Preface, *Midnight Court*, p. 7.

21. Preface, p. 7.

22. Preface, p. 8. In *Leinster, Munster and Connaught*, O'Connor says: 'Merryman had almost no feeling for Nature … But the moment the girl begins speaking Merryman is on familiar ground, and the whole mood of the poem changes' (p. 25).

23. In *Cúirt an Mheán Oíche*, ed. Liam P. Ó Murchú (Baile Átha Cliath: Clóchmhar, 1982), ll. 305–310. Further references to Woulfe's translation are to this text.

24. *The Midnight Court and The Adventures of a Luckless Fellow* (London: Jonathan Cape, 1926), p. 28. Further references to Ussher's translation are to this text.

25. *The Irish Statesman*, 9 October 1926, p. 114.

LORD LONGFORD: MERRIMAN AND THE THEATRE

1. 'The Midnight Court,' in *Poetry Ireland*, No. 6 (July 1949), p. 4.

2. *Poems from the Irish* (Dublin: Hodges, Figgis; Oxford: B.H. Blackwell, 1944); *More Poems from the Irish* (Dublin: Hodges, Figgis; Oxford: B.H. Blackwell, 1945); and *The Dove in the Castle: A Collection of Poems from the Irish* (Dublin: Hodges, Figgis; Oxford: B.H. Blackwell, 1946).

3. Peter Stanford, *Lord Longford: A Life* (London: William Heinemann, 1994), p. 32.

4. John Cowell, *No Profit but the Name: The Longfords and the Gate Theatre* (Dublin: O'Brien Press, 1988), p. 22.

5. In his brother's words: 'Edward in youth was certainly an inspiring rebel. I can see him now disappearing beneath a mass of persecutors at Eton while he shouted "Up the Republic" or some such Sinn Fein slogan' (*Born to Believe: An Autobiography*, by Lord Pakenham [London: Jonathan Cape, 1953], p. 22).

6. Stanford, *Lord Longford*, pp. 40–41.

7. Cowell, p. 32.

8. Cowell, p. 10.

9. Stanford, p. 79.

10. Stanford, p. 310.

11. *More Poems from the Irish*, p. x.

12. The translation was never staged, although a number of plays have been written, in Irish and in English, based on Merriman's poem. For a listing of plays inspired by Merriman's poem, see 'Partial Publication and Production History,' in *The Midnight Court / Cúirt an Mheán Oíche*, ed. Brian Ó Conchubhair (Syracuse, N.Y.: Syracuse Univ. Press, 2011), pp. 107–22.

13. An example from this translation:

> Oh! Had you seen how first I met the man,
> I know you'd love him as I only can.
> To church he came each day, with gentle air,
> And every day he knelt beside me there,
> And drew the attention of the congregation
> By the fierce ardour of his adoration. (Quoted in Cowell, p. 123.)

14. *Cúirt an Mheadhon Oidhche*, ed. Risteárd Ó Foghludha (Dublin: Hodges, Figgis, 1912), ll. 531–538. This is almost certainly the text that Longford was translating from. A revised edition of Ó Foghludha's text was published in 1949, but it seems unlikely that Longford, whose translation was published in July of 1949, would have had access to it when he was working on his translation.

15. 'Midnight Court,' *Poetry Ireland*, p. 18. All citations of Longford's translation are to this edition.

16. In *Cúirt an Mheon-Oíche*, ed. Liam P. Ó Murchú (Baile Átha Cliath: An Clóchomhar, 1982, ll. 707–10.

17. *The Midnight Court* (London, Dublin: Maurice Fridberg, 1945), p. 23.

18. *No Profit*, p. 155.

19. *Poetry Ireland*, p. 4. The passages in Merriman omitted from Longford's translation are ll. 757–78, 795–812, and 903–14. The printer is listed as Trumpet Books, in Cork.

DAVID MARCUS: MARGINALITY AND SEXUALITY

1. In the preface to his translation of Merriman's poem, Marcus said that he had been drawn to it 'by the surprising applicability of certain parts of the poem to contemporary Ireland' (*Cúirt an Mheadhon Oidhche: The Midnight Court*, trans. David Marcus [Dublin: Dolmen Press, 1953], n.p.).

2. *Oughtobiography: Leaves from the Diary of a Hyphenated Jew* (Dublin: Gill and Macmillan, 2001), p. 29.

3. *Oughtobiography*, p. 29.

4. *Oughtobiography*, pp. 246–7.

5. *Oughtobiography*, p. 165.

6. *Oughtobiography*, p. 25. Marcus also said that he was inspired to translate 'An Bonnán Buí' after reading the opening passages of *The Midnight Court* in a school anthology (pp. 25–6).

7. *Oughtobiography*, pp. 28, 29.

8. *Cúirt an Mehadhón Oidhche*, ed. Risteárd Ó Foghludha (Baile Átha Cliath: Hodges, Figgis, 1949), ll. 100–102. It's likely that this is the text, a revised version of Ó Fodhludha's 1912 edition, that Marcus used; it was published four years before his own translation appeared. All further references in this chapter to Merriman's text are to this edition.

9. *Cúirt an Mheadhon Oidhche: The Midnight Court*, p. 12. The translation was published in an expensive, limited edition, possibly 'a Liam Miller tactic,' Marcus once said, 'to forestall another ban' (*Oughtobiography*, p. 29). Marcus' translation was republished by Dufour Editions, Chester Springs, Pennsylvania, in 1968, and in *The Midnight Court / Cúirt an Mheán Oíche: A Critical Edition*, ed. by Brian Ó Conchubhair (Syracuse, N.Y.: Syracuse

Univ. Press, 2011). All references to the translation here are to the Dolmen edition.

10. *The Midnight Court*, trans. Frank O'Connor (London, Dublin: Maurice Fridberg, 1945), p. 16. Further references to O'Connor's translation are to this edition.

11. Marcus, *Midnight Court*, n. p.

12. *Midnight Court*, n. p.

13. *Midnight Court*, n. p.

PATRICK C. POWER: SCHOLARSHIP AND POETIC TRANSLATION

1. *The Story of Anglo-Irish Poetry (1800–1922)* (Cork: Mercier Press, 1967), p. 80.

2. *Cúirt an Mheán-Oíche: The Midnight Court* (Cork: Mercier Press, 1971), p. 11.

3. *A Literary History of Ireland* (Cork: Mercier Press, 1969), p. 133.

4. *Literary History*, p. 180.

5. *Sex and Marriage in Ancient Ireland* (Dublin and Cork: Mercier Press, 1976), pp. 6–7.

6. *Sex and Marriage*, p. 77.

7. *Sex and Marriage*, p. 48.

8. *Midnight Court*, p. 6.

9. *Sex and Marriage*, p. 48.

10. *Midnight Court*, ll. 309–18. All further citations to Merriman's text and to Power's translation are to this dual-language edition.

11. *The Midnight Court* (London and Dublin: Maurice Fridberg, 1945), p. 16.

12. In a note to his translation, Power says, 'an effort has been made to imitate the Gaelic assonance at the end of the lines in each couplet'. He also says that he set out to imitate the patterns of internal assonance as well, 'but this had to be abandoned because of the extreme difficulty of such an undertaking and the subsequent distortion which would inevitably result in so many cases' (*Midnight Court*, p. 11).

13. *Midnight Court*, p. 7.

14. *The Midnight Court and The Adventures of a Luckless Fellow* (London: Jonathan Cape, 1926), p. 34.

15. *The Midnight Court*, in *Poetry Ireland*, No. 6 (July, 1949), p. 15.

16. Power said that the primary source for his version was MS 23 M 8, in the Royal Irish Academy collection, in the hand of Seán Paor of Pickardstown, near Tramore, in Co. Waterford. The passages in Power's version that do not appear in the standard earlier editions are ll. 541–767; ll. 727–48, and ll. 767–82.

17. *Midnight Court*, p. 10.

COSSLETT Ó CUINN: THE FOOTPRINT OF SECTARIANISM

1. It's not clear why Ó Cuinn decided to translate *Cúirt an Mheán Oíche*, a poem he had first read in the 1930s, so late in his life. His biographer, Risteárd Ó Glaisne, says only that Ó Cuinn wanted 'é a choinneáil os chomhar an phobail mhór' ('to keep it in front of the public at large') (*Cosslett Ó Cuinn* [Baile Átha Cliath: Coiscéim, 1996], p. 273).

2. Biographical details are taken from Ó Glaisne, *Cosslett Ó Cuinn*.

3. Quoted in Ó Glaisne, p. 443.

4. Quoted in Ó Glaisne, p. 39.

5. Ó Glaisne, p. 302.

6. *Slánú an tSalachair* (Baile Átha Cliath: Clódhanna, 1978), pp. 12–13.

7. *Cúirt An Mheán Oíche*, ed. Dáithí Ó hUaithne (Baile Átha Cliath: Dolmen Press / Cumann Merriman, 1968), ll. 287–94. Ó Cuinn cites this edition, along with selections from his translation, in an essay that he wrote about Merriman: 'Merriman's Court,' in *The Pleasures of Gaelic Poetry*, ed. Seán Mac Réamoinn (London: Allen Lane, 1982), pp. 113–26.

8. *The Midnight Court* (Dublin and Cork: Mercier Press, 1982), p. 27. All further references to Ó Cuinn's translation are to this text.

9. Quoted in Ó Glaisne, p. 273.

10. Ó Glaisne, p. 273.

11. Ó Glaisne, p. 334.

12. *The Midnight Court and The Adventures of a Luckless Fellow* (London: Jonathan Cape, 1926), p. 15.

13. *The Midnight Court* (London, Dublin: Maurice Fridberg, 1945), p. 13.

14. *The Midnight Court*, in *Poetry Ireland*, No. 6 (July 1949), p. 6.

15. *Cúirt an Mheadhon Oídhche: The Midnight Court* (Dublin: Dolmen Press, 1953), p. 9.

THOMAS KINSELLA: 'A DUAL APPROACH'

1. 'The Irish Writer,' in W.B. Yeats and Thomas Kinsella, *Davis, Mangan, Ferguson? Tradition and the Irish Writer* (Dublin: Dolmen Press, 1970), p. 58.

2. 'Irish Writer,' p. 6.

3. 'Another Country,' in *The Pleasures of Gaelic Poetry*, ed. Seán Mac Réamoinn (London: Allen Lane, 1982), p. 177.

4. 'The Divided Mind,' in *Irish Poets in English: The Thomas Davis Lectures on Anglo-Irish Poetry*, ed. Seán Lucy (Dublin and Cork: Mercier Press, 1972), p. 209.

5. 'Divided Mind,' p. 209.

6. 'Preface,' *The New Oxford Book of Irish Verse* (Oxford and New York: Oxford Univ. Press, 1986), p. vii. Kathleen Shields has argued convincingly that Kinsella's translations are not essentially antiquarian in intention, as were many of the translations from the Irish done in the nineteenth century and earlier in the twentieth, but rather a 'seeking out of new points of contact between the two literatures in English and in Irish … allowing him to carry the literature of the past into the present' (*Gained in Translation: Language, Poetry and Identity in Twentieth-Century Ireland* [Bern: Peter Lang, 2000], p. 14). Thomas H. Jackson has argued that Kinsella's approach to the Irish tradition differs sharply from that of Yeats; whereas Yeats 'demonstrated that the stuff of Gaelic myth and legend or the fanciful lore of fairies, could be woven into major poems', Kinsella, Johnson says, 'knits that material to a sensibility, a consciousness, showing not how to make an Irish past something to write about, but how to make it truly part of yourself – your creative self, if you happen to be a poet' (*The Whole Matter: The Poetic Evolution of Thomas Kinsella* [Syracuse, N.Y.: Syracuse Univ. Press; Dublin: Lilliput Press, 1995], p. xi.) Unfortunately, Jackson's book does not address Kinsella's work in translation from the Irish.

7. *The Dual Tradition: An Essay on Poetry and Politics in Ireland* (Manchester: Carcanet, 1995), p. 5.

8. 'Introduction,' *An Duanaire, 1600–1900: Poems of the Dispossessed* ed. Seán Ó Tuama, trans. Thomas Kinsella (Portlaoise: Dolmen Press, 1981), p. xxxv.

9. *Cúirt an Mheán Oíche*, ed. Dáithí Ó hUaithne, (Baile Átha Cliath: Dolmen Press / Cumann Merriman, 1968), ll. 357–60. In *An Duanaire*, Kinsella cites this edition as the source for his translation. Further references to *Cúirt an Mheán Oíche* are to Ó hUaithne's edition.

10. In *Cúirt an Mheon-Oíche*, ed. Liam P. Ó Murchú (Baile Átha Cliath: An Clóchomhar, 1982), ll. 351–4. Further references to Woulf's translation are to this text.

11. *The Midnight Court and The Adventures of a Luckless Fellow* (London: Jonathan Cape, 1926), p. 31. Further references to Ussher's translation are to this edition.

12. *The Midnight Court* (London, Dublin: Maurice Fridberg, 1945), p. 25. Further references to O'Connor's translation are to this edition.

13. *The Midnight Court*, in *Poetry Ireland*, No. 6 (July 1949), p. 14.

14. *Cúirt an Mheadhon Oidhche: The Midnight Court* (Dublin: Dolmen Press, 1953), p. 21. Further references to Marcus' translation are to this edition.

15. *New Oxford Book of Irish Verse*, p. 230. Further references to Kinsella's translation are to this text.

16. 'Introduction.' *An Duanaire*, p. xxxvii.

17. Robert Welch, 'Poetry, Fear, and Translation: Versions of Merriman,' in *Brian Merriman and His World: Merriman ar an mbinse*, eds. Máirín Ní Dhonnchadha, Gearóid Ó Tuathaigh and Patrick Crotty (Dublin: Four Courts Press, forthcoming), says of the first two lines of Kinsella's translation: 'This translation was intended to assist the reader to understand the Irish, so its aims are circumspect, nevertheless "brink" is alert to the delicacies inherent in "ciumhais", which has suggestions of marginality as well as being-on-the-edge.' I am grateful to Professor Welch for letting me see this essay in typescript.

18. 'Introduction,' *An Duanaire*, pp. xxxvii-ix.

19. *Cúirt an Mheán-Oíche: The Midnight Court*, ed. and trans. Patrick C. Power (Cork: Mercier Press, 1971), l. 185.

20. *Cúirt an Mheon-Oíche*, p. 53.

21. *Thomas Kinsella: Designing for the Exact Needs* (Dublin: Irish Academic Press, 2008), p. 124.

22. *Thomas Kinsella* (New York: Twayne, 1996), p. 184.

23. Quoted in Harmon, *Thomas Kinsella*, p. xviii.

SEAMUS HEANEY: OVID, FEMINISM, AND THE NORTH

1. The most thorough assessment of the relationship between *Cúirt an Mheán Oíche* and various medieval texts is Seán Ó Tuama, 'Brian Merriman and his Court,' *Irish University Review*, Vol. II (1981), pp. 149–64; rpt. in *Repossessions: Selected Essays on the Irish Literary Heritage* (Cork: Cork Univ. Press, 1995), pp. 57–77.

2. 'Orpheus in Ireland: Merriman's *The Midnight Court*,' in *The Redress of Poetry: Oxford Lectures* (London: Faber and Faber, 1995), p. 53.

3. 'Orpheus in Ireland,' pp. 55–6.

4. 'Orpheus,' pp. 55–6. Sarah McKibben has argued for seeing Merriman's poem as promoting the empowerment of women at the expense of men: 'By making women fierce, strong,

and more than a little terrifying in their thwarted sexual longing, it relentlessly points up the sexual cowardice and incapacity of Irish men. *Cúirt an Mheán Oíche* punctures the image of masculine prowess promised by the *aisling* – always somewhat dubious given that the men of Ireland had yet to rescue their heroine or recover their lost sovereignty' ('Courting an Elusive Masterwork: Reading Gender and Genre in Cúirt an Mheán Oiche / The Midnight Court,' in *The Midnight Court / Cúirt an Mheán Oíche: A Critical Edition*, ed. Brian Ó Conchubhair [Syracuse, N.Y.: Syracuse Univ. Press, 2011], p. 75). The juxtaposition of Ovid and Merriman has also been interpreted in a considerably narrower context, but one that has to do with feminism as well, although in perhaps a less encouraging light: the controversy over the *Field Day Anthology of Irish Writing*. When the anthology appeared, in 1991, two years before the publication of *The Midnight Verdict*, charges were made by a number of writers and critics that it severely under-represented women's writing in Ireland, and it was pointed out that no women were on the editorial board of the project. Seamus Deane, the anthology's chief editor, had in fact been summoned to appear before an informal group at the Irish Writer's Centre, a situation that carries at least some correspondences to the position of Merriman's narrator, to defend the anthology against charges of sexism. As a director of the Field Day Company, and a close friend of Deane's, Heaney had a significant investment in the anthology. Declan Kiberd has argued that by arranging for the end of Merriman's poem to be followed by the death of Orpheus in *The Metamorphoses*, 'Heaney seemed to be offering his own verdict on the feminist verdict on the anthology' ('Merry Men: the Afterlife of the Poem,' in *Frank O'Connor: Critical Essays*, ed. Hilary Lennon [Dublin: Four Courts Press, 2007], p. 127). Heaney himself has said that once he started working on the section of Ovid's poem describing the death of Orpheus, 'the merry man in me couldn't help seeing the beleaguered Orpheus as a General Editor figure, being attacked not so much on the ground of a field as on the grounds of the Field Day Anthology' (Dennis O'Driscoll, *Stepping Stones: Interviews with Seamus Heaney* [New York: Farrar, Straus and Giroux, 2008], p. 313).

5. *Cúirt an Mheán Oíche*, ed. Liam P. Ó Murchú (Baile Átha Cliath: An Clóchomhar, 1982), ll. 185–190. All further references to *Cúirt an Mheán Oíche* are to this edition.

6. *The Midnight Verdict* (Oldcastle, Co. Meath: Gallery Press, 1993), p. 29. All further references to Heaney's translation of Merriman, and of Ovid, are to this edition.

7. In 'Orpheus and Ireland', Heaney says that through the bailiff's character, Merriman 'revised and implicitly criticized the *aisling* genre by burlesquing its idealized, victimized maiden' (p. 55).

8. 'Orpheus,' p. 60.

9. 'Orpheus,' p. 60.

10. McKibben, 'Courting an Elusive Masterwork,' says that at the end of *Cúirt an Mheán Oíche*, the male poet recovers from his abjection 'through this virtuoso poetic performance, with male prowess relocated to the arena of linguistic production. Similarly, the poet escapes from judgment and out of his dream, recovering the authorial control and completeness that he never in fact lost' (pp. 76–7).

11. Kathleen Shields has argued that Heaney's translations, because they are grounded in a trust in English as capable of absorbing external influences, enable him to move beyond dualities: 'Because English can absorb Scots, Irish, Norse and Latin words it can heal painful historical and sectarian differences' (*Gained in Translation: Language, Poetry and Identity in Twentieth-Century Ireland* [Bern: Peter Lang, 2000], p. 15).

12. *Seamus Heaney: Creating Irelands of the Mind* (Dublin: Liffey Press, 2002), p. 135.

13. *Stepping* Stones, p. 438. The dialect also appears, with fewer overt political implications, in Heaney's translation of *Beowulf* (1999). See Alison Finlay, 'Putting a Bawn into *Beowulf*,' in *Seamus Heaney: Poet, Critic, Translator*, eds. Ashby Bland Crowser and Jason David Hall (Basingstroke and New York: Palgrave Macmillan, 2007), pp. 136–54, for a thorough discussion of Heaney's use of dialect in his translation of *Beowulf*.

14. The definition of 'ganting', and those of the Ulster-Scots terms that follow, are taken from the online *Dictionary of the Scots Language*.

15. Quoted in 'Putting a Bawn into *Beowulf*', p. 136.

16. Robert Welch has pointed out that 'shrewd' in Heaney's translation of this passage, referring to 'críon le cianta', where 'críon' means 'withered' or 'worn-out', is also sensitive to another meaning of 'críon', which is 'canny' ('Poetry, Fear, and Translation: Versions of Merriman,' in *Brian Merriman and His World: Merriman ar an mBinse*, eds. Máirín Ní Dhonnchadha, Gearóid Ó Thuathaigh, and Patrick Crotty [Dublin: Four Courts Press, forthcoming]. I'm grateful to Professor Welch for allowing me to see this essay in typescript.

17. 'Orpheus,' p. 50.

18. 'Orpheus,' p. 51.

19. 'Orpheus,' p. 52.

CIARAN CARSON: 'WAVERING BETWEEN LANGUAGES'

1. 'Foreword,' *The Midnight Court: A New Translation of 'Cúirt an Mheán Oíche'* (Oldcastle, Co. Meath: Gallery Press, 2005), p.14.

2. *Ciaran Carson: Space, Place, Writing* (Liverpool: Liverpool Univ. Press, 2010), pp. 182–3. Referring to a translation by Carson of a poem by the Romanian poet Stephan Augustin Doinas, Stan Smith has argued that Carson's translations are 'crucially ambilocated, neither one thing nor the other – neither translations nor original poems,' inhabiting 'the space of the hyphen between Ciaran Carson and Stephan Doinas' (*Irish Poetry and the Construction of Modern Identity* [Dublin: Irish Academic Press, 2005], p. 218).

3. *Fishing for Amber: A Long Story* (London: Granta, 1999), pp. 203–4.

4. 'Foreword,' *Midnight Court*, p. 15.

5. *Buile Suibhne: The Adventures of Suibhne Geilt*, ed. J. G. O'Keeffe (London: Irish Texts Society, 1913), p. xvii. The poem is not actually part of O'Keeffe's text of *Buile Suibhne*, but is cited in his introduction as a poem attributed to Suibhne.

6. *The New Estate and Other Poems* (1976; Oldcastle, Co. Meath: Gallery Press, 1988), p. 62. See Alexander, *Ciaran Carson*, pp. 186–8, for the view that Carson's early translations often represent 'in part a gloss on the process of translation itself'.

7. 'Ciaran Carson,' in John Brown, ed., *In the Chair: Interviews with Poets from the North of Ireland* (Cliffs of Moher: Salmon, 2002), p. 141.

8. *The Star Factory* (New York: Arcade Publishing, 1997), p. 234.

9. 'Sweeney Astray: Escaping from Limbo,' in Tony Curtis, ed., *The Art of Seamus Heaney* (Chester Springs, Pa.: Dufour, 1985), p. 143.

10. See *Star Factory*, pp. 52–3, 191–3, for examples.

11. 'Carson's Carnival of Language: the Influence of Irish and the Oral Tradition,' in Elmer Kennedy-Andrews, ed. *Ciaran Carson: Critical Essays* (Dublin: Four Courts Press, 2009), p. 191.

12. This argument has been made by Alexander, *Ciaran Carson*, p. 8.

13. 'Foreword,' p. 14.

14. 'Foreword,' p. 14.

15. *Cúirt an Mheon-Oíche*, ed. Liam P. Ó Murchú (Baile Átha Cliath: An Clóchomhar, 1982), ll. 199–206. Carson says this was the primary text he used (*Midnight Court*, p. 62). All further references to Merriman's poem are to this text.

16. *Midnight Court*, pp. 24–5. All further references to Carson's translation are to this text.

17. *The New Oxford Book of Irish Verse* (Oxford and New York: Oxford Univ. Press, 1986), pp. 226–7.

18. *The Midnight Court* (London and Dublin: Maurice Fridberg, 1945), p. 20. Further references to O'Connor's translation are to this text.

19. The literal translation of the first line follows Patrick C. Power's edition, *Cúirt an Mheán Oíche: The Midnight Court* (Cork: Mercier Press, 1971), which has 'frith', an equivalent for 'fuarthas', rather than 'fríodh'. Carson says he occasionally consulted Power's text (*Midnight Court*, p. 62).

20. David Greene, for example, in *The Irish Language: An Ghaeilge* (Dublin: Three Candles, 1966), has argued that Irish is very much a 'noun-centred language', pointing, for example, to the use of verbal nouns in situations in which English would require an infinitive or a gerund, and the use of nouns in situations in which an adjective would be normal in many other languages (p. 31). Greene also says that perhaps the most distinctive feature of Irish is its 'reluctance to accept coinages common to most of the languages of Europe', particularly abstract terms derived from Latin (pp. 57–8).

21. *Star Factory*, p. 20.

22. Robert Welch, 'Poetry, Fear, and Translation: Versions of Merriman,' in *Brian Merriman and His World: Merriman ar an mBinse*, eds. Máirín Ní Dhonnchadha, Gearóid Ó Tuathaigh, and Patrick Crotty (Dublin: Four Courts Press, forthcoming), says of the opening two lines of Carson's translation: 'The "boots" are not in the Irish, but the heavy dew is. Carson brings them together, very effectively, so we get the motion of the walker.' I'm grateful to Professor Welch for letting me see this essay in typescript.

23. Robert Welch has said that 'líonta ó phianta' must be like what it is to have cardiac arrest' ('Poetry, Fear, and Translation').

24. 'Merry Men: the Afterlife of the Poem,' in *Frank O'Connor: Critical Essays*, ed. Hilary Lennon (Dublin: Four Courts Press, 2007), p. 128.

25. 'Ciaran Carson Interviewed by Frank Ormsby,' *Linen Hall Review*, Vol. 8, No. 1 (Spring, 1991), p. 7. In reviewing Carson's *The Irish for No*, Nuala Ní Dhomhnaill noted that the poems embodied many of the qualities of the *seanchaí* tradition ('The English for Irish,' *The Irish Review*, No. 4 [1988], pp. 116–7.)

26. 'Foreword,' *Midnight Court*, p. 11.

27. *Mouse or Rat? Translation as Negotiation* (London: Weidenfeld and Nicolson, 2003), p. 173.

28. 'Foreword,' *Midnight Court*, p. 15.

29. 'Poetry, Fear, and Translation.'

Index

Aeschylus, 45.

aisling (vision poem), xiii, 24, 37, 91, 192.

Alexander, Neal, 98, 193.

Árainn Mhór (Co. Donegal), 70.

Anglo-Irish Ascendancy, 4, 22–4, 28, 31, 45, 50, 52, 54.

Badid, Donatella Abbate, 88.

Behan, Brendan, 180.

Belfast, xi, 45, 69, 99–100, 109.

Bewick, Pauline, 'The Visual Translation of "The Midnight Court"', 182.

Binchy, D. A., 34.

Brehon Laws, 63–4.

Bright Wave, The / An Tonn Gheall: Poetry in Irish Now, 79.

Buile Suibhne (Mad Sweeney), 99–100.

Callanan, J. J., xvii.

Cambridge University, 23, 70.

Campbell College (Belfast), 69.

Cappagh (Co. Waterford), 23.

Carpenter, Andrew, 182.

Carson, Ciaran, xi, xvi, 98–108; *Belfast Confetti*, 100, 193–4; *The Irish for No*, 100, 106, 194; 'M'airiuclán hi Túaim in Inbir' ('My little oratory in Túaim Inbir') (translator), 99;

The New Estate, 99, 106, 193; *The Star Factory*, 100; *The Táin* (translator), 99.

Cashen, Yam, 180.

Catholic Church, xiv–xv, 32, 36, 41, 53, 58, 61, 63, 69–73.

Censorship Act of 1929, 27, 33, 41, 55, 186.

Censorship Appeal Board, 55, 185.

Civil War, 33, 37.

Church of Ireland, 69–70, 77–8.

Clarke, Austin, 79.

Collins, Michael, 45.

Colum, Padraic, xvii, 44.

Conradh na Gaeilge, 70.

Cork City, 33, 53.

Cork County Public Library, 54.

Corkery, Daniel, 9, 22, 33, 63, 183; *The Hidden Ireland*, 22, 183.

Cowell, John, 50.

Crann Faoi Bhláth, An: The Flowering Tree: Contemporary Irish Poetry with Verse Translations, 79.

Cromwell, Oliver, 27, 45–6.

Davis, Thomas, 14.

Deane, Seamus, 192; *Field Day Anthology of Irish Writing*, 192.

de Blacam, Aodh, 179.

de Vere, Aubrey, 14.

Dinneen, Patrick, 47, 57, 86–7, 100.

Dolmen Press, 53.

Dowling, Joe, 74.

Dryden, John, 9.

Du Bellay, Joachim, 186.

Dublin, xvii, 23, 34, 46, 77.

Egan, Bowes, 180.

Easter Rising, 33.

Eco, Umberto, xvii, 108.

Edwards, Hilton, 45–6.

Eglinton, John, 181.

Elizabeth, Queen, 46.

English-language tradition, xii, xv, 4, 6, 9, 12, 14, 22, 77–8.

Eton College, 45, 187.

Euripides, 45.

Feakle (Co. Clare), 181.

Feehan, Seán, 74.

Ferguson, Samuel, 79.

Finlay, Alison, 193.

Gabhla (Co. Donegal), 70.

Gate Theatre, 44–6, 50.

Goldsmith, Oliver, 55, 180; 'The Deserted Village', 55.

Gormanstown Internment Camp, 33, 186.

Great Blasket Island (Co. Kerry), 70.

Greene, David, 194; *The Irish Language: An Ghaeilge*, 194.

Griffith, Arthur, 45.

Great Famine, 13.

Griffin, Gerald, 14.

Harmon, Maurice, 88.

Hartnett, Michael, 79.

Heaney, Seamus, xi, xiii–xvi, 21, *89–97*, 100, 192; 'Orpheus in Ireland: On Brian Merriman's *The Midnight Court*', 90, 96, 192–3.

Hogan, James, 185.

Hyde, Douglas, xvii.

Irish Echo, The, 15, 18, 183.

Irish Free State, 24, 26, 32, 43, 70, 186.

Irish-language tradition, xii–xiii, xv, xvii, 3–4, 9, 12, 18, 22–4, 32, 53, 62–3, 77–8, 83, 111, 183.

Irish literary revival, xvii, 32.

Irishman, The, 4, 182.

Irish Poetry Now: Other Voices, 79.

Irish Press, 54.

Irish Times, The, 55, 70, 185.

Irish Writer's Centre, 192.

Jackson, Thomas H., 190.

Joyce, James, 23, 31, 35, 103; *A Portrait of the Artist as a Young Man*, 35; *Ulysses*, 23, 31.

Kelly, Eamonn, 74.

Kiberd, Declan, 105, 179, 181, 184–7, 192.

Kinsella, Thomas, xi, xvi, 76–7, *78–88*, 94, 99, 101–2, 190–1; *The Dual Tradition: An Essay on Poetry and Politics in Ireland*, 80; *An Duanaire: 1600–1900: Poems of the Dispossessed* (translator) 79–80, 83; *The New Oxford Book of Irish Verse* (editor and translator), 79–80; *Poems and Translations*, 79; *Táin Bó Cuailnge* (translator), 79.

Loch Gréine (Co. Clare), 104, 183.

Longford, Lord (Edward Arthur Henry Pakenham), 44–52, 54, 57, 62, 68, 74, 78, 82, 94, 187; *Yahoo*, 45.

Longford Productions, 46.

Mac Canna, Seoirse, 70.

MacDonagh, Donagh, 80.

Mac Gabhráin, Aodh, 'Pléaráca na Ruarcach' ('O'Rourke's Revelry'), 24, 109.

Mac Giolla Ghunna, Cathal Buí, 'An Bonnán Buí' ('The Yellow Bittern'), 55.

Mac Liammóir, Micheál, 45.

Mac Lochlainn, Gearóid, 99.

Mangan, James Clarence, xvii, 79.

Marcus, David, xv–xvi, 51, 52–61, 74, 78, 82, 88, 188.

Mathews, Jackson, xvii.

Matthews, James, 186.

McKibben, Sarah, 191–2.

Mercier Press, 74–5.

Mercier, Vivian, 180, 185.

Merriman, Brian, biographical information, 180–1; Cúirt an Mheán Oíche, bowlderized editions of, 34; and caint na ndaoine (speech of the people), xiii, xvi, 41–3, 106, 181–2; criticism of, xi–xii; date of composition, 179; diction, xii, xvi, 3, 9–11, 47, 103, 180–1; and drama, xiii–xiv, 44, 46, 49, 52; and dream-vision, xiii–xiv, 25–6, 37, 41; and feminism, xvii, 25–7, 64, 90–3, 192; imagery, xii–xiii, xvi, 19, 74, 82, 103, 180–1; manuscript copies of, xvii, 4, 180, 182; prosody, xii–xiii, xv–xvi, 3, 8–9, 18, 29, 42, 44, 48, 50, 66–8, 81–4, 94, 99, 108, 181; publication of, 22; reputation of, xiii; and rural life, xiii, 4, 14–15, 26; and sexuality, xiii–xiv, 10–12, 19, 27–8, 32, 34, 36–8, 43–4, 50–1, 54–57, 61, 65, 67–8, 73, 75, 91–2, 105, 191–2; and social and political issues, xiv, 3–6, 14, 44, 46, 55, 88, 100, 182.

Miller, Liam, 54, 188.

Modern Language Association, 79.

Moliére, Tartuffe, 46.

Murphy, Fidelma, 74.

Nation, The, 14.

Ní Dhomhnaill, Máire, 74.

Ní Dhomhnaill, Nuala, 79, 99, 194; Pharaoh's Daughter, 79.

Nic Dhiarmada, Bríona, 180.

Northern Ireland, sectarian violence in, 69, 77, 90, 93–4, 100.

O'Brien, Eugene, 93.

Ó Buachalla, Breandán, 179.

Ó Cadhain, Máirtín, 74.

O'Connor, Frank, xi, xv–xvi, 21, 32–43, 44, 50, 53–6, 58–60, 63, 66, 74, 78–9, 81–2, 86, 90, 102–3, 106–7, 179, 185–7; Kings, Lords and Commons, 36, 179; An Only Child, 33, 185–6.

Ó Crualaoich, Gearóid, 181.

Ó Cuinn, Cosslett, xv–xvi, 69–77, 78, 189; Slánú an tSalachair (Redeeming the Dirt), 70–1.

O'Daly, John, 183.

Ó Dónaill, Niall, 86.

Ó Foghludha, Risteárd, 87, 111, 185.

Ó Glaisne, Risteárd, 189.

Ó Murchú, Liam P., xv, 4, 86, 111, 179–83, 186.

Ó Rathaille, Aodhgán, 78.

Ó Rathaille, Tomás, 182.

Ó Ríordáin, Seán, 98–100; Eireaball Spideoige (A Robin's Tail), 98.

O'Shea, Michael C., xv–xvii, 14–21, 54, 69, 78, 183.

Ó Tuama, Seán, 179–80, 182–5, 191.

Ovid, The Metamorphoses, 89–90, 92–3, 192.

Oxford Union, 45.

Oxford University, 45.

Pakenham, Frank, 45, 187.

'Paddy's Panacea', xvi, 108.

Partridge, A.C., 180.

Pearse, Patrick, 33.

Phibbs, Geoffrey, 34.

Philo-Celtic Society (Boston), 15.

Poetry Ireland, 51, 54.

Poolbeg Press, 54.

Pope, Alexander, 9.

Power, Patrick P., xv–xvi, 62–8, 74, 78, 83, 86, 90, 94, 189, 194; *A Literary History of Ireland*, 62–3; *Sex and Marriage in Ancient Ireland*, 63–4; *The Story of Anglo-Irish Poetry (1800–1922)*, 62.

Proust, Marcel, 100.

Robinson, Lennox, 80.

St Columba's College (Rathfarnham), 69.

St Luke's (Cork), 33.

Sewell, Frank, 100.

Shakespeare, William, 46.

Shields, Kathleen, 190, 192.

Sinn Féin, 45, 187.

Sixmilebridge (Co. Clare), 4.

Smyth, Gerry, 184.

Sophocles, 45.

Spenser, Edmund, 46.

Steiner, George, ix, xii, xvii.

Stephens, James, xvii, 79.

Swift, Jonathan, xii, xv, 24, 45, 109, 180; 'Cadenus and Vanessa', xii, 24, 184–5; 'The 'Description of an Irish Feast', 24, 109.

Thompson, George, 70.

Tory Island (Co. Donegal), 70.

Titley, Alan, 34, 179, 181, 185–6.

translation, and colonialism, xii–xiii; as critical interpretation, xii; criticism of, xvii; as cultural and historical negotiation, xii–xiii, xv; and fidelity to original texts, xiii, xv, 11, 82, 87.

Trinity College Dublin, 23, 69–70.

Tullynally Castle (formerly Pakenham Hall) (Co. Westmeath), 45, 52.

Ulster-Scots dialect, 93–4.

University College Galway, 62.

Ussher, Arland, xiv–xv, xvii, 22–31, 33, 40–3, 50, 54, 67–8, 74, 78, 81, 85–6, 88, 184–5; *The Face and Mind of Ireland*, 23, 27; *Three Great Irishmen*, 23.

Ussher, John, 23.

Ussher, William, 23.

Verling, John, 75.

Welch, Robert, 109, 185, 191, 193–4.

White, Jack, 55.

Wicklow Town library, 34.

Wilson, Sir Henry, 45.

Woulfe, Denis, xv, xvii, 3–13, 14–15, 17, 19, 27, 29, 40–3, 48, 54, 78, 81, 86, 94, 109, 182–3.

Yeats, W.B., xii, 24, 79, 180, 184, 190.